The Rule of Three
and the
Evolution of Governance

Temple of the Rule of Three

Incongruity: Things do not match—as in our cover design where a Chinese Pagoda-style roof sits upon a neoclassical American temple of government inside which a traditional Chinese three-legged *ding* standing for stability and harmony replaces a Western hero statue. Things get all mixed together! East and West, in all cultures, people are pretty much the same the world over. So, we mix the cultural artifacts of architecture together to communicate our belief that peace and plenty—harmony—may yet rule upon earth, overcoming our surface cultural differences and the dark forces of totalitarian violence. In our book, we show you how.

Ding: Originally an ancient Chinese cooking cauldron or storage vessel possessing three legs for stability even when set upon irregular surfaces. It evolved into employments in ceremonial observances. For us, the *Ding* symbolizes national stability, as it stands upon three legs representing the Rule of Three.

Cover image designer: Eric Jiaju Lee <ericjiajulee@gmail.com>

The Rule of Three and the Evolution of Governance

Temple of the Rule of Three

Charles Tsungnan Lee
Peter deH Caldwell

World Scientific

NEW JERSEY • LONDON • SINGAPORE • BEIJING • SHANGHAI • HONG KONG • TAIPEI • CHENNAI • TOKYO

Published by

World Scientific Publishing Co. Pte. Ltd.
5 Toh Tuck Link, Singapore 596224
USA office: 27 Warren Street, Suite 401-402, Hackensack, NJ 07601
UK office: 57 Shelton Street, Covent Garden, London WC2H 9HE

Library of Congress Cataloging-in-Publication Data
Names: Lee, Charles (Charles Tsungnan), 1940– author. | Caldwell, Peter deH, author.
Title: The rule of three and the evolution of governance / Charles Tsungnan Lee, Peter deH Caldwell.
Description: New Jersey : World Scientific, [2021] | Includes bibliographical references and index.
Identifiers: LCCN 2020051741 | ISBN 9789811228261 (hardcover) | ISBN 9789811228278 (ebook) | ISBN 9789811228285 (ebook other)
Subjects: LCSH: Government accountability--United States. | Government accountability--China. | Human rights--United States. | Human rights--China. | United States--Foreign economic relations--China. | China--Foreign economic relations--United States.
Classification: LCC JF1525.A26 L44 2021 | DDC 320.951--dc23
LC record available at https://lccn.loc.gov/2020051741

British Library Cataloguing-in-Publication Data
A catalogue record for this book is available from the British Library.

For any available supplementary material, please visit
https://www.worldscientific.com/worldscibooks/10.1142/12041#t=suppl

Desk Editors: Aanand Jayaraman/Lixi Dong

Typeset by Stallion Press
Email: enquiries@stallionpress.com

Dedication

We dedicate this book to our families, parents, and ancestors for fulfilling the purposes of some master designer to bring us all together into this one place. We meet here now not by *chance* but by *design*. Authors and readers alike, we are all *learners*, and now we set off together upon a voyage of discovery through many years of time.

We also express gratitude to those great philosophers past and present, the original learners to whom we owe so much.

Biographical Summary

Dr. Charles Tsungnan Lee has had a lifelong interest and successful career in global Information Technology businesses. He has a proven track record as a successful venture capitalist, and a 40-year rolodex of cross-border business relationships. He authored *Cowboys and Dragons* (2003) and, "The Code that Changes China" (2012, 2014). He founded and chaired the Department of Management of Technology at Peking University (2006–2016). He also served as a Visiting/Adjunct Professor at The National University of Singapore, Zhejiang University, and The University of Southern California (2002–2014). Dr. Lee was a frequent speaker to many MBA/EMB programs focusing on Entrepreneurship.

Born in China (2/18/1940), raised in Taiwan, and educated in the United States, Dr Lee has more than forty years of experience in the Information Technology industry with operating expertise in venture capital, product development, and marketing and general business management on both sides of the Pacific. He possesses long and deep experience working with young technology entrepreneurs to help them optimize their companies' growth. Dr. Lee became the first Asian American Venture capitalist in 1977 and founded Abacus Ventures in 1985 with investors from both domestic U.S. and Far East sources. In 1979, he became the second investor in Steve Job's Apple Computer.

Dr. Lee attended National Taiwan University (BSCE, 1962) and the University of Minnesota (MSCE, 1965, MSAE, 1967 and Ph.D., 1969 in Applied Mathematics).

Peter deH Caldwell began a teaching and writing career a bit late, after several decades in business—including being a part of a team taking a high-tech start-up public in the early 1980s. He then began pursuing a long-term interest in Economic History, taking a PhD degree (1994) in Economics at the University of Connecticut that was quite inter-disciplinary with a special interest in Scottish history, political economy, and philosophy. He did undergraduate studies in English Literature at Dartmouth College and a MA at Tufts University—as well as an MBA at the Amos Tuck School. During a twenty-year teaching career, he filled assignments at Providence College and several other schools and authored several business books. He and co-author Charles Lee earlier teamed up in producing *Cowboys and* Dragons, a book on East-West cultural differences affecting business relations. *The Rule of Three* stands as their first lengthy book together—once more merging their Chinese and American knowledge and insights.

Annotated Contents

Prologue

Queen Elizabeth and Her Three-Legged Stool

He gave his Flesh, and Blood in Bread and Wine:
For if his Body he did then divide,
He must have eat himself before he died.

A Meditation How to Discern the Lord's Body in the Blessed Sacrament, Lady Elizabeth Tudor, 1688

A Faerie Tale

Once upon a time there was a young virgin queen named Elizabeth who ruled in a very hilly land. She found her father's old, four-legged throne to be very tippy. No matter how on her land she placed it or leaned in it while sitting on it, one leg was always up in the air, making it very hard indeed for her to keep her composure—or for that matter her head, as there were naughty lords in her kingdom who wanted to remove it. In fact, she would choose never to marry, because she feared that she would then have to take one side against another amongst the numerous rebellious lords and peoples facing her. And then, she might very well lose her head in fact.

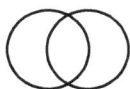

So, she thought about having a special, two-legged throne made just for her, and she consulted the Carpenter Royale. But he warned her that a two-legged stool would be even worse, because it could tip over two ways rather than only one. So, next she consulted the Court Geometer. "Pray tell, Sire, how might I build me a throne that will not tip over?" She was, in fact, very big on prayers generally. Being a very theoretical man, the Court Geometer replied, "I know nothing about building thrones, your Highness, but I can tell you that in a hilly, three-dimensional world like the one in your kingdom, only a throne with three legs could be perfectly stable. The legs would not even have to be equal in length, but there must be three of them. In a flash of pure female intuition, she once more beckoned her Carpenter Royale to her and said: "Make me a three-legged throne! That would make my throne completely non-tippy!"

"But your majesty, that would be so inelegant! I do not know how I could make a three-legged stool look like a throne. In your kingdom, only milkmaids sit upon three-legged stools."

"Very well then," quoth she. "I will rule my kingdom like a milkmaid!"

And she did. And in all the following some 40 years of her reign, she never tipped over, not even once.

This story, of course, is only a faerie tale. But, nevertheless, it has some profound truth to it, as we shall now see.

The True Story Behind the Faerie Tale

The real Elizabeth Tudor ruled England for 45 years—from 1558 to 1603. And in a certain sense, she did rule seated upon a three-legged stool. Here's the short version of the real story: It begins a generation back, as most real stories do. Her father, Henry VIII, who ruled from 1509 to 1547, had become enamored of the Protestant revolution initiated by a German monk named Martin Luther in 1517. Henry fancied himself as something of a theologian, and when the Pope in Rome refused him an annulment of his first marriage, he found Luther's own rebellion against Rome to be quite a helpful guide for action. He simply took the Catholic Church in England "private," to borrow a current business phrase, and sold off the nonproductive assets of that church. Of course, he then became the CEO of the renamed Church of England. This move did not work out well for either him or his kingdom.

Following the founder's death, a total of three family members sat upon Henry's throne—two daughters and one son—not all at once, of course. As appears so often within "blended families," the resulting progeny grew up within conflicting cultural surroundings. The first, Edward VI, was being raised as one of those new Protestants when, as a sickly child, he died shortly after his crowning as king. Mary Tudor succeeded him, and being much older than he had been, and having been raised in the Catholic Church, she proceeded to kill off those dreadful Protestants who had influenced Henry and Edward. For this, she rightly earned the sobriquet "Bloody Mary."

The second daughter to become queen, of course, was the heroine of our story here—Elizabeth Tudor. She, also, had been raised a Protestant—and had in fact only narrowly escaped her older half-sister's bloody rages. So, as a precocious child grown into a highly intelligent young woman, when she received the crown, she set out to avoid the pitfalls of the Catholic–Protestant conflict raging in her kingdom. In order to do so, she did indeed for many years sit upon a three-legged stool—metaphorically, of course, not literally. The two political factions seeking to pull her to their respective sides could be called the Traditionalists and the Reformers. One demanded that she force the Church of England to follow Roman Catholic practices—and eventually yield to the Pope. The other demanded that she follow the Puritan faction that wanted to purge her Church of everything Catholic—and even yield to England's becoming a theocratic state. What to do?

With a truly brilliant stroke of intuition, such as only very intelligent women may do, she created a third, mediating position. That position would come to be called, in the jargon of her era, *right reason*—thanks to the Church of England's only great theologian Richard Hooker. Today, we would call this sort of reason *common sense*. So she, with biting wit, simply threw out demands posed by each side when they seemed a bit silly to her—and did seem so to most of her people. Thus, in her early poem quoted above, she made the Catholic doctrine of transubstantiation seem silly—but not something to outlaw—while carefully avoiding the opposing Calvinist doctrine held by the Puritans. In short, the third leg of her three-legged stool was common sense, which she exercised with uncommon ability. Her genius was to chop up the extremes of the factions facing her, while avoiding taking biased positions that would inflame one side or the other.

One should note two basic matters here: One, the Good Queen's successors reverted to type and did take one side or the other—ultimately engaging in a horrid civil war and then reaching a peace between the factions based on a totally new concept for the world: *tolerance* of all sides that did not actually threaten the state. And two, these were not merely "religious" squabbles, for religious beliefs then underlay the manner in which government controlled the behavior of the people. Indeed, until Henry's takeover, the Roman Church in England had its own laws and courts where wrongdoers were tried, and usually convicted. So, too, with the Scottish Presbyterians whom the future King James royally hated. Eventually, in the English-speaking world, social control would move from exterior means to interior means: A culture of liberty and tolerance would grow, and that culture would create individuals who controlled themselves so that government goons would not have to. But this is getting ahead of our story.

There is, of course, a Chinese version of the rule of three governing a social order, but that is too big a subject to place in a simple prologue and will be taken up later. So, here we will stick with the Virgin Queen and her three-legged stool.

Principles we Know so Far

The Rule of Three. Dyads are inherently unstable; triads may prove the opposite.

The Rule of Mediating Institutions. The Rule of Three works when one of the three institutions functions as a mediator, a peacemaker between fighting factions. For the West, tolerance evolved into such a mediating institution. In the East, harmony filled that role.

Outer and inner space. Human discipline may get applied from either without or within. It is far cheaper and more effective to use ordered liberty than to use goon squads.

Peter deH Caldwell

Introduction

1979

An Auspicious Year

> It matters not whether the cat is black or white, as long as it catches mice.
>
> Deng Xiaoping

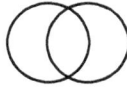

Nineteen-seventy-nine began a most auspicious period for The Peoples' Republic of China (PRC), and for other nations as well. This period has lasted roughly 40 years now. Before getting into this period's characteristics, we might first want to consider the first-order matters of change that 1979 marked. For China, the initiating event occurred in 1976 when Chairman Mao Zedong died. Mao himself had come to power in 1949 when he had forced the Nationalists under Chiang Kai-shek to flee the mainland for Taiwan. Following his death, a period of instability occurred, for in a sense a new dynasty was evolving in the age-old Chinese imperial system replacing the Mao dynasty that had only lasted some 30 years. The new emperor, Deng Xiaoping, emerged in late 1978 after a prolonged political struggle within the Party. The great change motivator: Chaos triggered by the Cultural Revolution and its aftermath. Nineteen-seventy-nine would see the beginning of truly astonishing changes within the PRC as Deng began a process of opening the Chinese economy to intercourse with the rest of the world. In a sense, Deng's policies were a rerun of the 1911 Chinese Revolution that also sought to modernize China economically, but without democracy. Opening the imperial system to some market forces without yielding Party rule—that was the essence of the thing.

Without going into any great depth here, we should recognize that Deng's "reforms" came about piecemeal rather than as a grand five-year plan in the Maoist and Soviet traditions. A Chinese form of pragmatism became the order of the time: "It matters not whether the cat is black or white, as long as it catches mice." The whole thing began innocuously enough with the order of three Boeing 747s. In 1979, reacting to the abuses of the Maoist Cultural Revolution, Deng's government began recreating the legal system that the Red Guards had destroyed, thereby providing some protections for the people against the abuses of single-party government. Some protections for foreign patent holders got legislated. A degree of religious freedom appeared. Mildish criticism of Chairman Mao became acceptable. In what would become a long-term big deal for China, the government commenced paying government officials and students alike for their costs of acquiring western education.

Along with Western education would come some engineering knowledge of how to make things. The Chinese government desired to export consumer goods to the West, capitalizing on its cheap labor. Doing this would require more and more Western know-how—technology. This stricture created intense unease amongst Party leaders, for Western companies wanted to sell China their own products, while the Party wanted the companies' know-how. What should be the price of know-how acquisitions? The Chinese have very long memories; those related to onerous treaty terms extracted by the West in the 19th century still haunted Chinese memories. The groundwork thus got laid for current conflicts, East versus West. Toward the end of 40 astounding years (1979–2019), reacting to perceived threats from the West, the Chinese imperial system reasserted its authority over Deng-based pragmatism: Xi Jinping declared himself ruler for life, casting aside any Western-derived democratic fig leaves.

Also in that auspicious year, 1979, rumblings in the United States political order began, like the first shock tremors preceding an earthquake: Ronald Reagan would initiate his pursuit of the American presidency. The triggering events: The two Arab oil embargoes. Winning election in 1980, Mr. Reagan, too, began an evolutionary change process, in his case aimed at restoring American financial health and killing runaway inflation, tax-cutting to stimulate economic growth, and legislating limitations to another runaway government effort—the welfare state. The advance of the liberal welfare state slowed for a time. By the mid-1980s, American wealth and prosperity had created companies eager to make money doing business in China, and consumers eager to buy cheap Chinese consumer goods—thanks in part to the strong Reagan-era dollar. Forty years on now, the incomplete Reagan Revolution has a new leader determined to pursue to logical ends the conservative principles that Mr. Reagan had first boldly advanced back in 1976—the year that Mao died. Donald Trump's American conservatism now runs up against Xi's authoritarian strictures. The great wheel of international relations has come a full turn. And the liberal Western push for a globalized economy and society has returned to competition amongst nation-states, great and small. At least for now

Continuing on, in 1979 the "sick man of Europe" started to show signs of new life: Margaret Thatcher became Prime Minister of Great Britain. The triggering events: severe labor unrest and its resulting economic, social and political chaos. The "shopkeeper's daughter" saw things in the light of 19th-century English liberalism, with its emphases upon laissez-faire economics, free trade, and individualism. In Thatcher's neoliberalism, that translated into privatizing large and inefficient British public corporations, neutering unions, and encouraging wealth creation and discouraging government meddling. Mr. Reagan and Mrs. Thatcher became best friends.

Our next 1979 event meriting mention occurred in the Middle East although, once more, the opening actions happened in late 1978. In this case, two nation-state enemies actually became friends! The Israelis had been facing an Arab-sourced existential threat ever since their country's formation in 1948. They earnestly desired an agreement that would split off one of their surrounding enemies, so that, in the likelihood of another war, they would no longer be surrounded by attackers. Egypt, meanwhile, very much wanted territory back, specifically the Sinai Peninsula. Some pretty formidable barriers to Israeli–Egyptian peace presented themselves, however; perhaps the stumbling block being the Israeli pioneer settlements in the Sinai. An agreement appeared hopeless: once more, two conflicting sides that promised only continuing low-level conflicts, or a winner-take-all defeat for one side. Then, quite unexpectedly, the American President Jimmy Carter inserted himself between the two angry parties—inviting both of their leaders to meet at the American Camp David presidential retreat (at the suggestion of Mr. Carter's very intuitive wife, Rosalind, one must add). Seemingly against all odds, the strategy worked! Egypt and Israel made peace. The Middle Eastern world turned upside down.

The other major Middle Eastern event of 1979, of course, was the revolutionary overthrow of the Shah of Iran, replacing that country's modernizing government with a radical Islamic theocracy. That event, along with America's refusal to give succor to the Shah's regime, gave birth to a great threat to world stability in our present time.

A major lesson from these five occurrences has sadly attracted little notice: In all cases, the situation involved conflicting and competing dual entities. Four of these may be described as domestic old regime/new regime in nature: China, United States, Britain and Iran. The first two unwittingly laid the groundwork for a two-state future conflict that we now see as existential in nature. The fourth event involved cultural/religious regional conflict and triadic entities. Crudely stated, four events were win-lose; the fifth event, involving Israel and Egypt was win-win—thanks be to the dedication of the Carters. This is because dyadic relations possess an inherent instability. Triadic relations where one element of the three behaves as a peacemaker possess inherent stability. Like a three-legged stool. Three cheers for all three-legged stools! In what follows, we will call this principle of the Three-Legged Stool or the Rule of Three. Both terms mean the same thing.

Immersed in a Great Sea of Change

Forty years later, look backing upon auspicious 1979, how might we evaluate the present, and how might we regard the future? This becomes a major task of our book. For that matter, what might we say about the extraordinary changes effected by such dynamic small countries as Singapore and Israel? China's changes since 1979, of course, cannot be evaluated in a vacuum. These changes have a direct relationship to actions and reactions taken by the West—particularly the United States. After all, the American President Richard Nixon in a sense began the modernization trend in China way back in 1972 when his actions began the process of opening China to the Western world for a second time.

I should like for a moment to look at all of these matters from my own personal perspective. I do not do so as an egotistic exercise. I have actually *lived* this 40-year period—as an American corporate executive and venture capitalist, international business consultant, and Chinese and American university professor. Many have paddled about on the surface of this great sea-change time; I have *swum* about, immersed in it.

My Western friends always say, "Charles, you are so Chinese!" My Chinese friends always say, "Charles, you have become so American!" I am both; I contain two worlds within me. Born in Chiang Kai-shek's Republic of China just before World War II, fleeing mainland China for Taiwan with my family just after the Communist takeover, raised and educated in Taiwan, earning a PhD in America and subsequently becoming a United States citizen, returning to China and Singapore to teach—I am so thoroughly both East and West that I cannot separate the two; most of the time, I do not know which I am. Oil and water sometimes do mix.

My writing brother in this endeavor is also a PhD. We like to tell people that we are actually brothers—just not twins! He is the progeny of New England Puritans, but we are still best friends. He knows America very well. I know China very well and am still learning about America. We learn together! So you see, under the skin we are brothers.

As I see it, the 40-year period that I wish to converse with you about conveniently breaks down into two 20-year parts. The first period Westerners might call the *Wild West*. For American entrepreneurs and businessmen, China seemed like a new frontier—and one to be conquered just as the American West was in the 19th century. The second period might be termed the *New Dueling States Period*—a term possessing great meaning for the Chinese, as we shall see. We currently still live in this second period—and will continue to do so for quite some time. One should recognize that these periods and their natures did not arise out of planning so much as they evolved over time—without hard beginnings or endings.

I certainly could not have predicted when I wrote my first book, published in 2003, that we had already entered into this second emerging new era in Chinese-American relations—the New Dueling States Period. I have now lived in this second brave new world for nearly 20 years, and I am just beginning to see what it is all about—a frightening new world for China and America that has reared up its ugly head. It involves a new form of competition, no longer between cowboy and dragon *businesses*, but competition between the Chinese and American *nations* for dominance. How will this all play out?

Hindsight is not a great thing—unless you possess both the knowledge and the wisdom to make sense of it for the present and the future.

This raises a very interesting question: Using hindsight as a tool, can we identify certain basic principles from the past that will help us comprehend better our current circumstances, and even project how things may evolve in the future? We believe that we can use hindsight in this manner—to discover from the past those principles that will bring understanding to our present circumstances, and in turn yield likely outcomes for the future.

In hindsight, I had some intuitive sense for living within the new Wild West when I wrote my first book, *Cowboys and Dragons*, for that title in retrospect seems most appropriate for that time. Following the "opening up of China", the Americans really did begin behaving like Wild West cowboys. They figured that American know-how and aggressiveness would conquer the new frontier named China. That the Chinese would behave like offspring of the old Imperial Dragon would also prove to be the case—but in a more subtle manner than the Cowboys who always wear their hearts on their sleeves. The Imperial Dragon could be very dangerous, but also defensive in nature. Some sense of his nature can be gathered from old Western images of the dragon's lair or cave where the dragon lay hidden, but was very dangerous when approached. So, the Americans figured that all they had to do to win Chinese business would be to make a power presentation of a rational business proposal. Little did they understand that American-style marketing presentations would come off as overbearing and offensive to their Chinese counterparts. The Americans also did not understand that Dragon sensibilities focused upon trust far more than immediate profits.

Being both Chinese and American, I could understand more quickly why it was that so many American firms found it very difficult, or even impossible, to deal with the Chinese. This is why, in the 1990s, I found myself drawn toward international consulting, largely on behalf of American firms seeking to do business deals in China. A short story should give you a living sense for the Cowboy–Dragon dynamic of the time.

A Short Story Dealing with Long Memories

The year? 1992. A U.S.-based international telecommunications venture called the San Francisco Moscow Corporation (SFMC) with Soros Group funding had approached me about help in forming a joint venture in China. FSMC was the world's first international cellular communications firm.

The American firm's executives saw this as the best way to penetrate the Chinese telecommunications market that was at the time woefully behind the Western world. To the Americans, this seemed like a natural "fit"—where the Americans would supply the technology and capital and a Chinese organization would "open up" a market segment. The specific technology involved satellite communications. We would eventually form a company called Shanghai VSAT to serve Chinese entities, but that is getting ahead of the story.

In the early market research phase, we had identified Chinese media industries as one of the target segments. So, I arranged a meeting with the Chinese *People's Daily*—the official state newspaper and the most authoritative outlet in China then and up till today. The meeting as arranged would, among others, include the SFMC President, Ray Marks, and, surprisingly, the Secretary-General of the *People's Daily*, Mr. Ma. I say surprisingly, because Mr. Ma was the Communist Party's overseer of its newspaper—a political, not an operational official. For Western minds to grasp this, look to the American movie *Hunt for Red October* and you will see the importance of a political commissar within an operating unit—in that case a submarine. It would become very clear very quickly that Marks and Ma would be the chief, if not the only, active participants in the meeting. The Americans had brought along technical people to bolster the power presentation that they intended to make. The Chinese presented an entourage of officials meant to give weight to their side and bargaining position.

Both sides in the meeting asked early on that I translate for them—and in effect become their interpreter communicating what the other side meant. This was highly unusual for the Chinese who would normally find such an arrangement very suspect. But, as I have already told you, I am both very Chinese and very American. The meeting, being in China, involved a luxurious meal first—Chinese food of course. (Western hosts would offer their Chinese guests a choice of cuisine; Chinese hosts always offer Chinese cuisine. After all, it is the best.)

Once requisite pleasantries had been exchanged, we began to consider how to move forward in establishing a joint venture. The Americans took the lead and advanced a proposal for a joint venture, made in the American form of a power presentation that involved several team members. Chairman Ma said, "No." The American team was taken quite aback, held a quick discussion amongst themselves, and then Ray Marks made another proposal aimed at doing what the Americans would call "sweetening the pie." Chairman Ma said, "No." This became like a programming "do-loop"—American suggestion, Chinese refusal.

The Chinese have great patience in negotiations; the Americans have little. After going through the proposal do-loop a number of times (how many I cannot say; I lost track of them all), the American leader finally lost patience and blurted out in a frustrated tone of voice, "Why is it so difficult to do business in China?" Now, up until this moment, Chairman Ma had worn the face of the Chinese Panda—listening carefully, smiling beneficently. The Americans, of course, were behaving like Cowboys, trying to herd the Chinese into the joint venture corral they had constructed before the actual meeting. Now, their faces had come to project what they felt—great frustration at the Chinese refusal to be roped in. In a sense, the two parties had unwittingly created a powerful, dramatic scene.

The drama erupted when Chairman Ma dropped his Panda face and suddenly became the Dragon before his lair: In a manner very stern but with a straight face he spoke angrily, as I recall it: "I will tell you why! You Westerners have been stealing from us for two hundred years! You forced your way into our empire when we were weak. We were peace-loving; we had many fine things that you Westerners lacked. And what did you have to trade with us in order to "do business"? Opium, to destroy the Chinese people, brought in by the East India Company. And when we resisted, you used military force to defeat the Qing Dynasty. You then forced us to sign unequal treaties with you. When we tried to resist, you demanded huge capital compensation. This became the beginning of China's demise that launched the Peoples' Revolution and brought about the establishment of modern China in 1911. We then endured decades of civil war in which Chairman Mao's revolutionary forces finally conquered those of the Western puppet Chiang Kai-shek. This ended with Mao winning and forming the Peoples' Republic of China in 1949!"

"Because we had been so badly hurt by foreigners, especially from the West, Chairman Mao closed our doors to these foreigners and severed interactions with you so that China could rebuild and once more become self-reliant. So, for the past 50 years, we have not had much experience in dealing with you, other than for limited contacts with our Chinese diaspora since Chairman Deng reopened the door to usher in the current policy of 'Market Economy with Chinese Communist Character' in 1979!"

At this point, the American Mr. Marks interjected: "But that was all history! I am an American businessman who is sincere in coming to China to establish mutually advantageous relationships. I understand that to you and to the Chinese I am a foreigner. However, I humbly desire to learn. But every time I make an offer, you reject it." Chairman Ma replied: "After all these years of what you call history, we Chinese do not have any experience negotiating with foreigners. How can we know that you are not just taking advantage of us again?" Marks replied something like: "So, you are just waiting for us to give up, pack up and leave China for good!" Chairman Ma replied, "No. How can we know that we are getting the best deal from you? We keep saying 'no' until you get angry and threaten to leave. Then we know that we have gotten your best offer. Then we can consider doing business."

The West, and particularly America, engages in give-and-take bargaining: I give a little here; you give a little there. Eventually we reach an agreed-upon compromise—a "win–win" that both sides can feel comfortable with. The Chinese do not do "win–win"; they do "no giving in" unless forced to—a legacy from past dealings. Also, while the Americans value peace, the Chinese see unremitting conflicts as perfectly normal—attack–defend, *yin* and *yang*. Very significantly, the business behaviors of the Chinese, as symbolized by my Chairman Ma story, have now become nationalized.

The Chinese have very long memories; the Americans think history is bunk. The Dragons clearly have very different approaches to negotiating from those of the West. It is like how auctions are run: Americans participate in auctions where the auctioneer accepts the *smallest* offer that anyone will make, and then encourages bidding up from that offer. But in a Dutch auction system, the auctioneer begins by asking a high price, and then progressively lowers the asking price until some taker raises his or her hand. The asking price, of course, cannot go lower than the seller's reserve price. The Chinese, in effect, operate a Dutch negotiation strategy. Dragons always wait for the Westerners to make an offer; they can then always keep saying "no" until the Westerner threatens to walk away. Then, the Dragon knows that he has driven the offer down to the Cowboy reserve price.

The American President Harry Truman famously once said that "history is bunk." A counter to this classic American thinking comes from the 19th-century American philosopher Georges Santayana: "Those who do not know history's mistakes are doomed to repeat them." What, then, does the past teach about the present?

Past, Present, Future: The Six First-Order Questions of Life

Mankind cannot stand very much reality.

T. S. Eliot, *The Four Quartets*

What, where, when, who, how, and why: These are the fundamental, first-order questions of life that reasonable people should be asking about the past—in the same way that good reporters compose a news article. We can readily find answers to first the five questions. So much of human history we may now quickly access online. We can also readily find answers to these first five questions for the present time that we live in—but not for the sixth, *why*. We cannot know the answers to the same five questions for the future. Mr. Santayana's famous comment on past and future, then, has only limited value: If we do not know *why* things happened as they did in the past, how can we avoid the same mistakes today and in the future? What, where, when, who and how are easy; *why* is tricky.

The manner of proceeding in this book will be to search out answers to the *why* questions from out of the what, where, when, who, and how that we do know about certain events from the past. But for which events? Because the conflicts between China and America dominate our present time, our database will be certain historical events involving East and West, although not necessarily East versus West. I say East and West here, because events in the corporate lives of people in small countries East and West such as Singapore and Israel also have value in our analysis. So, this answers part of the *which* question—which events. Not all past events are equal.

A very good guide to which events to focus upon comes from the *world turned upside down principle*, which will receive attention in our work. At any level of analysis, something earthshaking deserves special attention and a serious effort to locate the *why* of it. Why did the last Chinese dynasty fall? Why did the following Republic of China fail? Why did the American Revolution succeed? Why did British common law become the basis for the rule of law in the new American Republic? Why is it that most revolutions revolve back to the same state that existed before them? Why does China appear to be heading toward another very authoritarian dynasty?

The *why* question involves the *discovery principle*. If you only need to know *what* happened in the past, you deal with a simple bind: if I do not know the *what* of something that I know is known, I can find the answers, or hire someone to do that for me. For instance, if I know from my study of China in the 19th century that the Boxer Rebellion had great importance, I can study about the Boxer Rebellion; much has been written about it by experts. But what if I do not know that I do not know something, something from the past that matters for past, present and the future? There may be some unknown cause behind the Rebellion, but I do not know if there is something that I should know. Now, I am faced with a double bind.

A double bind cannot be broken strictly by one's power of rational thinking; it can only be broken through discovery—which is an intuitive undertaking. I put all the knowns on a table in my mind's eye, and then perhaps something appears that I have never seen before—a pattern, a discovery. I check this new factor out against the factors I know, and yes!, it fits, and it is so profound that it assumes a high place in the hierarchy of ideas within my own mind—the *space principle*: You can choose to explore outer space, the world around you, and you can explore inner space, the world that you have been creating within you. You need both. However, most of us do not want to explore inner space, perhaps for fear of what we may find there. "Mankind cannot stand very much reality." I do not know what I do not know; once I do know, I will never unknow.

Power, Know-how, and Love

We all live with memories of the past, fears for the present, and hopes for the future: a triad of complex emotions. The halcyon days of the 1990s have passed us by. For the Cowboys, they were a heady time of conquering new frontiers. For the Dragons, they were a time of recovering long-lost honor and prosperity and for seeking equality with the West. But we are deeply into the second 20-year period following that most auspicious of times: 1979. The focus has been shifting for quite a while now from a business rivalry to a geopolitical one. Prosperity has only led to a renewal of international conflict. Mankind cannot stand very much reality. Why has this happened? It seems to me that the world, both East and West, has gained in two factors since 1979—and lost in a very important third. The three great factors that should lead to worldwide happiness are: know-how, power, and love. We have the first two in abundance: stunning new technologies within energy, bioengineering, and information. We have great cultural, social/political, military, and economic power. There is one thing we lack: love, or what the Chinese call *harmony*. Our basic human building blocks for maximizing harmony have failed us. Why have they failed to deliver peace?

As you may have noted in the Prologue, there is a basic principle that lies out in the open for us to follow, yet we do not see it; *it is hiding out in the open*. It is called the *Rule of Three*. We shall be exploring history—past, present and prophetic—throughout the rest of this book, using a number of basic principles, but above all, following the Rule of Three and something related to it that we shall term the *Third Way*.

Third Way

How shall mankind finally achieve some general level of peace and harmony, a condition that would place us upon an upward-leading pathway to something we might well call *joy?* Recently, Western culture has evolved from kinship sovereignty toward radical individualism; Eastern culture (including the old USSR) has evolved from radical equality toward radical authoritarianism. Might there be a third way?

In this book, we make the argument that a third way does exist, something between two radical extremes. The Third Way that we identify and espouse involves hierarchies of communities as the essential building blocks for harmonious living—rather than the individualism of the Western liberal tradition or the authoritarian tendency of socialistic/communistic enterprises. We see the principle of the Rule of Three (or, more colloquially, the Three-Legged Stool) as the multifaceted and multilevel bridge between otherwise conflicting human organizations. The Three-Legged Stool becomes the ultimate peacemaking weapon. In making the fundamental argument to follow, we add one more basic principle at the outset: It is far easier to build a bridge than to rebuild a country. At the extreme, a one-world government would require ruthless command and control forces to construct—if such a global monster could ever be built at all. Much easier by far to build bridges, from each community to every other community. Then, human communities may evolve out of crude, gut-level passions, to self-interest, to common interest. The goal? To reach the high and joyous plateau of common love.

As a simple visual symbol for what we will propose late on in our book, we have adopted an overlapping, two-circle Venn diagram, where the circles stand for any two communities—each with its own institutions and culture. The overlapping area is the physical and virtual space where the two communities meet to foster good relations and harmony. The overlap is *mediating space*—the third leg of the Three-Legged Stool. So, you will see the symbol of our enterprise throughout this book, as a gentle reminder of that we are about.

Why Have We Three Met?

One last thing; one more important question: Do you, the reader, meet us here on this page by chance, or by design? If you say "by design" then go to the head of the class, and keep reading.

***

PRINCIPLES:

Long Memories: Sometimes events that occurred hundreds, or even thousands, of years ago remain hidden in inner space where they may still cause disharmony today.

World Turned Upside Down Events: These events do occur, and they can be opportunities for reversing conflict and creating harmony.

Space Principle: Do not only explore outer space; explore inner space as well. Solutions to our outer space problems lie in inner space—within us.

Discovery Principle: You do not know what you do not know. What you need to know that you do not know lies within you. Once you do know, you cannot unknow. You have then been changed forever.

The Rule of Three: The secret to harmonious living lies in the turning of dyads into triads. The first condition is always unstable; the second may lead to harmony—the high uplands of human living.

The Rule of Why: No one can withstand more than six *whys*—just as no adult can cope with more than that many *whys* from a child. The Rule of

Why says that you should continue to ask of any situation why it is so. In doing so, you will strip away each false *why*, until you can see the truth of the matter.

The Rule of Bridges: It is far easier to build a bridge than a country.

The Rule of Love: Only common love will save us from ourselves.

Charles Lee

Part One

Anno 30,000 BC to 1,500 AD

The Deep Past: The Evolution of Human Governance and Humankind

History is little more than the register of crimes, follies, and misfortunes of mankind.

Edward Gibbon

A nation can survive its fools, and even the ambitious. But it cannot survive treason from within.

Marcus Tullius Cicero on the Roman Republic, 1st century BC

Who controls the past controls the future.

George Orwell, *1984*

The WHY of Violence and Poverty

Why has human chronicle been so replete with stories of violence and grinding poverty, rather than of peace and plenty? Why cannot species *homo sapiens*—Wise Man—form means of governance amongst members of our species so as to achieve a progress to the high plateau of joy? What constitutes the most promising form of governance, so as to make the best promise of peace and plenty? Lastly, what basic principles will best yield the full measure of joy for the world's citizens?

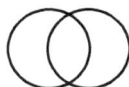

The answers to these three existential questions regarding endemic violence, governance, and the principles for peace and plenty constitute the subject matter of our book. Because we do not know the answers *a priori*, and because we do not even know that we do not know regarding critical factors behind the answers, our work necessarily involves a process of discovery. And, we might add, discovery itself constitutes a process of spontaneous evolution involving intuition far more than logical deduction. This must necessarily be the case, for the human quest for peace and plenty itself has been, and continues to be, a spontaneous evolutionary process. And we are all learners.

Our method involves the intuitive examination of the past in order to learn what principles work, and do not work, for peace and plenty to arise amongst us. So, this Part of our book details our process of discovery from out of the deep past. In doing such discovery work, we find that we run up against problems in history itself.

The Problems of History

> Time present and time past are both perhaps present in time future, and time future contained in time past. If all time is eternally present, all time is unredeemable. What might have been is an abstraction, remaining a perpetual possibility only in a world of speculation.
>
> T.S. Eliot, "Burnt Norton" *The Four Quartets*

It appears that most people regard history as a collection of *what, where*, and *when* facts—very dull facts indeed. The problem lies not with peoples' perceptions, so much as with history's definition of itself. *What, where*, and *when,* in fact, do not yield history; they yield what used to be called chronical: "In the *x*th year of the reign of our noble Emperor such-and-so, he lost his head fighting the heathen come upon him from Northern Mongolia." That sort of thing. History to be history must answer the *why* things of life. *What, where* and *when* are the easy bits; *why* is tricky.

Unfortunately, historians tend to be better at writing chronicles about the *what, where* and *when*—with an occasional *how* thrown in for good measure. *Why* what happened receives less attention and may simply regurgitate a commonly held explanation amongst historians writing in and for the same era. For instance, in the 19th-century Western world, the "great man" hypothesis held popular sway. Wellington won the battle of

Waterloo because he was a great general. This really will not do; it simply begs another *why*: Why was he such a great general? Fortunately, a simple tool helps us cut through all such silliness: Ask another *why*! Eventually, repeated *why* questions will get to the bottom of matters. No one can withstand more than six "whys." If you do not believe this principle, try answering more than six *whys* thrown at you by a three-year-old. *What* has to do with the professional historian's delight in perceiving every event as possessing uniqueness rather than belonging to a part of a pattern. Why should this be so?

Perhaps the quest for uniqueness merely peeks forth from humankind's desires to matter in a seemingly purposeless universe. Whatever the root cause, the quest for uniqueness blinds us to patterns existing in the historical record, patterns that often take the form of stories. What if we studied a number of similar events occurring over time, for instance the rise of different types of nations? Might a pattern emerge from such a study? We have all often seen this in the stories that our own families and friends live out. There are just a few of such stories, such as: "So-and-so slept with what's-his-name's wife, and what's-his-name killed him." Happens all the time—a pattern of existence. We simply live these few stories out over and over again—and will continue do so until the "last syllable of recorded time," as the Bard has Macbeth speak. So it is, too, with larger groupings of individuals—tribes, empires, and nations. Examine the *why* behind the constantly recurring stories, and you will approach the truth of a matter—a process of discovery. There are just a few stories, and they replay themselves, over and over, like a bad dream.

Historians tend to learn only the historian's craft, and so deprive themselves of helpful models from, for instance, economics or cultural anthropology, political economy, or property rights law. This situation is like teachers only learning how to teach and remaining largely ignorant of their subject matter. With all of this in mind, we take up our focus upon the evolution of human governance, and humankind as well—both East and West, particularly China and America. What might the few basic stories of human and corporate lives repeated over and over again tell us about why certain outcomes occurred—indeed why they happened over and over again, why they will happen again in our own time, and why they will happen again in the future.

In this part of our book, we explore three broad categories based within the ancient past related to how our species, *homo sapiens*, came to govern and be governed—specifically, the factors exterior to government (hardware), interior to each member of a *polis* (software), and finally the first two as mediated by the many applications of the Rule of Three to human life in community (the Three-Legged Stools of a social order).

Our look at the stories of nations' evolutions shall begin in antiquity and end in roughly 33 AD for this first Part of our book. We shall examine closely ancient China, ancient Israel, the Greek city-states, and the Roman Republic. In each case, we have discovered that just a single story, or myth, dominates all others: "A nation can survive its fools, and even the ambitious, but it cannot survive treason from within."

Chapter One

The Evolutionary Forms of Human Governance

OVERVIEW: The three basic forms of human organization evolved spontaneously, from the earlier and more primitive (and more violence-prone) to the larger and more complex: from tribe to empire to nation. Critical technological innovations—*hardware* effects, if you like—chiefly lie behind this evolution, especially the first Agricultural Revolution. Centrifugal forces continually threaten the centripetal for all larger social arrangements. The three critical areas: *spontaneous organizational evolution, the Agricultural Revolution,* and *the nation-state's emergence.*

Introduction

The Great Delusion

> More human beings had been killed or allowed to die by human decisions than ever before in human history.
>
> Eric Hobsbawm

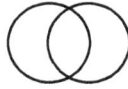

The Great Delusion states that the 20th century was the most violent in world history, murdering a record number of people through war, starvation, and related plagues. The Delusion still holds in the popular mindset of most Westerners, and probably most Easterners as well. But is it true? In terms of simple numbers, yes. Something like 120 million 20th-century deaths may be attributed to organized war and genocide—far exceeding other periods. Nevertheless, some recent scholarship has examined the claim in a different light. The revised look at the matter begins with this observation: Of course, 20th-century violence in absolute terms exceeded all other periods. The human population had grown far larger than in previous periods. But what happens when rates of such violence get examined *relative* to population size rather than in *absolute* numbers? The result according to the new quantitative analysis offered by Stephen Pinker of Harvard: Early human history was far more bloody than the 20th century in relative terms, where *relative* refers to overall population size. We submit that Dr. Pinker's book—*The Better Angels of Our Nature: Why Violence Has Declined*—overwhelmingly makes the case for the hypothesis that violence has indeed declined since human prehistory and early recorded history.

We find ourselves, however, in disagreement with the good Dr. Pinker over the critical matter of *why* the noteworthy decline occurred, and also what may be done to deter future organized violence. His explanation for the decline adds up to something of a Whig history in our opinion—a story linking the decline to the emergence of his own, Western liberal beliefs. We believe that the decline has occurred due to a much more complex set of evolutionary and revolutionary occurrences that began, not some 500 years ago but more like 5,000 to 10,000 years ago—or more. We also believe that a serious look at humankind's violent past has been derailed over the past 300 or so years by the propensity of philosophers and polemicists to create and sustain the myth of the noble savage—a myth that in modern times has been promoted by such figures as Jean Jacques Rousseau in his *Confessions*. Most recently, in 2018, Yuval Noah Harari wrote a book entitled *Sapiens: A Brief History of Humankind* which argues that life was just grand in the hunter-gatherer Neolithic world, with all humankind resting under palm trees munching vegetables and chatting up one another, but subsequently declined precipitously with the advent of agriculture-based cultures. This is simply the recycled noble savage meme that fails a simple test: With little exception, historical anthropologists have found no persuasive examples where the noble savage myth holds.

In reality, the Noble Savage was indeed savage, but not noble. Putting to rest the noble savage, we should like to discover the real causes for the decline in violence, as a prelude to discovering what might prevent a rise in future violence. Ultimately, we ask: *Can humankind reach a high plateau of human happiness and joy? Does such a pathway to it exist?*

The Human Story—A Neglected Look into the Past

Human intercourse determines history, yet apparently by a common consensus, stories about human interactions do not constitute legitimate sources for our knowledge about the past. Rather, they receive treatment, if at all, as myths that operate at a psychological level or as legends dismissed out of hand as fanciful. Stories may embroider real history, but they do not reveal it, say the historians. We should like to redeem storytelling, making stories a valuable way to see into why the past unfolded as it did.

Two initial observations about the human story: One, there are relatively few story plots, although there may be many unusual details within individual tales. There are only a few stories: of sexual attraction, theft, and murder; of desires for peace, harmony and joy; of heroic action, sacrifice, and conquest. The same few stories simply get repeated over and over again throughout thousands of years of recorded history: Jeff Bezos today and Anthony and Cleopatra around 40 BC. Different times; same storyline. Doubtless these same few stories occurred many years before any of them got recorded. Regard the Greek poet Homer in this light: His grand epic got passed down orally by bards for 300-some years before being recorded in a formal written form. Two, stories do not get determined by culture—that over-determining current categorical fascination that modern thinkers think determines everything and itself gets determined by nothing. As a cautionary matter, we must remember that a hypothesis that explains everything explains nothing. Culture does not determine storylines; stories partly determine culture. Story and culture feed incestuously upon each other. Regard the present-day *National Enquirer*.

Another principle emerges from the just-mentioned one—that stories do not get culturally determined: The same stories occur in all societies and cultures. This principle holds because all human beings have fundamentally the same makeup. We are all fundamentally emotion-driven beings capable upon occasions of both rational thought and of extremely cruel behaviors. The implication of these principles: We can be very sure that stories recorded in one time or place also occurred in other times and places. Similar evolutionary processes in human organization and history occurred pretty much in every place and time, and stories document this. There are just people. Having said this, let's have a look at a particular example.

Shui Hu Zhuan (The Water Margin) and Robin Hood

> …the noble robber begins his career of outlawry not by crime, but as the victim of injustice, or through being persecuted by the authorities for some act which they, but not the custom of his people, consider as criminal.
>
> Eric Hobsbawm, *Bandits*

There are only a few stories. The same few stories occur again and again in every nation, race, and ethnic grouping. Human nature is human nature, and a subconscious yearning for some form of cosmic justice and human harmony underlies many stories. A very popular such story running throughout much of human history is the tale of the good outlaw or the noble robber. The tale of the good outlaw works because people have very long memories of perceived wrongs committed against them by ruling elites. The stories live on, sometimes through many generations, as kernels of truth. The tale of the noble outlaw satisfies innate desires for revenge or retributive justice. Take, for instance, the tales told within one of the four great ancient Chinese literary works, *The Water Margin*, also translated as *The Outlaws of the Marsh*. While frequently termed a novel, *The Water Margin* has more of the nature of a collection of popular folk legends pieced together by a far-fetched plotline and conveyed in vernacular rather than classical Chinese—the *what* of the matter.

What happens in *The Water Margin* begins with the collapse of the Qin Dynasty, perhaps the world's first nation-state, in 220 BC. In the ensuing chaos, a great Taoist sage secures under a stone monument 108 demons or spirits of destiny who had been set loose upon the earth. According to Taoist beliefs, each person has a spirit of destiny. These spirits have a relation to the overarching ancient belief in the Mandate of Heaven, wherein unworthy rulers are to be overthrown. The 108 demonic overlords remain in captivity under the stone until another, much later, period of crisis for the Chinese nation-state—the later Song period in the 1120s, some 1,300 years after the initial event. A long time indeed. We learn that the 108 demons—36 heavenly spirits and 72 earth fiends—have been sent to earth on a divine mission. When an arrogant Song court official orders the stone monument to be opened, the demons become reincarnated as bandits who will seek to right the wrongs committed by a corrupt dynastic rule. The *when* of the matter.

The leader of the reincarnated bandits, Song Jiang, had been a god but was sent to earth by the Emperor of Heaven as punishment for some lingering demonic tendencies. He is now expected to enforce Tao, or the right pathway on earth—first by becoming the leader of an outlaw band to ensure that justice and loyalty will prevail over a corrupt government, and then to become the imperial subject acting to help the common people by bringing peace on earth. All very convoluted.

The entire work received the name *The Water Margin* because Song Jiang and his band of brothers, and several sisters, retreat for safety into the Liangshan Mountain, in turn protected from government forces by a huge, watery marsh. The *where* of the matter. From there, they come out to execute depredations upon evil government officials—and also to engage in riotous and frequently bawdy behaviors. The *how* of the matter.

Eventually, the 108 bandits are restored to lawful positions when evil government officials fall and the bandits' actions become seen to fulfill the Chinese philosophical principles of Ren and Xiao (benevolence and filial piety). Now we can enter more deeply into the core of the matter—the *why* if you will. The roots for the good bandit tradition go back to the pre-Qin nation-state time—the Spring and Autumn period (770–476 BC)—when some men, and women, began placing small group relationships along with personal codes of conduct ahead of the existing state laws. So, the outlaw state of affairs comes to be seen as an answer to the question "what do honorable men do?" when the moral order of the universe comes under dark threat. In the vernacular of ancient times, such men become *hoo han*—literally the *good guys*. The good guys challenge the evil that has overtaken a moral nation-state and thereby help restore a moral order. As such, the hoo han bands constitute a centripetal force maintaining a nation-state by rebalancing the civil authority's relation to the people—a *safety valve*, if you will.

How universal is the story? Well, Westerners find *The Water Margin* reminiscent of England's Robin Hood tales. Robin Hood, too, lived as an outlaw—in this case in Sherwood Forest, the dry land equivalent of the Liangshan Mountain marshes—and robbed the rich to help the poor. The earliest records of such a man and his band of brothers date to the 14th century and may reference events from two centuries earlier. That makes the time period contemporary with *The Water Margin* events. The legends surrounding Robin Hood set the scene in some period of great unrest within the English kingdom—such as the time in which the rightful King

Richard I the Lion-Heart had gone on crusade. Every such tale must of course have a villain, and in the Robin Hood sagas, that villain appears as the Sheriff of Nottingham.

Another, less well-known bandit-hero appears in the historically factual tales told around Hereward the Wake (1035–1072), an Anglo-Saxon lord fighting to resist the Norman French conquerors of England. In a fascinating parallel to *The Water Margin* tales, Hereward located his base of operations for his band of resistors in the fens area of East Anglia—in other words, in a large marsh. The fenlands also served as a base for rebellious outlaws during the chaotic competing reigns of King Stephen and Queen Maude during the first English Civil War in 1135–1153 AD. The English parallels to *The Water Margin* tales do really grow.

One of the aspects of *The Water Margin* that intrigued and frustrated so many readers over many centuries involves the complex and convoluted story line. Looking at the whole thing from 30 thousand feet up rather than from the ground, one can unwrap the tale into three separate *root* or *Ur* stories—where *Ur* is derived from the German meaning *earliest* or *most primitive*. In addition to the bandit-hero *Ur* story, *The Water Margin* contains the *Ur* story of a figure or figures from the deep past re-emerging to come to the aid of a country in current crisis.[1] It also bundles into the main plotline the *Ur* story of the redemption of the outlaw. In all, the convoluted story lines contain the shadowy history of human organizations far more primitive than the nation-state or empire: the *Ur* stories that facilitate the evolution of human arrangements that eventually led first to the empire and then to the nation-state. Centrifugal

[1]In a curious little story entitled "The Grey Champion" published in *Twice-Told Tales* (1837), the American author Nathaniel Hawthorne tells a tale of an aged Puritan who appears seemingly from nowhere to confront the tyrannical Governor-General of New England, Sir Edmund Andros, and his army who march through old Boston in a show of force meant to quell a brewing revolution. The year is 1688. The Grey Champion cries out, "Stand!" The British halt. Then he speaks to Andros, "I am here, Sir Governor, because the cry of an oppressed people hath disturbed me in my secret place." He then informs Andros that King James II has abdicated, cutting the legs out from under Andros' actions. The aged Puritan then simply disappears. The news of the king's abdication comes by ship the very next day. Who was this patriarch inspiring such fear? One of the regicides who joined the judicial execution of King Charles 40 years earlier—and then fled to New England? Perhaps. How did he know about James II ahead of the ship's news the following day? We do not know.

forces from warring tribes and outlaws aiming to tear a structure apart become converted into centripetal forces pulling the structure more tightly together under the human desires for justice and for peace. All three *Ur* stories have simple plot lines; combining all three creates the delightful complexities of *The Water Margin*. So, beneath its surface simplicity lies deep meaning from the distant past.

With regard to the redemption *Ur* story, within Germanic tribes a most curious institution evolved called *Wergild*, from the Old English for *man payment*. Under *Wergild*, a man might make a money payment for a crime—up to and including murder—and then be regarded as having redeemed, or atoned for, his bad behavior. Tribes or clans making depredations upon others might similarly be forced to make restitution in some form. Redemption/atonement stories abound in ancient literature.

To capture the full sense of what *The Water Margin* conveys, one must develop a sense of how shadows of *Ur* beginnings appear below its surface meaning. To use a modern medical analogue, consider what appears on the MRI brain images for patients who have suffered strokes. Very often, the images not only show the areas of the brain affected by the present stroke, but also something like shadows of previous very minor stroke-like episodes. An apparently simple picture holds complex history leading up to a cataclysmic event. *The Water Margin* serves as a microscopic view into the deep past.

So, too, stories from the deep past underly much of what presently goes on between West and East—between the Cowboys and the Dragons. As we suggested in the Introduction, contemporary conflicts originate in the deep past.

"Home on the Range"—American Cowboys

Modern American international entrepreneurs can be called the *cowboys*—largely due to their actively seeking out new frontiers and new cattle, and profits, to herd back home. They are boastful, high-spirited, adventurous and determined to make a deal. Americans believe that the cowboy is a peculiarly American invention, but in this they are very wrong. The American cowboy actually began arriving in America when England owned the 13 colonies. Immigrants from Scotland and Northern Britain brought cattle herding and rustling traditions with them when their mass migration began in 1715.[2] The matter of cattle rustling—stealing a neighboring clan's cattle, and women, and driving them home—has a much more ancient heritage dating back some 4,000 years at least. It could well be that cattle rustling came to the British Isles when Germanic repopulation occurred following the retreat of the last great ice age. The antiquity of cattle and sheep rustling becomes confirmed when one reads the Hebrew scriptures where the practice appears, probably dating back at least 4,500 years. The biblical shepherd is the earlier version of the cowboy.

Did the Chinese Dragon indulge in Cowboy-like behaviors as well in the deep past? Very likely. But by the time of the American Wild West, dominated by Cowboy culture imported from Scotland, China had long been a very civilized domestic culture, and so the Dragon appears defensive in Chinese–American relations—at least until very recently.

All of these stories and all of the history recounted so far have their roots in hunter–gatherer tribal and clannish organizations of the dim past. The question: Why did something so civil as the nation-state evolve from the earlier brutish and lawless dark period of human prehistory?

Spontaneous Organizational Evolution

The history of humankind has involved the formation of numerous organizational structures—band, clan, tribe, nation, empire, kingdom, republic, city-state, nation-state. This list is surely not exhaustive, but adequate here. We maintain that none of these structures resulted from some form of central planning "system" beforehand. It would be a fallacy of functionalism to maintain otherwise. Even the "new world order" organizations of the 20th century—national socialism and international communism—first developed organically, although philosophers have had a role in formulating ideas for organization. It would be equally silly

[2]Long-distance cattle herding for them had begun right after the 1707 Act of Union that joined England and Scotland. Four hundred-mile–long cattle drives of immense size soon began bringing Scottish beasts to London's protein-hungry population. So, the cowboy was an imported good, and the original American cowboys spoke with a Scottish burr.

to maintain that human organizations simply happened, without any causal forces at work. What forces might have driven the progressive evolution of forms, finally to result in the nation-state?

Zhengming or Rectification of Terms

> If names be not correct, language is not in accordance with the truth of things. If language be not in accordance with the truth of things, affairs cannot be carried on to success.
>
> Confucius, *Analects* XIII, 3, tr. Legge

If we wish to understand how the nation-state particularly came into being in a spontaneously evolutionary manner, we must first follow the sage Confucius regarding *zhengming*, or the naming of things—in this case the evolutionary way-stations on the way to the nation-state—according to the truth about them. Two overarching categories should be defined; first, nomadic versus fixed settlement groups. At some critical point in human history, some groups switched from migratory patterns of living, driven by the quest for foodstuffs each year, to geographically fixed-location groups. Second, three sorts of migratory groups appeared: In order of their numerical size, bands, clans, and tribes appeared amongst migratory groups. Bands might number as few as 6 to 12 members and formed spontaneously within clans for such purposes as hunting and raiding. Clans consisted of larger groups, perhaps something like 30 to 150 members—distinguished by a claimed common ancestry, and usually by a revered founder about whom *Ur* stories got told. Lastly, groups of clans could form into tribes. Tribes consisted of several clans joining together whose members all shared commonalities such as general ancestry, language, culture, and history. Tribes usually had single leadership, perhaps with a counsel composed of clan elders aimed at producing unifying decisions. In this taxonomy, none of these entities truly comprised a state, although some tribes might through annexation or conquest acquire additional tribes so as to constitute a nation—once more, driven by certain commonalities of ancestry, language, and culture. Nations began as accumulations of tribes, organically unstable in nature. A nation does not necessarily comprise a state; a state requires a professional administration.

Clans and tribes usually form and strengthen the spiritual and emotional bonds holding them together as centripetal forces by composing and storing heroic stories of their founders, such legends comprising one sort of the few stories that exist. In pre-literate ages, of course, such stories were saved in the memories of bards, the most famous being the blind Greek poet Homer. The ancient bards used certain techniques as assists to memory; after all, the reciting of a founding legend might take several days. The memory techniques included speaking in lines of equal syllables, rhythm within lines, and end-rhymes—in other words, legend stored as oral poetry. The correct answer to the old question as to which came first, poetry or prose, is "poetry."

Next up the evolutionary ladder come the three forms of human organization that do comprise nations: empires, feudal kingdoms and city- and nation-states. They have a permanency in fixed location and economic activity, and they can create much larger organizations than nomadic and semi-nomadic tribes can achieve. We can define a *nation* as being a "large body of people, associated with a particular territory, that is sufficiently conscious of its unity to seek or to possess a government" (from *Dictionary.com*). A *state* means "a compulsory political organization with a centralized government that maintains a monopoly on the legitimate use of force within a certain geographical territory. Some states are sovereign; some states are subject to external sovereignty or hegemony where ultimate sovereignty lies in another state" (from *Wikipedia*). Nation, then, is a more general term than state. Combining the two terms, nation and state, into one distinguishes larger units with significant hinterlands from city-states which have limited or no hinterland areas as a part of them.

In very general terms, *empires* come into being when one state conquers other states or nations and rules them by force. Empires arise from ruthless rulers willing to exercise extreme power. In the poem *Ozymandias*, the poet regards the broken, desert statue of a fallen ruler of empires. So much for an empire's ruler in the long run. *Feudal kingdoms* attempt to reduce enforcement costs of empires over a number of tribes by creating hierarchies of obligation—frequently involving family members set up to rule in subordinate states, nations and tribes. Lastly, *nation-states* differ from the more general categories of nation and state by possessing or creating the combination of cultural, economic, and political commonalities within a bounded geographical area and a monopoly on the use of force to enforce a rule of law—not of powerful men.

Why such organizations as nations, empires, feudal kingdoms, and city-states—and eventually nation-states—developed from primitive clannish and tribal relations now concerns us here.

Humankind's First Great Revolution—Agriculture

The Necessary Conditions for Nation-Building

Once upon a time, there was no such thing as the nation-state, or for that matter the nation, the empire, or the feudal kingdom. There were only hunter-gatherer tribes scratching out a bare existence with primitive tools and technology. We know this because we know the stories such tribes-people tell cultural anthropologists even today. Because it is frequently less costly to murder, rape and then steal than it is to hunt and harvest and raise livestock, hunter-gatherer life was in Hobbes' language "nasty, brutish and short."[3] Violence was endemic amongst human beings in such organizations. Then, everything changed in a matter of only a few thousand years—a miniscule period compared to all human existence up until then, or even until now. Real human progress began variously in the period from roughly the 10th century BC to the 2nd century BC with the advent of the First Agricultural Revolution.

The First Agricultural Revolution did not just suddenly appear, cut and shaped out of whole cloth. Nobody planned it. We should regard the small steps leading toward the agricultural revolution as being an ongoing spontaneous evolutionary process generating all sorts of experiments and led by that most valuable of all human resources: intuitive creativity driving experimentation. The process no doubt proceeded somewhat like this: Hunter-gatherer tribes had learned nomadic patterns of existence, led by animal migration patterns and by the seasonal geographic occurrences of naturally growing vegetable matter, most notably primitive cereal crops. Technology and tools were also primitive; the most complex technology probably involved animal husbandry and primitive efforts at selective breeding. Then some Neolithic geniuses began experimenting with artificially seeding otherwise naturally-occurring plants. A resource-rich area could be seeded, left to itself for a tribe's own seasonal wanderings and then returned to for a hopefully increased cereal grain food supply, perhaps for the winter months. Tribes then became semi-nomadic, and less dependent upon the hunt for evading starvation, and at some daring point in this process, some tribes made commitments to remaining all year long in agriculturally-rich locations—reversing the hunter-gatherer order to gatherer-hunter by making agriculture their food basis, sending hunting

---

[3] See Thomas Hobbes, *Leviathan* (1651) for his view on how and why nations develop.

bands out far afield for supplemental protein nourishment. Agricultural improvements in seeds and soil enrichment followed. None of this was planned for. These experiments changed everything. And the stories told to anthropologists confirm this pattern.

In terms of both technology and economics, settled tribes inadvertently created something totally new on the face of the earth: fixed assets. Prior to the developments leading to life fixed in one place, all things of value—assets—that a tribe or individual possessed were, quite literally, movable ones: cattle and sheep and goats and herding dogs, seasonal hunting and fishing rights held by tradition, and seasonal gathering rights. [The much later tragedy of the Native Americans came about because the advent of the Europeans pitted Neolithic seasonal hunting and harvesting rights against modern Western fixed property rights in land. Neither side really understood what property rights meant to the other.][4] When threatened by a more powerful tribe, a weaker tribe could simply run away—driving its chief forms of communal wealth ahead of it. Once people made sweat and tears, and blood, investments in the soil, everything changed. People had to stand and fight thieves—or starve later on. We know about this proto-historical experience because of the shadows of it left in the stories of a more developed time possessing the art of writing.

Fixed asset accumulation made possible by the First Agricultural Revolution was the necessary condition for all advanced human organizations. Only asset accumulation could reduce the precariousness of human existence and thereby create a surplus to fund the beginnings of civilization. Cereal crops could be accumulated and stored as insurance against starvation. The Hebrew Bible's story of Joseph and the seven years' accumulation of food against a famine period fits right into this reality. Prior to this, hunter-gatherer people could only tighten their belts and pray for game or rain. But the advent of security founded in food stocks also introduced the cruel Paradox of Prosperity: Food supply security creates greater incentives for theft by rival tribes. Efforts at security multiply insecurity. Many stories record the truth of this problem.

Nomadic, semi-nomadic, and settled tribes lived in an uneasy co-existence for several millennia. Violence did not abate, but, if anything, grew worse.

---

[4] See William Cronon, *Changes in the Land* for insights into how different definitions of property rights doomed the native Americans faced with the sudden appearance of the English.

The costs of protecting fixed assets threatened the very underpinnings of larger human organizations. Nomads and empires overlapped considerably; for that matter, nomadic tribes lived in Arabia until nearly our present time, frequently raiding vulnerable empire outposts. The finest record of such a world appears in the Hebrew Torah and histories. The Abraham story documents the eventual settling down of a semi-nomadic tribe who make their first land purchase, a fixed property right, in the form of a grave plot for a founding father. The histories also record the violent and frequently chaotic evolutionary processes leading toward feudal arrangements and empire, and eventually a new nation-state called Israel. We may date this period as running from roughly 2500–500 BC for Israel—and perhaps beginning in something like 4000 BC for other places in the fertile crescent. After the Israelite invasion of the land of Canaan in roughly 1300 BC, Hebrew documents record the history of how a loose-knit group of tribes fought other, more technically-advanced tribes and nations for possession of an already-settled place. Roughly the same experience shows up in ancient Chinese writings, along with a not dissimilar timeline, but with perhaps a heavier accretion of mythological elements.

Security Versus Theft: Defeating the Paradox of Prosperity and the Exponent of Distance

In the spring, at the time when kings go off to war....

2 *Samuel* 11:1 NIV

With hindsight, we can identify three basic institutional attempts at maximizing security whilst minimizing violence following in the train of the Agricultural Revolution: empire, feudalism, and the nation-state. By 500 or so years into that revolution, this was the typical situation: In order to guard an agricultural community's possessions, particularly foodstuffs, the construction of fortified villages became the norm. Soon, fortified villages evolved into cities, where valuable trade could occur, in addition to the provision of protective services related to trade. The peasantry around the villages could flee into the enclosures in time of threat—which became very frequent. Fortified cities, however, demanded considerable forces of armed men to keep watch over them, particularly during the night. From this period, the somewhat romanticized stories of night watchmen on towers appear—another one of the few stories. The failure of a single watchman could precede slaughter for the whole tribe or nation.

Without realizing it, the revolution in foodstuff security created the conditions for what were in effect standing armies, men with much time on their hands—food being provided them as part of wages. Partly to keep such men from capturing the fortified towns they nominally guarded, warfare against other fortified towns became normative. Creating contention outside the city to assure domestic peace became another strategy for survival, even into our present time. To keep the peasants in order, create a new international war. The line from the *Samuel* historian precisely captures the nature of things: "In the spring, at the time when kings go off to war...."[5] Kings needed war each spring in order to keep their crowns, perhaps even to keep their heads on. Warfare became the endemic situation everywhere that agriculture flourished. What to do about such a situation?

The first, and most obvious, attempts at breaking the Paradox of Prosperity involved the direct use of force: A king would use his army of idlers to conquer another walled village and then force its occupants into submission. Because an occupation force could get costly, the usual pacification strategy involved extracting a forced payment in foodstuffs, timber or other such valuables from the conquered village or city each year. The system is a venerable one, still existing today where mafia-style gangs extract "protection" money from their neighbors. Pacification might also involve demands for hostages against future bad behavior. The protection racket only worked under a credible threat of harm for failure to pay. A subject village, then, waited until the threat appeared less credible, perhaps because of another war being fought by its conqueror—and then revolted. Once again, read the Hebrew histories for sterling examples of betrayal and violence.

A threatened or conquered village might pay a stronger village to become its "white knight" and save it or free it. Of course, then the white knight might turn black and simply consume its client. Or, several weaker villages might gang up on the strong village in order to defeat it. Clearly, the simple submission-to-force model had many weaknesses and could yield huge transaction costs. Very interestingly, medieval terms such as "white knight", "poison pill", and "raider" reappeared in the form of the takeover sharks of 1980s American business buyouts. Some things never change.

---

[5] 2 *Samuel* 11.

Strategies would eventually become more complex, and they would inevitably lead to attempts to build larger-scale organizations controlling growing numbers of weaker territories. Conquered villages could then be forced to become mercenaries helping to enforce peace at spearpoint or make additional conquests for the dominant ruler. This pattern eventually became the means by which Rome grew from a small, independent republic to an immense, and eventually vulnerable, empire. Rebellion still remained a constant threat, however. A final strategic twist to this game was wholesale forced population relocation: A portion of a rebellious tribes' population—usually its elites—would be removed to another land to live subject to a people and culture foreign to them. The Hebrew histories record just such a string of events following the 586 BC conquest of Jerusalem by the Babylonian empire. As recently as the first half of the 20th century, whole ethnic populations received such treatment within the Soviet empire.

The most significant 20th-century contribution to the art of maintaining empire evolved in Soviet Russia and Maoist China: Set a part of the proletariat to watch the rest; have them snitch on their neighbors at the slightest whiff of unauthorized speech. Complain about the vodka ration, and it's off to the gulags. At its height, some 20% of the total populations in both empires watched over the other 80%. The military was particularly suspect: Military force, after all created the empires, and military force could overthrow them. The recent Western movie *Hunt for Red October* illustrates that necessary watchfulness: The Russian submarine in the movie has its own party commissar, and a snitch amongst the crew, watching the behaviors of the captain, his officers and the crew, lest they should attempt to defect to the West. That 20/80 ratio assured the economic failure of the Soviet experiment, and nearly that of Communist China.

The difficulties in making an empire work include the obvious, and the not-so-obvious: Obviously, the costs of an enforced peace worked against building up resource security and reducing the inefficiencies of violence. Less obviously, problems of scale presented themselves. Smaller empires could be beaten by larger ones. But large empires possessed a serious, though less obvious, flaw: Conquest proceeds linearly, whereas challenges to conquest grow exponentially as the square of the distance to the next conquest. Conquering armies learn this quite frequently over time. For example, during the American Civil War, the Union armies had great difficulty holding cities that they captured well inside enemy territory; the farther the army advanced, the worse guerrilla warfare became—sometimes forcing stasis, or even retreat.

As a general rule, empires have always had to strike a rough balance between plunder from territories annexed by force and the marginal additional costs of holding those territories. Centripetal versus centrifugal forces. In a famous dramatic scene from the Hebrew Bible's *Book of Daniel*, disembodied fingers mysteriously appear at the great feast given by the King of Babylon, and the fingers write: *Mene, mene, tekel, upharsin,* meaning, as interpreted by the prophet Daniel: "God has numbered the days of your kingdom and has brought it to an end; you have been weighed on the balance and found wanting; today your kingdom is divided and given to the Medes and the Persians."[6] That very night, the great city of Babylon fell to a secret attack coming from an unexpected and unguarded quarter. Exponential increases in threats at some point become realities—often at a time when an empire begins shrinking. Shrinking empires face more enemies while they themselves have fewer defenders. Consider in this regard what happened to the retreating Nazi regime in 1944.

Something clearly needed to get done to deal with the paradox and the exponential factors making empire so costly and unstable. Here early Chinese experience becomes an instructive case.

Zhou to the Rescue: The Power of Gong

> The winner becomes king; the loser becomes outlaw.
>
> Old Chinese saying regarding the Mandate of Heaven

> If there's any money to be made, for God's sake keep it in the family.
>
> An old New England saying

There are only a few stories. Sometimes a story has its reciprocal: For every story of a good outlaw, there is a story of a corrupt ruler. Both of these stories find their root source in the new wealth generated by the First Agricultural Revolution. Around 1000 BC, a new story emerged from out of the growing Zhou Dynasty (1046–256 BC): the story of the *gong* or feudal lord who places other ruling family members in under-lordship, lord to vassal, thereby facilitating loyalty whilst expanding a power

---

[6]Daniel 5:25.

base—thus founding an early feudal state. Eventually a reciprocal to the feudal state story does emerge: the usurper who challenges a family overlord. We may see the lordship story as documenting the attempts to overcome the weaknesses revealed in both ethnically homogeneous smaller states and in larger empire-states.

The first Chinese dynasty to leave a legendary shadow of itself in the written historical record has been called the Xia, spanning roughly 2000–1600 BC. [The Xia period thus spans roughly the time of the patriarchs to Moses in Near Eastern Hebrew history.] It appears that the dynasty's legendary founder Yu—somehow a deified lord of harvests who drained the waters of a great flood—possessed the power and authority to make his nation's rule hereditary, thereby establishing China's first imperial regime. Legend has it that 15 rulers within his family line followed him, before the last one made the tragic error of falling in love with a beautiful but evil woman—itself one of those few stories repeated over and again. Presumably this last ruler's reign favored his consort rather than the people, who soon revolted. A hero named Zi Lu led the revolt that, according to legend, became Tang, the first ruler of the next dynasty, the Shang Dynasty (1600–1046 BC). The Xia Dynasty's hereditary structure suggests that its likely had elements of an early state that could enforce a ruler's will by laws and a monopoly of force—until the usurper story appears in the form of Zi Lu.

We should remember here that we can only observe a few still shots in the great evolutional movie of human organizational forms. With the advent of the Shang, something like historical records of a dynasty began. That is one change. But also, elements of what would become China's great feudal period would begin emerging. The Shang historical record has nothing like the narrative detail of, for instance, the *Chronicles* of Ancient Israel (*circa* 400 BC), but the recordings in burial records suggest a dynasty of 17 generations, each ruler being known as *wang*. The ritual records related to religious beliefs in themselves represent the earliest known examples of Chinese writing, and something like an annual calendar driven by days identifying the "cult" to be offered to for whom. Ancestor worship and the propitiation of gods and powers shaped the major events of each year, fed by both animal and human sacrifice. Being a ruler at this time certainly meant success in implementing brute force against resisters, but also in enforcing a monopoly in ancestor propitiation, thereby supposedly gaining good harvests and such.

The Shang, then, was a dynasty dominated by ancestor worship and a religiously driven political reality, a leadership practicing divination, and a ruling aristocracy exercising some degree of bureaucratic control. Overall, a sense of general social obligation gave form to everyday living. The highest recognized power came in the form of the deity *Di*, or *Shangdi*—the Lord of High—controlling victory in battle, the harvest, and the weather. The ties of obligation descended downward from *Shangdi* to king to former kings to ancestors to superiors to everybody else—a condition that would become a hallmark of early Chinese society. A social evolutionary process led from kinship ties within tribes to a web of personal dependencies throughout an entire nation. Eventually, a feudal nation, small at first, began to emerge.

The ties that bound the Shang nation together, however, remained at the personal level. So, the Shang kings found it necessary to live peripatetic lives, traveling much of the time amongst the subservient tribes and states that comprised the larger national dynasty—a sure sign of an emerging feudal empire. Two factors appear to have necessitated this nearly nomadic governance: First, loyalty coming from personal relations with each tribal or state ruler needed to be enforced at the personal level in order to minimize the chances of a usurper stealthily arising. Second, the costs of the kingly retinue, and the weakness or absence of a tax collection institution, made cost sharing through traveling about necessary: Living off not the land but one's kinspeople. The great weakness of this proto-feudal nation lay in its lack of either an effective controlling bureaucracy or some means of social control over distances. One might note, parenthetically, that the same conditions pertained to medieval England, and indeed the entire European continent.

The Shang apparently experimented with a novel approach to gaining cohesion within a nation potentially riven by the two most powerful tribes: Generationally, the *wang* or ruler would rotate between those tribes. Perhaps the breakup of the Shang peoples occurred when one rotation got blocked by the tribe about to lose the next leadership. One might note that such arrangements have occurred from time to time in human history—perhaps most notably in Switzerland where the headship of a ruling council rotates annually. One should note that in the Swiss example, the head of state position does not convey individual power but rather something akin to a moderator-ship for a committee. In reality, rotating leadership offers no real gains to a nation poorly integrated internally; instead, it merely creates another opportunity for theft—in this case of kingship.

So far, we have a picture of China before the Zhou Dynasty as a number of small states and tribes, some with agricultural economies, in continually churning conflict, with outside invaders appearing spasmodically as well. The Shang state only partly reduced warfare. Harmony existed only marginally. The transition from the Shang to the Zhou Dynasty, predictably, involves the usurper story. The king of one of the subject states, Wu of the Zhou kingdom, successfully revolted in 1046 BC. The Zhou captured the Shang capital and effectively ended the dynasty. The Zhou justified their overthrow by claiming that the last Shang king had been evil and had lost the mandate to rule that descended from the *Di*, the lord of heaven.

The Zhou Dynasty lasted a very long time indeed—from 1046 BC to 221 BC. However, all was not smooth sailing. Historians break the 800-some years into three distinct periods: an initial period of internal peace as the Zhou utilized growing ties of obligation to build up a feudal kingship, then a period of inner conflict called the Spring and Autumn Period (770–476 BC) as the feudal web of relationships fragmented—partly from external threats—and a final Warring States Period (475–221 BC) when a balance-of-power evolution yielding four major states itself fell apart. Why the feudal nation created by the Zhou eventually failed shall concern us here, rather than all of the details of what happened where and when.

Geography explains something of the situation on the ground in 1046 BC and thereafter. The somewhat ramshackle Shang nation had never been able to create a contiguous set of tribes and states in order to form one land. Instead, much of the landscape was largely wild and challenging, and populated by hostile tribes, interspaced by small states under Shang control. The Shang, then, always faced the linear distance/exponential area-of-threat problem. Attempts to extend control to more distant statelets in order to minimize threats merely grew exponentially the areas where ruffians lived in an uncivilized state of nature and were only too happy to shatter a fragile peace.[7]

Within this forbidding geography, areas with agricultural advantages had formed into city-states or *guo* that included surrounding hinterlands that could be controlled by a local lord or *gong*. In each case, an alliance

---

[7]See George Macdonald Frazier's *Steel Bonnets* for a marvelous description of such a condition as it existed in the border region between England and Scotland in the 16th century.

between a local lord, the diminished Shang state, and the Zhou state could be formed. The big change came as the early Zhou kings undertook to gain control over the lawless tribes separating the major city-states by creating ties with tribal leaders through marriage or through forcing vassal status upon them. Eventually, the Zhou Dynasty exercised feudal control over a relatively contiguous area and created a large measure of internal harmony—partly through cultural assimilation. Centripetal forces were thus created to tie the feudal relations closer and closer together; inner peace and harmony made people in the various states comprising the Zhou nation desire to stay within what might be termed a league of states.

During the first 250-some years, then, the Zhou Dynasty achieved growing harmony within the nation and pushed back external threats from the northern nomads that would from time to time threaten China—nearly up until to the modern era.[8] The Zhou also extended their control southwards during the first period. At the same time, however, older parochial ties between the several city-states could work against the newer ties as a centrifugal force tending to pull areas away from the center, the dynastic ruler. The story of the rebellious or the breakaway tribe captures this reality—even to this day, as places such as Catalan on the Iberian Peninsula illustrate. The relative strengths of the opposing centripetal and centrifugal forces determined the conditions pertaining to the Zhou Dynasty from roughly 770–475 BC. This very long time period was hardly harmonious, however, and has been traditionally broken down into two eras following the initial honeymoon period.

Beginning around 770 BC and extending to 476 BC, the Zhou entered into a period of failing feudal ties and disharmony termed the Spring and Autumn Period. The feudal harmony breakdown had its beginning roughly 100 years before, driven by a rebellion amongst some of the feudal lords against a reigning Zhou king, Liwang, whom the nobles called a tyrant. Liwang's overthrow created a power vacuum as his genealogical successor was not of age. So, in the interim, the two most powerful nobles of the royal family ruled in the young man's place, making him a ward of theirs—a very common story and one having great import for early modern nations as well—in nations such as Scotland,

---

[8] The most famous nomadic tribe to threaten China, of course, was the Mongol hoard led by Genghis Khan who conquered the Song Dynasty in 1279 AD—a hundred and some years after the time of *The Water Margin*—and ruled China as the Yuan Dynasty for nearly 100 years.

that suffered through a string of child kings-to-be. Eventually, the young prince came to power. While the Zhou form of feudalism survived this time period relatively intact, an event that occurred in 771 BC led directly into the Spring and Autumn time when the royal family line was again broken. This time, the triggering event came as an outside threat rather than an inside revolt: The then-ruler Youwang died while leading an army to block a barbarian invasion. The feudal lords could not agree upon a replacement for Youwang, causing a division of the nation with two rulers at two separate courts. The feudal leadership once more coalesced around a single leader upon the death of one of the pretenders to the throne.[9] The period of leadership vacuum, however, had destroyed much of the regime's legitimacy by successive fractures of kinship ties. For the next 300-some years, a pattern of peripheral states within the Zhou confederacy loosening bonds with the parent dynasty became the norm. The breakdown of the feudal system was once more driven by barbarian threats from both the north and south that could not be met by the nominal head of state. In efforts to defend against foreign invaders, groups of small peripheral states began recognizing overlords who in effect became war leaders. They paid lip service to the central government but fought their own battles. While initially participation by border region states came voluntarily, eventually the warlords extracted support in the form of paid tribute and forced services of war chariots—much like the recent period in the Middle East.

Why did such a breakdown within overall feudal loyalty occur? It appears that the root cause was an example of what might be termed the size/balance dilemma: In every nation, territorial expansion appears an attractive way to both suppress threats from the outside and to capture more resources—all aimed at increasing regime security, a net positive. Increasing territory, however, in turn adds new threats, also from two sources. The outside threats appear as the cultural weaknesses of the newly acquired peripheral states' bonds to central authority—a centrifugal effect. The other effect arises from the very nature of feudal arrangements: Feudalism relies upon loyalty to superiors—a potential centripetal force. Such loyalty can be attained either through blood ties or through purchase, or both. Purchased loyalty has obvious weaknesses, falling into the realm of politics: The buyer of such loyalty may at any time be outbid

[9]If this sounds like the condition of the Catholic Papacy at one point in medieval time, it was.

by a rebellious overlord.[10] Within the high feudalism of Plantagenet England (1154–1485), a number of powerful families competed against one another for the prize of the overall kingship of the realm. Allegiances constantly shifted as the major players in the game sought out power positions to capture overall rule. A particularly brutal period running from 1455 to 1487 became etched in Englishmen's minds as the War of Roses. One might term such sequences of events the treachery story.

For the Chinese period encompassed by the Zhou Dynasty, another factor worked to create both centripetal and centrifugal forces: kinship. In feudal systems, kinship always had some role to play. In the Western world, the sovereign normally came from the ruling family—a political tradition of ancient lineage that hardened into the dogma of the divine right of kings to the throne by the late Middle Ages.[11] Other, powerful lordly families from time to time overthrew a weakening ruling family—always seen as a usurpation. The Western system thus allowed for a degree of freedom for enterprising challengers who might stave off an enervating stasis. In Zhou China, kinship and political rule were coterminous—both a feudal strength and a weakness. The overall rule of the nation was not, however, seen as a divine mandate for absolute family-line rule. Instead, a dogma called the Mandate of Heaven—long in developing—permitted the overthrow, by another family, of a ruler who had through some corruption of the body politic lost the right to rule.

The Zhou feudal system, at every level from nation to smallest states, evolved into a four-part social-political structure with the ruler at the peak of the pyramid. Feudal lords or *gong*, men who served as counselors and ministers in the ruler's court, fell under the overlord. Next came the *shi* (sometimes translated as *gentlemen*) who filled the roles of state functionaries and officials. The *shi* linked the lords to the last and most populous element in the social order: commoners and slaves. Eventually, the *shi* would become the class critical to developing a stable political economy and to harmonizing the entire social order—but not until after the fall of the Zhou Dynasty. The ministerial lordship class evolved into two, or even three, levels of authority and rule, so that lordship–vassal relationships grew in number and complexity.

---

[10] It used to be said during the American Gilded Age of the 1870s to 1900 that an honest politician was one who, having been bought by another politician, stayed bought.

[11] See Appendix A for a description of Anglo-Saxon England as a naturally evolving precursor to bloodline kingship.

The unraveling of the Zhou Dynasty had its root cause in the very strength of its kinship bonds. Its feudal hierarchy spread downward and outward from the king who was the eldest brother within his family to the eldest brothers of each state's ruling family within the overall nation. Even to this day, family names in China have far greater importance than individual names. Families may have millions of members at any one time—the family name Lee, in anglicized form, being one of the largest! Did the Zhou period's emphasis on feudal family relations have something to do with the tradition of emphasizing the larger family at the expense of recognizing individual relations? We likely will never know.

The ruling families then, in states below the national level, did not necessarily have the same family name as that of the overall ruler, but very often did. From each of these eldest brothers, whether close kin or not, lower level eldest brother rulers controlled smaller units of government down to the least significant. Seniority, then, ruled both family lines and political authority. All in the family. The head of each family in the feudal hierarchy also had the authority for offering sacrifice and worship to ancestors who it was believed would reciprocate with blessings and the assurance of a continued mandate from heaven to rule.

This belief system had powerful centripetal force early in the Zhou Dynasty, but as territory grew by conquest or lesser forms of persuasion, senior brotherhood ties became very distant indeed, and scarcely more than formulaic. At the same time, the peripheral states most recently acquired suffered the most from nomadic raiders. Eventually, the linear-distance/exponential-area-to-defend relation would go decidedly against the regime. Then, too, the emphasis upon seniority all throughout the hierarchy surely must have presented some very sclerotic leadership, incapable of either creative problem-solving or forceful action. Nepotism versus politics: The rule of kinship would eventually get replaced by the rule of law as a way of making politics less bloody—but that remained for later dynasties than the Zhou.

The situation on the ground after roughly 720 BC, then, saw diplomatic soft-war and armed hard-war events in the core states of the dynasty—a continual churning in which no core state could exercise sufficient power to overwhelm the others and seize overall leadership. Among the stories driving this whole period were those of usurpation, rebellion and treachery. The real drivers for change appeared amongst the peripheral states—states too far removed to receive effective defense from the central government against nomadic raiders. It is easy to see how groups of peripheral states began making common cause against northern aggressors, and eventually, against southern aggressors, too. The first overlord of a number of peripheral states, Huangong of the Qi state, came to power in 685 BC. He paid lip service to the overall rule of the Zhou ruler of his time but acted in effect as an independent lord, organizing interstate resistance to the barbarians of the north. Not surprisingly, after Huangong died, his successors progressively lost leadership strength, until the Qi state lost power to the more northern state of Jin, led by Wengong (636–628 BC) who created a more efficient confederation of states than did Huangong.

The Jin *gong* took the place of the original Zhou monarchy, institutionalizing a system of compulsive feudal support from smaller states against enemies in the form of required numbers of soldiers, war chariots, and supplies—again very much like the conditions pertaining in the recent Middle East. Lord and vassals. The southern state of Chu then saw its own *gong* appear who consolidated smaller southern states and began threatening the Jin overlord. That left two nonaligned states of some power—Qin and Qi—that also absorbed smaller states about them to ward off the unfriendly wooing of Jin and Chu. Thus, over a period of some hundred years, the once centrally administered nation broke effectively into four—the states of Qi, Qin, Jin, and Chu—creating a tense balance-of-power situation. The four-state power balance itself then changed when a similar pattern of breakup occurred within the states themselves, particularly Jin. This pattern of events continued until seven major and a number of smaller states finally emerged by 475 BC.

During the entire time of the Spring and Autumn Period, warfare might be said to have been stylized and not undertaken with brutal efficiency for the goal of decisive victory—rather more like Sun Tzu's writings than Bismarck's. The pattern that sets in appears to have been a prime example of the ancient Chinese philosophy of two opposing but balancing forces—the *yin* and the *yang*—constantly striving one against the other. Dating to at least 3000 BC, if not earlier, the Taoist philosophers had developed this dualistic religious and philosophical belief regarding the dark and lightsome forces of nature and the natural world. War and peace by the time of the Zhou had become regarded as a continual and perpetual interplay between harmony and disharmony. Peace and war—with no possible winner-take-all outcome. But then, something very disturbing followed.

The Emerging Nation-State

After some 270 years of intermittent conflict, the Spring and Autumn Period yielded to the Warring States Period. For some 250 more years China was to consist of these seven states living in fairly constant conflict with one another. Perhaps from eventual exhaustion of the will to fight and the material ability to wage technology-driven warfare including costly war chariots, and perhaps also due to the destruction of basic food supplies, a reconsolidation into one nation occurred. Remember, armies always kill people and break things. Reconciliation did not happen through diplomacy; it happened through brutal force—no-holds-barred and to the death. The precarious *yin-yang* balance got smashed.

It stands as a fair question to ask: Why did the Chinese engage in some 550 years of chaotic conflict? Why continue in a lose–lose condition? Sunk Costs? Why did Chinese lord–vassal feudalism fail so spectacularly? Perhaps all the reasons for this downward spiral of events can never be fully identified, but at least three factors appear relevant. First, geography. Following the Agricultural Revolution, populations tended to concentrate in areas of rich soil and good rainfall—in lowland food bowls often bordering river floodplains. That made the seekers of foodstuffs very vulnerable to nomads from higher, more difficult terrain and weather, who of course, quite literally, hungered for what the rich agriculturalists could accumulate. The costs of defending from invasions progressively weakened a central government's ability to maintain the loyalties of all its states, particularly around its periphery. As peripheral states peeled off, the core monarchy weakened, and then died. Eventually, a new equilibrium comprised of four states resulted—which then fell apart under similar forces. Centrifugal forces overwhelmed the centripetal for each governing core.

Second, downward spirals increased. People today have been lulled into a false security by several generations of apparently linear, upward economic growth and progress The reality for most of recorded human history until the Industrial Revolution commencing around 1720 has been that events run in spirals, not linearly, and real economic growth scarcely occurred at all after the initial agricultural gains. Downward spirals overcome upward spirals, because it is far easier to destroy things than to produce them: the production/destruction relation. Last, the Sunk Cost Theorem may have had something to do with persistent warfare carried on by states doomed to lose, because the losers felt that they needed somehow to recoup their investments in blood, sweat, and tears—and war chariots. The Sunk Cost Theorem states that decision-making regarding future actions should never be made based upon past investments. Disregard the theorem at your peril: Consider World War II and how long Germany and Japan fought on, with tremendous loss of life and treasure, when the final outcome was so obvious.

Of Spirals

> Turning and turning in the widening gyre/The falcon cannot hear the falconer.
> Things fall apart; the centre cannot hold/Mere anarchy is loosed upon the world.
> The blood-dimmed tide is loosed, and everywhere/The ceremony of innocence is drowned.
> The best lack all conviction, while the worst/Are full of passionate intensity.
> Surely some revelation is at hand/Surely the Second Coming is at hand.
> Turning and turning in the widening gyre/The falcon cannot hear the falconer.
> Things fall apart; the centre cannot hold/Mere anarchy is loosed upon the world.
> The blood-dimmed tide is loosed, and everywhere/The ceremony of innocence is drowned.
> The best lack all conviction, while the worst/Are full of passionate intensity.
> Surely some revelation is at hand/Surely the Second Coming is at hand.
>
> W.B. Yeats, *The Gyres*

An understanding of circles, lines, and spirals deserves more attention. For most of human history, both in the East and in the West, time was seen as circular—just like the seasons. To borrow from Hebrew Scripture's King Solomon, there was nothing new under the face of the sun. History, such as it was, was the chronicling of circular happenings. Such thought was perhaps more dominant in the East; perhaps this is why Chinese verbs have no tense: Everything gets spoken as though it happens now. In the West, however, something remarkable regarding how we see history occurred around 2500 BC: Hebrew thinkers began to write about a linear nature to history. Generally speaking, it also happened that Western languages, all originating in the Middle East around 4500 BC and from an Indo-European root language, had complex verb tenses—seemingly right from the beginning. Western thinkers frequently saw history as linear—having a beginning and moving toward an end. These very different ways of regarding human history can produce great disagreement, with the East and the West each arguing for its own philosophical viewpoint. In reality, each side is both right and wrong; or perhaps we should say that each side's model is incomplete. History does repeat itself; chronicle goes in circles. Great gains and losses do occur simultaneously, giving the short-term appearance of linear progress or regress. The geometric form called the spiral captures both the circle and the line: Upward-trending circles merely create the illusion of a linear advance. Human history rightly seen consists of both upward and downward spirals, and events both great and small cause the upward and downward movements. In the W.B. Yeats poem quoted above, the falconer's term "gyre" describes a spiral. Inflection points in human history caused by "world turned upside down" events bear close watching—for they may foretell a new spiral.

Of Intercourse: The Qin

> Intercourse: Latin "between" + "run." Communication or dealings between individuals and groups. After late 18th century, sexual relations as well.
>
> *Oxford English Dictionary*

In 221 BC, Ying Zheng, the ruler of the State of Qin proclaimed himself *Qin Shihuangdi* or *First Sovereign Emperor of Qin.* With that proclamation, the Zhou feudal empire officially ended. That the Zhou had been on life support for several hundred years had been obvious; perhaps less obvious, Qin had begun its final power consolidation following the boy king Ying Zheng's coming to rule in 246 BC. Within 25 years, everything changed for China.

A little history: At the founding of the Zhou Dynasty, the Qin constituted a small tribe on the Chinese northwest frontier. Defending that frontier against nomadic tribes naturally fell to them as a consequence of geography. Also as a consequence of geography, and pressure from barbarians, the Qin had moved eastward into what had been Zhou lands—lands naturally more defensible—while the Zhou shifted more eastward as well. Located in what is now Shaanxi Province, the Qin had protective mountain ranges to their eastern backs and access to the broad northern flood plains of the Yellow River before them. As a result, the Qin became talented and ruthless fighters, people whose own territory was never successfully invaded, but who easily invaded others, particularly the lands of the damned foreigners.[12] They also had developed kinship relations with the Zhou through favorable marriages—and with those relations, titles to valuable titles and estates. Power shifted away from the Zhou and to the Qin.

So, during the Warring States Period, the Qin became a state dedicated to ruthless warfare, much like Sparta in ancient Greece at roughly the same time period (4th–5th century BC). They did not go the way of earlier conquering states, however; instead, they created the first in some sense modern nation-state in China, encompassing roughly one-third of the people and land then under cultivation. While the Qin Dynasty itself lasted only 15 years, it set the pattern for all successive Chinese dynasties—right up until modern times. The big question is why? Why did not the Qin evolution go the way of all previously warring states?

A proximate answer points to the Qin way of warfare. It can be argued that Chinese warfare had resembled Japanese Kabuki theater—very stylized with elaborate rules that mitigated against horrific violence. The Qin apparently restored brutality to human combat. This, however, while it accounts for conquests, does not explain how the Qin built a nation from the chaos of war. Here we must note a development that first bloomed in the house of Zhou: the group called the *shi*, the professional bureaucrats, engineers, and legal personnel. For the Qin leadership was about to do something totally new, at least within Far Eastern experience to that date: building an efficient administrative state.

Emperor Ying Zheng's chief minister, a man named Shang Yang, had been recruited from abroad, for the Qin as a warrior cult lacked a bureaucratic skillset. One might say that Shang Yang was the East's first business consultant. He rapidly turned into an administrative genius. The Qin already had a strong tradition of a no-nonsense enforcing of strict rules for individual conduct (a Chinese tradition then called *legalism*): You will be made to care about the law. With an obedient, and

[12]The English region called *Cornwall*, literally, in the Celtic tongue, *hill of the damned foreigners*, challenged the Anglo-Saxon invaders for centuries, and remained undefeated—all at roughly this same time period.

probably very cowed, population, the genius part then involved employing the new professional class in creating a network of human intercourse that would eventually bind all of agricultural China together: by written language to instruct and order people far distant from the dynasty's center, by roads and canals—including the monumental Grand Canal project connecting north and south—permitting goods to be traded quickly and cost-efficiently, by other great engineering projects, by coinage and printing—and by a regimented army of tax collectors that forced payment for the whole thing. The bureaucracy initiated the now long-standing tradition of indoctrinating the people into a notion of collective responsibility for the whole. Of course, the bureaucratic structure also included the enforcers whom we call the police. After all, Qin China was something of a police state: The beatings will continue until morale improves. The Great Wall would protect this intricate intercourse from disruption by the barbarians in the north. The interplay of technology and power at work.

The Qin system reduced the inherited aristocracy and rewarded the professionals, and condemned mere laborers to something like slavery enforced through legalism. To ensure that the populace would not become inflamed by seductive philosophies, all but the most practical of writings went literally up in physical flames. No new thought, please. The actual builders of the great civil engineering projects were callously worked to death, much as the Romans treated slaves in the lead mines of that empire. The genius part of what we might call the whole "system" gets well-captured, then, in the early sense of that great English language word *intercourse*. If the old saying has truth to it—"God and the devil are in the details"—then intercourse comes from the Godly. The devilish part comes from the sheer, mindless brutality built into the "system." *Yin* and *yang*? In the end, for Qin rule, the devil won out. A revolt arose in reaction to the people's heavy burdens, and after a short period called the Chu-Han Contention, the great Han Dynasty began.

While the original sense of the word *intercourse* had to do with trade and commerce, the sexual meaning should not be overlooked. After all, feudalism at its very heart relied upon webs of intermarriage to promote harmony within a nation, and amongst nations. The logic behind the whole feudal structure was that "family"—frequently greatly extended—would yield loyalty to the dominant patriarchy. It did not work out well for the Zhou. And consider: The British Queen Victoria's progeny sat upon all the thrones of Europe, and that did exactly nothing to prevent World War I.

Does all of this remind you of how one of the more remarkable modern nation-states, or perhaps we should say city-states, formed? The answer is post–World War II Singapore. There has been, of course, no working people to death or total subversion of thought, but the dynasty founding the new Singapore did use very strictly enforced rule-directed laws to overcome a history of truly nasty internecine feuds between the four religious/ethnic groupings comprising the country's populace—a modern version of the four Warring States period just before the Qin assumed control. Singapore has grown dramatically, through intercourse—a city-state that has few natural resources but a strong propensity for gains from trade. The sexual part of such intercourse, apparently not so much. Like the Swiss.

Conclusions

Natural human desires for peace and prosperity drove the rulers and the people of the Agricultural Revolution to experiment with new forms of human group organization—an evolutionary process lasting thousands of years and ending with early examples of the city-state and nation-state. In the process, institutions got created that made possible hitherto unknown gains in human welfare emerging from advances in technology and trade. Many of the most remarkable gains appeared first in China, where the technologies for writing and canal building enabled great prosperity and population control to bloom.

The failures of the era, both East and West, came in the form of abuses of newly-created power by rulers. The "strongman" problem has persisted to this day. More on these matters in Chapter Three.

Half a Loaf of Bread

In a sense, the explanations so far for the rise of the Chinese nation-state have been narrow in focus: We might say that they have been based in "hardware" intercourse, the physical-world things only that bind a nation together. Half a loaf of bread. The Chinese Qin efforts to encourage collective responsibility point us toward the whole realm of "software" efforts to bind a nation together—the other half of the loaf and the subject of our next chapter.

***

Discoveries:

There are only a few stories. Behind this seemingly simplistic remark lies the natural law truth that, across the entire spectrum of cultures and races, people are people—with very similar propensities for both good and evil conduct toward one another. Conduct has only limited possibilities, so there are only a limited number of plotlines to stories. It is a little like horses, who as a species have only so many tricks in their bag. Therefore, the stories that people tell and recall—throughout all recorded time—offer open windows into what people may do. If a story first appears in poetry of the blind Greek poet Homer, it will inevitably reoccur in later stories, and all of these similar stories will occur within the annals of human history. In this manner, stories old and new offer us windows into why history happened. Anger and murderous rage, lies and thefts, rebellions and coups—these constitute the nuts and bolts of destructive human events. Lovingkindness and peace, harmonious relations, forgiveness—these make up the all too infrequent events that we wish to foster and strive for. Stories offer a microscopic view into these matters. Strip away romantic overlays: This is what we get—Cowboy and Dragon behaviors. Cowboys herd and raid; that's what they do. Dragons guard their lairs; that's what they do. They possess in common the desire to increase or at least to keep wealth. Cowboy and Dragon stories throughout recorded time reflect these basic propensities.

Spontaneous evolution. The nexus of creativity, technology, and power over others constitutes the great engine of human progress—almost always involving discovery and proceeding from incremental endeavor. Our present work in discovering *why* what happened in the past happened mirrors the original discovery of advanced forms of government and technology.

The great fixed asset change. Incremental discoveries at one critical turning point in human history yielded the fixed asset revolution—a monumental discontinuous factor in human progress.

(*Continued*)

(*Continued*)

The paradox of prosperity. Paradoxically, the material prosperity wrought by the fixed asset revolution yielded increased lawlessness and violence—because it is frequently more laborious to produce than to steal.

The exponent of distance. This principle expresses the inherent limitation to empire. The principle both limits the expansion of authoritarian empires and increases the threats that extended empires always face. This is because expansion has as a goal the capture of another nation's capital—its nerve center—a linear undertaking. Threats and resistance, however, come from a circle surrounding the linear undertaking—and therefore always increase as the square of that distance.

Lord-vassal failure. Feudal structures always fail due to the inherent uncertainty of organizations based in human relationships—agency failures. The continuing success of intercourse does not extend to feudal arrangements. The rebellion and/or theft stories always kick in.

State-directed intercourse. Such intercourse utilizes a nation-state's creative bureaucracy, engineering talent, and administrative skills to weave together synergistic communications networks that generate physical ties binding a state's various entities together as one. Such intercourse, along with trade intercourse, represents the most effective manner of uniting disparate parts of an overall nation together known to date.

The spirals principle. Human history is at once both circular and linear. The spiral geometric form best captures the interplay between circles and linear movements. All great changes in human history have been marked by events that convert circular chronicle into linear movement—sometimes up and sometimes down with regard to productivity.

(*Continued*)

(*Continued*)

"The world turned upside down" principle. Singular great events should receive exceptional scrutiny, for they mark the great transitions in the affairs of tribes and nations.

Inner space versus outer space. In the search for why tribes and nations succeed or fail, the answer will never lie strictly in the outer world; it will first develop in the inner space of the human minds of critical thinkers. See the next chapter.

Chapter Two

Schools of Thought and Human Evolution

Overview: The *hardware* for forming a peaceful and harmonious human order includes law and order, the tax man, and much technical and administrative capability. This, however, will never suffice to explain *why* humankind got on the institutional development path that we did. Another dimension to creating peace must get discovered—which means that the quest for a peaceable kingdom begins when tribes and nations have been acting out chaotically and violently for some time. *Software* contributions involve changes in the human heart—the matter of replacing Hero Warrior beliefs with peaceable beliefs. In this process, the true hero of the story becomes not the Warrior but the Philosopher, and only the philosopher who persuades people to change beliefs toward harmony, which then changes culture. Downstream of the Philosopher comes the Brave Reciprocators of human history who create and teach new founding myths to replace old Hero Warrior cultic beliefs. The three critical areas: *the perception/beliefs/culture paradigm*, *game-theoretic discoveries,* and *philosophy and founding myths.*

Introduction

The Quest for a Peaceable Kingdom

Every battle is won or lost before it is ever fought.

Sun Tzu, *The Art of War*

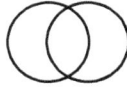

> Every race is first won or lost in the human mind, before it is ever played out on the field of human conflict.
>
> Peter deH Caldwell

We have established that most of human history comes replete with stories of terrible conflict; indeed, pre-modern history was far more bloody relative to population size than even that of the 20th century in which by some estimates over 120 million people died, either at the hands of ruthless invaders or at the hands of their own rulers.[1] What then shall we do about the human propensity for violence and for bad conduct? It is a first-order question of life, this perennial propensity for harm, this matter of even the good we try to do turning out as bad.

Chapter One dealt with the outer dimension, the *hardware* issues for achieving what the East calls harmony and the West calls peace. Humans have tried various forms of government with the aim of reducing human carnage and suffering—of protecting the good guys from the bad guys, if you will. Early on, however, let's say by 1000 BC, a new breed of men—we can call them philosophers—began considering the inner dimension causing human conflict. To varying degrees, the ancient philosophers who took up this matter recognized a fundamental reality of human nature: Rather than being driven strictly by blind instinct, human beings have the capability for thought-driven outward behaviors, a capability that has evolved over millennia. Yes, we do possess very ancient instincts for survival—flight, fight, or freeze for instance—that drive our actions in *extremitas*. But mostly, our beliefs about the goodness or badness of our choices in conduct determine our actions. Our beliefs, the ideologies that we hold to be true, represent the ragged ground whereon such men as Confucius and Plato sought to change our propensities for violent conduct. Thoughts, and emotions attached to thoughts, comprise beliefs. So, changing beliefs can get quite challenging. Emotions are messy stuff. But, change our beliefs about the goodness of an action, and maybe change the world. How might this work?

"Every race is first won or lost in the human mind"—at precisely the same single point in time. Just before any human action, a point always emerges—a momentary thing like flickering lightning—when the human actor in a scene in the great Play of Life may choose amongst two or more courses of conduct. The scene before him becomes enlightened by his

[1] Stephen Pinker in *The Better Angels of Our Nature* provides the groundbreaking evidence for the general decrease in violence in the modern era.

own beliefs about it. Perception is subjective; perception gets determined by belief. Whether the conduct relates to a great battle planned for months, or it relates to a personal insult just received, there exists this single, momentary time of choosing. It is here, in the blindingly short time between perception and our action exploding outward into the world, that the great philosophers have sought to engage every individual actor in the great play of human history.

Examine carefully the simple principle: Every race is first won or lost in the human mind, before it is ever played out on the field of human conflict. Now, consider a morally neutral example of the workings of the principle: The classic movie *Chariots of Fire* replays the 1924 Paris Olympics' 400-meter race, in which the Scottish hero, Eric Liddell, walks up to each of his rival runners, shakes each man's hand, and says to each: "Good luck." When he approaches his last rival, a brash American named Jackson Scholz, he adds something: He says, "Good luck. I won't be seeing you again until the end of the race." Movie watchers of the original, uncut film then see the American's face fall, for he knows intuitively that in footraces only one man never sees his competitors after the start—the man who leads from the sound of the starter's pistol until the finish line. Eric Liddell has told Scholz what will happen, and the American's face falls. Right then, seconds before the starting gun, he has lost the race. Every battle is first won or lost in the human mind.

What might this have to do with something freighted with moral meaning? A footrace, even at the Olympics, can rarely rise to the level of great events in world history. So, adding a moral dimension, imagine for a moment that in the immediate aftermath of an ancient great battle, in a time of superheated passion, the officer in charge of the enemy soldiers who surrendered asks his commanding officer for permission to kill them. It calls for a split-second decision—yes or no. What if that permission were denied? How would that change things? Potentially, rather radically—as we shall see.

The Perceptions/Beliefs/Culture Paradigm

Of Perception

> ...perception, cognition, thoughts and feelings; personal relationships; they are all a projection of you.
>
> Deepak Chopra

The perception of beauty is a moral test.

Henry David Thoreau

You can observe a lot by watching.

One of many sayings by the great American baseball player Yogi Berra

In primitive cultures, my tribe attacks another tribe because we know that they are wicked, and we see that they are about to strike us. But what if they are not? What if, perchance, they have gathered together for a game hunt? Perception always comes before action. And there's the rub. Perceptions are in reality highly subjective matters. Actions, and reactions, all depend upon beliefs about the goodness or badness of a situation. What I see partly depends then upon what I want to see. My sight works less like a camera and more like a paintbrush wielded by an interpretive artist. Perceptions work to reinforce the beliefs we already hold.

Here's a simple example—from an American college football rivalry of the 1950s studied by a group of sociologists. In one game played by the two rivals—Harvard and Dartmouth—the Harvard fans became very upset at what they "saw" as unnecessarily rough play by the opposing team, which had won the game. The Dartmouth fans did not see this at all. Some sociologists found this intriguing and ran a survey with a simple questionnaire going to both sets of fans: Was the game "fair" or "rough"? The Harvard fans overwhelmingly saw the game as too rough. The Dartmouth fans invented their own third option—"rough but fair"—and overwhelmingly chose that option. It appeared that the two sets of fans "saw" two different games. So it is with much of what we believe we see—run through our belief software of the mind.

Perception, then, hardens beliefs—making us predisposed to see what we believe, rather than take in new information. Perceptions may block social learning. Resolving the dilemma of the self-defeating violence endemic in the world really must begin at the level of influencing beliefs. And here it is important to remember that a belief has two components: a judgment about reality (subjective of course) reinforced by a feeling response to that judgment. The great challenge for humankind, then, goes deeply into the thought-heart of the matter.

The Formation of Culture

So much is written and said about *culture*. Everything living is said to possess a culture, and culture is said to explain pretty much everything. Culture, it is commonly believed by our present elites, determines politics and the economics that trickle down from it. But theories that explain everything are not theories at all; they represent tautologies. For our purposes here, of course, we limit *culture* to human interactions only. That excludes many things, such as laboratory bacterial cultures or styles in food preparation. Now, let's operationalize the culture concept: Culture is the sum total of a human group's beliefs and resulting behaviors. Beliefs—about the goodness or badness of any action—determine behaviors. Perceptions, in substance very subjective, feed back to reinforce or modify behaviors: Culture is ever-changing—and sometimes quite rapidly. The whole package adds up to the ever-evolving culture of any group. It may yield an extraordinarily rich and great society replete with spectacular advances in the arts, sciences, and technology, or great advancements in economics and human welfare—societies such as existed in classical China and 19th-century Europe. But broken down into its smallest units, human cultures consist simply of evolving patterns of giving out "goods" and "bads" for all perceived conduct. Culture is potentially circular, and not hierarchical.

Culture is also "sticky": The circular feedback loop that should modify beliefs often fails, and a tribe may hold the same self-destructive beliefs for centuries, or even millennia. Mestizos believe that the evil Spaniards stole their lands back in the 1500s. Mexicans believe the Yankees stole their land in the 1840s. Many Chinese believe that the evil Westerners forced unequal treaties upon them beginning in the late 17th century, treaties responsible for China's sharp descent into poverty. Everybody possesses the propensity for believing that personal failures come from somebody else. Sticky beliefs add up to fated outcomes. Fate is then the ruler.

There are just a few stories, and one of them is the victim's tale: "I am the victim of a great wrong imposed upon me or my ancestors." This is a lie. Nobody is a victim who does not choose to be one. At that momentary flash in time between belief and conduct, a time for choosing appears. "Am I a victim, or a hero?" Do I react out of self-pity, or out of righteousness? And this same choice regarding our personal situations also applies to my reactions to the situations of others. "He deserved what he got," we may say. Perception becomes destiny.

The giving of a "good" or a "bad" does not have to take the shape of a thumbs up or thumbs down in the Roman Coliseum, however. Consider that we humans respond to outside events in one of three ways: from the gut, from the heart, and from the head. Gut-level responses have deep history in clannish and tribal cultures, commonly going back many thousands of years. As a result, violence was and is much more prevalent within these forms. Passions rule; there are no interests. In great societies, it may take nothing more than an expression of *disapprobation*—a great 18th-century term meaning mild disapproval, an emotion—to affect a change in a behavior, private or public.[2] This is not to say that great societies are always harmonious and peaceful. Propaganda plays upon emotions, and thinking can be the tool of the devil. Propaganda is twisted perception. Or third, we may think things through before forming an emotional response to a situation, thus forming a *sensibility* that may lead toward harmony rather than violence.

Beyond our three propensities for behavior, there is the whole matter of the responses of individuals directed at our behavior toward them—a response function or *feedback loop* in the model, if you will. All great societies have complex feedback loops: We may, for instance, pour out approval of a great public figure or the works of a great artist because our friends do so, and we seek our friends' approval. We may also become captured by a mass hysteria regarding an economic event or a political figure. We may stand up to a majority opinion and change public opinion for the good, or we may suffer public outrage.

Within a feedback loop, my behavior toward you very likely will get determined by what I believe you may do to me, or for me, in return. Take a simple example: If I witness a crime and believe that the criminal poses no threat to me, I will very likely testify against him in court—good citizen conduct. But if the criminal belongs to a mafia gang, I may refuse. Trust/distrust. Squeal/go silent.

One might now suspect that in our model there are limited strategies to be played out in the great game of life, and this is so. Remember: There are only a few stories.

---

[2]Adam Smith, *The Theory of Moral Sentiments* provides key insights into the role of public opinion emerging within the early modern era.

Game-Theoretic Discoveries

Tit-for-Tat and the Prisoners' Dilemma

> In the spring, at the time when kings march out to war, David sent Joab out with the king's men and the whole Israelite army.
>
> 2 *Samuel* 11

> Why can't we all just get along?
>
> Rodney King

There are only a few stories. How do a group's leaders react to an overt threat or an actual attack? There are only three strategies, and each has played out countless times in the stories of actual history: attack back; surrender; absorb the punishment. Throughout all human history, the strategy most often followed has been to attack back: Tit-for-tat. You attack me; I attack back. You live at peace with me; I do the same with you. Tit-for-tat has yielded near-constant warfare among tribes large and small for nearly all of human history, for the other alternatives appear to yield worse outcomes.

Social scientists have even created a model for this sort of thing: The Prisoners' Dilemma.[3] In the simple, non-iterative version, the Prisoners' Dilemma comprises two men arrested for a crime. Both men are guilty. They are kept separate and each offered a deal: Squeal on your partner in crime and get spared a prison sentence—no time in jail. But, if your partner squeals on you first, you get a long prison sentence—let's say, three years. Oh, and if neither man squeals, you both get convicted of a more minor crime and go to jail—let's say, for one year. The most efficient outcome as regards the two partners is for neither to squeal: total time served by both men, two years. In reality, in a *non-reiterative* game, both men squeal on the other: total time served, six years. This explains why amongst crime gangs some form of Omerta, the mafia code of silence,

---

[3]Quite a large body of literature exists regarding the Prisoners' Dilemma as a game theoretic device to model a number of socio-economic conditions. Originally invented by Flood and Dresher in 1950, Robert Axelrod provides a superb understanding of the Prisoners' Dilemma in his *Evolution of Cooperation*.

gets adopted. The Rule: Never, never squeal on a fellow gang member. To enforce that rule, kill any gang member who does squeal—or appears likely to.

In a *reiterative* game, played for some large, indeterminate number of rounds, the model becomes far more expressive of many situations—for instance, for the above-mentioned behavior of individuals in criminal enterprises. There is good reason for Omerta, for a criminal enterprise operates a reiterative game, and in such a game, the least costly way of dealing with law enforcement is for every gang member to swear never to betray a fellow mafioso. At most, then, gang members may serve out small sentences. Of course, the murder of witnesses who may testify at trial helps enormously.

The reiterative version of the game also applies to the relations of tribes and nations, and this is why the Prisoners' Dilemma model matters here. As we have seen, for all of human history tribes have attacked other tribes. In the spring, kings march out to war. This is what they do. Warfare appears as nearly continual even today in parts of our globe dominated by hunter-gatherer tribes. Why is this so? Tit-for-tat. The perceived cost of responding to an attack with an attack is lower than the costs associated with capitulation or with turning the other cheek in an effort to bring about peaceful behavior from one's enemies. Perhaps the finest narrative history ever written about the outcomes of the three strategies appears in the history books of Hebrew Scripture. Here we also learn of the fatal complexities of betrayals, power alliances, and the outcomes for tribal and national failures. Unspeakable horrors appear in these pages, along with smaller mercies.

In the games of violence and war, what other strategies exist besides tit-for-tat? We might well look at the results from a computerized version of an extended Prisoners' Dilemma game of long but indeterminate iterations played by high-powered Western academics in the 1980s, as reported in David Axelrod's *Evolution of Cooperation*. One other factor in the game: Every player out of dozens, or even hundreds, has *memory* for what every other player does, for every round of play. This simple factor creates a model that includes the *deep memory* possessed by all of the world's peoples: "Back 50 years ago, you attacked us, and we fear you will again." In fact, the Prisoners' Dilemma reiterative model captures a stunning amount of real-world depth within its simple parameters.

As applied to tribes and nations, two pure strategies may be adopted by each player for each round in the game: peace or war, good or bad. Player strategies are either weighted toward cooperative altruism, or individual greed or defensiveness. In an ideal world, every player would choose peace, and no destructive aggression would occur. It would be a very nice thing indeed if the peace strategy would win out, but can it? The peaceniks get defeated by the players who always choose aggression, the empire builders. In a world of peaceful cooperators, a sole aggressor always wins, but at a huge overall social cost. We might say that, in the shape of a computer program that always chooses aggression, the Prisoners' Dilemma model creates a simple form of *evil* within its code. The basic lesson: Peacemaking usually involves a credible threat of retaliation—in other words the willingness to play tit-for-tat. What other strategies might be played then—either than pure altruism or unremitting war?

Here's the thing: With a large number of players and an indeterminate number of rounds played, mixed models become more successful than pure conquest models, or even tit-for-tat. Thus, I might write a program that plays the peace move initially, but then switches to a retaliation mode when an opponent chooses to attack. I might accept attacks for more than one round without retaliating, in the hopes that my opponent would *learn* from this not to attack me. I might add in a measure of *forgiveness*—accepting a *truce* if my opponent backs away from an attack strategy. Out of all these mixed models, the most successful turns out to be simple tit-for-tat—four lines of Basic coding back in the 1980s. Complex mixed models with hundreds of lines of code did worse.

Only one strategy in the 1980s games outdid all the others, including tit-for-tat. That strategy might be called *The Brave Reciprocator*. The Brave Reciprocator always plays "nice"—always choosing peace over war. Tit-for-tat programs quickly learn to first wipe out the aggressors and then to follow the Brave Reciprocator's lead and opt for peace. The Prisoners' Dilemma game points us all toward the higher uplands of peace and plenty. The big question for us all: In the physical world, can a Brave Reciprocator succeed?

As a somewhat cynical conclusion to the lessons learned from game theory, allow us to recount to you the result of an international relations game created by some American college students back in the 1970s. The game allowed the teams playing it to invest in their countries' futures through a number of strategies, both domestic and foreign. Permissible investments included nuclear weapons. All of the students playing the game were anti–Vietnam and nuclear war, and believed fervently in peace. They were very certain that no team would ever opt to use nukes. The game that they played became very competitive, and tempers grew hot. The game ended when one team destroyed the world—in a mushroom-shaped cloud. This caused great angst amongst them. The game highlighted, negatively, the core problem that the Prisoners' Dilemma had been designed to study: Why do rationally-motivated people fail to cooperate even when it is in their mutual best interest to do so? Perhaps we might call this outcome the Dr. Strangelove Effect?

After game theory, enter philosophy.

PHILOSOPHY AND FOUNDING MYTHS

Schools of Thought

> It was the best of times; it was the worst of times. It was the age of wisdom; it was the age of foolishness. It was the epoch of belief; it was the epoch of incredulity. It was the season of Light; it was the season of Darkness. It was the spring of hope; it was the winter of despair.
>
> Charles Dickens, *A Tale of Two Cities*
> About the French Revolution

> When the root is firmly established, the moral law will grow.
>
> Confucius, *Analects* 1:2

> There is government, when the prince is prince, and minister is minister; when the father is father, and the son is son.
>
> Confucius, *Analects* XII,11

> Everybody has to serve somebody.
>
> Bob Dylan

Some 3,000 years before Flood and Dresher at Rand Corporation first conceived the Prisoners' Dilemma (1950), ancient philosophers both East and West, had already determined the nature of the cooperation problem and begun generating solutions to it. It appears quite fascinating that this radical movement began at roughly the same period in human history in East, West and Middle East. The solutions to the cooperation quandary came from disparate sides of the globe, but they had a number of similarities. And they did occur at roughly the same period of human history. In ancient China, the Hundred Schools of Thought movement began around 600 BC. In Greece, the earliest philosophers appeared around 600 BC as well. For ancient Israel, the beginnings are confusing, for its prophets largely served as its philosophers for cooperation amongst nations. That said, we might date the beginning time with the prophet Isaiah at around 750 BC.

Parenthetically, a time period similar to the Chinese Hundred Schools of Thought emerged in the West beginning around 1600 AD. This Western evolution in thinking about how to achieve peace comprises part of Chapter Four in this book. This does not mean that Chinese thinking was superior to Western thinking because it came first. It does mean that by around 1600, the West produced something new under the face of the sun when Eastern thinking had stagnated.

To continue, philosophy East and West all began at roughly the same period. Why might this be so? The answer is so simple! One, all people are fundamentally the same: emotionally-driven beings capable periodically of very rational thought. Two, many tribes and nations faced similar threats during this time, and also tremendous violence—all having roots in the Agricultural Revolution. Three, there are only a few stories: The choice set is quite limited.

We might begin this quick tour through ancient philosophy with a very rational interpretive principle: Thinking like a Westerner, the cooperation problem breaks down into two parts: One, the theoretical. Two, the operational. The problem's solution involves understanding the problem and then crafting a way to change the actual world of men to conform with the idea of the *ideal*. Within this basic interpretive framework, what happened in the minds of the men involved? While the narrative history of Israel is by far the richest, the story of what transpired in China during its Golden Age works best for our purposes here.

It was the best of times and the worst of times. It was during the time of the great Zhou Dynasty (1046–256 BC). It was also the time of the Spring and Autumn Period and of the Warring States Period (770–221 BC). It was the time of great human creativity shaping a cultural blossoming in arts and applied sciences—truly a Golden Age. It was a time of struggle for survival amongst the ruling but competing feudal lords making up Zhou rule, and for its peasantry bearing the brunt of conflicts. Within this overall, churning, creating, destroying period, China's greatest philosophies took root and gave flower. Why was this so?

Remember, as the Zhou regional lords, or *gong*, extended a feudal empire, they ran up against the need for talented engineers, administrators, teachers, and tax collectors—administrators who might be assigned and reassigned as demands varied. Hardware stuff. This in turn required creating an educated and literate bureaucracy linking state directives to local communities. Software skills: our concern here. Without apparently ever intending to do so, the *gong* called into being a group of wandering, itinerant intellectuals—men who were both professional gentleman servants of the state and itinerant observers of the moral problems behind the methods of government, engineering, accounting, and war. The most famous, of course, was Shang Yang of the Qin, a professional gun-for-hire who found a home there. What they observed was pretty upsetting: outrageous official corruption, raiding, betrayals, murders, invasions by foreigners and other Chinese lords alike—perhaps all of the relatively few stories packed into one time and place. Lords actually became warlords. The itinerants' experiences converted them into what the West calls philosophers and the East calls students of "heart-mind." And they as students influenced more students. Perhaps there really are no teachers in life, only learners—voyagers upon oceans filled with awaiting discoveries.

Classical Chinese philosophy-religion possesses massive complexity, far beyond this book or its authors. Literally hundreds of itinerant feeler-thinkers emerged from their wanderings, both physical and spiritual. What we hopefully can agree upon here takes the form of a basic structure or outline and its most prevalent practical expression. This means beginning with the concept of *Tao* and applying it to the matter of building a harmonious society. So, here we go! *Tao* stands for a natural and holistic ordering of the entire universe. It cannot be known through Western-style thinking, but rather through Eastern intuitive experience. The West blurts out an IBM mantra and says, "Think!" Be objective. The East says, "Heart-mind." Be very subjective. From *Tao* comes the Mandate of Heaven and a cascading fountain of harmony.

Consider the beauty of it all from an Eastern perspective: The entire universe of all things and sentient beings possesses orderliness. Orderliness flows downward like a brilliant waterfall from the very top of the universe which is *tian* or heaven. Human moral nature, *xing,* has its transcendent source in *tian*. Therefore, the way to human harmony must also involve orderliness that complements and completes the natural order. The working out of transcendent and impersonal *Tian* through *xing* in the human world unfolds through the working of the spirits or gods of this world, the *shen*. The task of the "heart-mind" learner is to discover and apply that orderliness that brings human harmony out of the natural order. In Western thought: Operationalize the concept of *virtue*.

Turn to that foremost of all heart-mind learners of the East: Confucius, or Kong Qui (551–479 BC). Certainly, he was a learner of the *Tao* that contained the relationships of all things each to each other in one grand wholeness. If follows, then, that the source for human harmony with man and nature involves relationships. For Confucius and his followers, this means that *tian* and *xing* must also be in harmony: the sacred and the secular merge. Parenthetically, Western monasticism and Anglo-American Puritanism also made the sacred and the secular one. Monasticism tended to stress the sacred; Confucianism stressed the secular; Western Protestantism descended into the Protestant work ethic. About the same time, Confucian thought boiled down to work ethic as well. But that goes far beyond our story here.

Descending the superstructure of Confucian thought, the great learner identified first the five basic ethical concepts involving virtue descending from the heavens: *ren, yi, zhi, xin, li*. These comprise the theoretical component to his thought—the idea of the ideal. *Ren* has to do with basic benevolence, or humaneness—the virtue that manifests as compassion for others. *Yi* represents the moral disposition to do good and is comprised of *zhong* or doing one's best, and *shu* or altruism or consideration of others. Confucius himself penned a very early, cryptic version of the negative Golden Rule: "What you don't want yourself, don't do to others." *Zhi* is the intuitive knowledge of the right, or the wrong, in one's own behaviors and those of others. *Xin* stands for the twin virtues of faithfulness and integrity. *Li* signifies the ritual of behaviors defining how each person should act in harmony with the rule of heaven in everyday life. Followers of the great learner held in absolute contempt those who failed to uphold these fundamental moral virtues found in *ren* and *yi*. They define the pathway of *Tao*. "Heaven is always kind to the virtuous."[4]

Next in order descending the Confucian superstructure comes the first operationalizing component to the overall plan: the three Confucian values of filial piety, humaneness, and ritual consciousness. Some writers refer to these as being like unto the three legs of a tripod. As such, the three Confucian values represent a very early version of the Rule of Three,

[4]Attributed to Confucius.

which shall comprise this book's next chapter. Suffice it to say here that dyads make for unstable relationships. Without humaneness, one may display filial piety and perform appropriate rituals, but nevertheless treat parents and others with extreme cruelty. A very teachable example of this occurs regarding the Pharisees, as taught by Jesus in the Christian Bible in *Mark* 7:11–12:

> For Moses said, "Honor your father and your mother," and "Anyone who curses his father or mother must be put to death." But you say that if a man says to his father or mother, "Whatever you would have received from me is Corban (that is, a gift committed to God), he is no longer permitted to do anything for his father or mother."

The Pharisees earned a bad name for good reason.

Humaneness, this third leg, balances and perfects the other two. Parenthetically, the Christian version of the Confucian three-legged stool comes from 1 *Corinthians* 13:13 where St. Paul writes: "And now abideth faith, hope, charity (love), these three; but the greatest is charity." For the Christian tradition, love humanizes the other two.

The three Confucian values have a fascinatingly organic nature to them, for they all emanate from the child's relation to his or her parents, beginning with the bond to the mother. Out of this motherly bond comes everything else. *Xiao* or filial piety grows and extends from that most basic of bonds. You see this visually in the Chinese character for *xiao*: The top portion of the character pictures an old man. Underneath him, upholding him, a young man appears. So, from filial piety grows the sense of support by the young for the older generation. Reciprocity pulls the entire character into one meaning: As parents nurtured their progeny when young, so their progeny support their parents when they grow aged—and revere them. The sensibility extends to sacrificing to them after their death as an integral part of due reverence. Then, by a further extension, ritual reverence and awe become due to previous generations. Filial piety and ancestor worship thus join hands as two parts to a single whole. Parents use ancestor worship to teach their children filial piety—even after their own deaths. And so it came to pass that in China one's family name, such as "Lee", took precedence over one's given name, such as "Charles."

Parenthetically, a similar thought appears within the Christian Bible: "By faith Abel offered unto God a more excellent sacrifice than Cain, by which he obtained witness that he was righteous, God testifying of his gifts; and by it he, being dead, still speaketh."[5] Very different cultures/similar idea. There are just a few stories. Failures to live up to virtuous conduct, then, not only bring shame to one's self and family, but also to one's entire line of ancestors. Cain killed Abel and subsequently became an outlaw in the land.

Expanding organically out of filial piety comes *ren*—benevolence, or humaneness. The Chinese character resembles a human figure to the left and the number two to the right, conveying relationship one to the other. Dyads. Then comes *li* or ritual awareness. At a trivial level, it has something of the English idea of "good form"—doing what is correct and proper. The Chinese character links proper conduct to a symbol for a religious vessel. The original sense grew out of courtly rites performed to sustain on earth the whole cosmic order of the universe. Under Confucian thought, *li* rises above politeness to join the human to the cosmic order. The three basic values thus become one whole—a Three-Legged Stool. The overall purpose: To inculcate moral precepts and values into the human heart so that people will govern themselves. Make each heart a school for virtue.

Confucius explicitly argued against the *law and order* mentality dominating the Chinese *legalism* tradition that came to a full head under the Qin: Try to govern through laws and threat of punishment, and people will find ways of evasion; they will also become shameless in their breaches of propriety. The Qin Dynasty lasted scarcely a dozen years. Teach people virtue and they will practice self-discipline, enforced by personal shame when doing wrong. Law and order versus Virtue—a never-ending one of humankind's few stories.

One more level down in the superstructure then comes the foundation for the workaday nitty-gritty of forging harmony out of human selfhood and willfulness—the method, in Western terms, of operationalizing the theory: "Everybody has to serve somebody," as the Bob Dylan song goes. The five Confucian pairs begin at the top of the human existential superstructure and descend downward to capture all of political and social life: Ruler/Subject, Father/Son, Husband/Wife, Elder Brother/Younger Brother, Friend/Friend. And at the very apex of things, the highest pair, not completely human at all, involves Heaven/Emperor. The first four define authority; one member of the pair is superior to the other. The inferior always owes obedience to the superior. Only the last pair—Friend/Friend—works between equals,

[5] *Hebrews* 11:4, KJV.

thereby strengthening loyalty and humaneness. Throughout some 2,500 years or so, through many dynasties and even through materialistic communism, the five pairs have bound individuals to larger society within a Chinese culture formed by countless individual behaviors acted out according to this basic belief set.

Set against the rigidity of the five Confucian pairs, the Heaven/Emperor metaphysical pair introduces a single permitted degree of freedom into the whole set-piece tragi-comedy of Eastern life. The five human pairings may only be upheld if the supreme, metaphysical pairing also holds. When the Heaven/Emperor paring fails due to an Emperor's wrongdoing, violating the Mandate of Heaven, then the duty of the lesser rulers becomes that of overthrowing a sitting Emperor. Then, a new Emperor, and a new dynasty, forms—restoring the Mandate.

What About the West?

> It is the mark of an educated mind to be able to entertain a thought without accepting it.
>
> Attrib. Aristotle

> By the time a man is forty, he gets the face he deserves.
>
> Abraham Lincoln

> Righteousness and peace kiss.
>
> Psalm 85

What about the West? On the surface of things, East and West seem like polar opposites. In Eastern heart-thought, the whole is greater than its individual constituents. In the West, the individual reigns supreme. The East constrains individual action; the West, particularly in America, glorifies it. While the East produced many schools of thought, only one came to predominate—the Confucian. In the West, two traditions emerged as dominant—the Greek and the Hebrew— and they tussled with one another for two millennia. Despite these vast cultural differences, classical Western thought as a whole has fascinating parallels to the classical East. Are we not all of the same flesh and blood? Are there not just a few stories?

Very simply, we might say that the Greeks invented objective, dispassionate observation and thought, and in the process also invented Western science. The tool that the foremost Greek thinker—Aristotle—used to pry open all areas of interest? Logic. Logic expels the subjective. Even the greatest Greek thinker about the ideal—Plato—communicated in logical analogies, most famously by writing in *The Republic* of men shackled in a dark cave, unable to see the light, but only the flickering shadows on the facing cave wall caused by idols of men and beasts dancing behind them, created by fires in turn behind those idols. In all, a conjuror's trick. Now, by analogy, see that the condition of these imprisoned men shows the reality of the uneducated ignorance of mankind generally: Men, shackled to superstition, cannot see the inherent beauty of the ideal. Aristotle, in particular, made many appeals to the concept of virtue and desired that men live by it, but did Greek philosophers operationalize virtue in order to make a peaceful nation? Not really. Rational thinking may dispel ignorance, but only for a few. Nothing in classical Western thought pushed an ideal down to the level of the humdrum.

While the East tightly joined philosophy and religious sentiments together into one whole possessing little of the sacred, the Greeks believed in many, many gods—all of whom consisted of psychological projections of human propensities onto beings given mythical status. How much like Plato's physically-blinded men in a cave seeing only flickering shadows on a black wall were the Greeks? Psychological blindedness misshapes perception.

In the East, the Chinese had created a large, viable nation-state by roughly 220 BC—when Confucianism moderated Law and Order. What about the Mediterranean West, the birthplace of much of Western civilization? Significantly, Greece remained a land of warring city-states—until 1831, when a national government finally succeeding in quelling most unrest, but only after some nasty fighting. And Italy? With warring city-states or simmering hatreds until around 1860, Italy became a completed nation-state only in 1871. Why might this great disparity have occurred?

Before searching for answers to the conundrum, we should consider that other leg of the Western civilizational biped—the Hebrews. While Greek thinkers engaged in dispassionate, objective thinking, Hebrew kings, priests and prophets always perceived reality subjectively, in terms of relationships—the how-it-relates-to-me point of view. While the Chinese concept of *Tao* regards an impersonal natural order of the universe, the Hebrew beliefs in a supernatural order of all things attribute to this order a personal creator—the YHWH of Hebrew scripture. Some modern writers see this as the Hebrews discovering or inventing an omnipresent and omnipotent being given personhood. Some see the whole matter as one of psychological projection—man creating God—resembling the creation of gods by the Greeks. The ancient Hebrews, however, saw it as God revealing himself to *them.* Confucians conflated the sacred and the secular into the secular. The Hebrews made the sacred absorb the secular.

The genius of the ancient Hebrews can be seen in one simple word frequently occurring in Hebrew writings: *paniym* or *face*. Meanings have consequences. The words for *face* possess far different meaning and consequence Greek to Hebrew, and for that matter East to West. For the ancient Greeks, the word *prosopon* signified appearance—that which allows me to distinguish you from someone else. From it we receive the English word *person*. The sense of the Greek word follows from the Greek propensity to make logical categories of all things. We should recognize this Greek propensity as, unsurprisingly, comprising the first step in forming the objective science of anything: That first step involves identifying and categorizing the things about which one wishes to do science. The Greek *prosopon* may also convey the idea of a mask, from early Greek theater. Change appearance in order to change the character in a play. The source of stereotypes?

For the Hebrews, however, the word *paniym* carries very different meaning. *Prosopon* is singular; *paniym* is plural—plural because it conveys many meanings. Its plurality captures its sense of something set in continually changing motion—between expressions of mood, emotions, and thoughts inherent in the changing states that our faces communicate about the inner makeup of each individual. Yet, out of all that facial expressions convey about the inner person, *paniym* also conveys a sense of the inner wholeness of the individual. Out of many, one. Look with a spiritual eye into the face of another and know his or her identity as an individual.

For the Chinese, during roughly the period we have been considering, two words for *face* emerged: The first, *mainzi*, came earlier and dates back to ancient Chinese literature. It connotes an individual's status or social position. It may also have meant something akin to the English word *appearance*, but that seems secondary. *Mainzi* is a possession, not an endowment. *Lian*, on the other hand, appeared much later, let's say 1200 or so, and has a meaning more aligned with social psychology and connotes social obligation. A son with *lian* displays filial piety. Without *lian*, a man brings dishonor upon family and the social order. Lack of *lian* stands out as a negative—a sense of shame related to social standards. Summing it all up, in ancient China a man might possess great *mainzi* but no *lian*. The entire sense for Chinese *face* took the form of a social construct related to the collective conscience of the Confucian state.

The proper analogue to Chinese *face* for the West, particularly the Hebrews, would be *honor*. One of the Mosaic commands speaks this directly: "Honor they father and they mother, that thy days may be long upon the land which the LORD thy God giveth thee."[6] In the social sphere, then, Hebrew sensibility saw God as offering conditional promises for future wellbeing: Do this, and all will go well for you. Very different from the Confucian pairs. The entire social promise of the Lord God for the Hebrews gets summed up in just four words from Psalm 85 in the Hebrew Scriptures: "righteousness and peace kiss."

Hebrew scripture has this linear sense: Do righteous acts, and the Lord God promises peace to come. Righteousness makes peace. One of the hallmarks of all Hebrew, and Jewish, thought regards the doing of good deeds for the most vulnerable and helpless of people among you as defining virtue. The tradition eventually come to full fruition in the positive Golden Rule of Jesus found in *Matthew*: "Do unto others as you would have them do unto you." Heal the sick; lift up the downhearted; rescue the lost; offer hospitality to strangers. Eventually, under the teachings of Jesus, the doing of good reached its furthest development: Love your enemies. Return good for evil. Brave Reciprocator stuff.

All traditional cultures include measures of patriarchy and elder obedience. In the classical era, only Chinese tradition linked all human relationships together through the vehicle of the five Confucian pairs. Even in China, of course, our common human nature still remained to work ill. Classical Israel and China shared some elements of a potential wholeness descending down from heaven to bring peace or harmony.

The Free Rider Problem

> And the serpent said unto the woman, "Ye shall not surely die: For God doth know that in the day ye eat thereof, then your eyes shall be open, and ye shall be as gods, knowing good and evil."
>
> *Genesis* 3:4-5, KJV

---

[6] *Exodus* 20:12, KJV.

> Moral Virtues are the Political Offspring which Flattery begot upon Pride.
>
> Bernard Mandeville, *The Fable of the Bees*, 1723

There are just a few stories. All attempts to enforce honor and virtue upon human beings run afoul of the Free Rider Problem: Some people will always find vice more attractive than virtue, and thus strive to appear virtuous in public affairs whilst practicing deceit in private. Always beware of what men do in the name of good. In this blatant manner, corrupt politicians may gain great rewards for little honest effort—thereby riding free on the public railroad to prosperity. While the five Confucian pairs provided great stability to the Chinese state, political corruption frequently took a great toll upon both material progress and rulers' integrity. The chief reason for the turnover amongst Chinese ruling dynasties took the form of massive political corruption—at various points so blatant as to remove the Mandate of Heaven from a reigning emperor. Corruption was the Chinese storyline, as well as the West's.[7]

Appeals to honor and virtue always fall short of success, because some men believe that no one will see what they do in the dark: the Hebrew storyline. It began with the serpent and Eve in the garden, where the serpent, "more subtil than any beast of the field", assures Eve that God does not really mean what he says, or perhaps He merely changes his mind. Or, maybe he is simply sleeping.[8] The whole trajectory of history driven by God's desire for people to live at peace gets violated again and again. Righteousness and peace do kiss—but only for a handful. Harmony driven by the sacred fails far too often. God won't see, most people reckon. At the extreme, the Hebrew prophet Elijah suggests to the prophets of their god Baal that perhaps he is not actually sleeping during their self-flagellating appeals for rain; perhaps he just stepped out for a piss.

---

[7] See Chapter Nine and Appendix C for a judgment upon both East and West regarding political corruption.

[8] *Genesis* 3:1, KJV.

Of Blood and Soil

> Blood and Soil (*Blut und Boten*) is a nationalist slogan expressing the 19th-century German idealization of a racially defined national body (blood) united with a settlement area (soil).
>
> *Wikipedia*

> *Hwaet! We Gardena in geardagum....* [Hear! We the Spear Danes in days of yore...]
>
> *Beowulf,* Prologue

A clear reason exists for why Herr Hitler adopted the 19th-century German ideological statement *Blood and Soil*: It works to unite a people, and to focus anger upon the "other." Every advance in human organization spills out of that slogan. Blood unites a present generation to previous ones—a most basic element to human identity. Long before Westerners came to possess surnames, the most common way to distinguish one person from another was to attach a phrase meaning "son/daughter of so-and-so" to a personal name. For ancient Israel it was *bar*—as in "Simon bar Jonah"—"Simon son of Jonah"—as found in *Matthew* 16:17. For the Scots and the Irish it would be *Mc* or *Mac*—somewhat interchangeably. So, the lead character in William Shakespeare's tragedy *Macbeth* actually in history was named "Macbeth mac Findlaech." The Chinese still to this day maintain the surname followed by the personal name formulation: Blood is more important than individual identity. In the finest Early English literary work, *Beowulf,* the Spear Danes recount their folk mythology as founded in blood in a particular location. Soil links blood to geography.

All human sensibility of belonging of course stems from the mother-infant relation. For every infant, relations of belonging extend outward from mother to father, relatives, fellow villagers. It may extend farther to include clan members and tribal relations. That is about as far as it goes as a matter of direct human limitations. Once an organization goes beyond an extended family, some other glue becomes necessary if comity amongst the larger group is to form and survive—some form of common history. Sometimes that history becomes shaped by one brilliant poet, as in the Greek Homer's *Iliad* and *Odyssey*. Or, the *Beowulf* poet. Blood and soil join hands to form tribes: blood initially and then soil as agriculture set in. And the order of things matters here: Heroic Myth comes before the tribal union of families and clans; Heroic Myth fixes people's beliefs about who they are and where they originate. Then beliefs change behaviors of each one toward the others. A new culture becomes conceived and born.

This works fine for uniting people of common ancestry into a tribe—but not so well for larger organizations of unlike-minded folks. Inevitably, as a tribe seeks to control more land, non-tribal members become unhappy and tend toward revolts. Force only works for so long and so far, and so empires eventually crumble. Things can get very messy in the meantime, because underlying every tribe an *Ur*-story still lives—a Heroic Legend that remains deep within the tribesmen's souls. *The Water Margin*.

Blut und Boten. The evil genius of Herr Hitler intuitively tapped into the Germanic *Ur* story that had already been stoked by Richard Wagner's 19th-century operas. *Blut und Boten* thus would yield *Das Tausend Jahr Reich*—a criminal enterprise that, in the end, lasted but 12 years. From this debacle—which hurried the most civilized and highbrow country on earth into barbarism—we should recognize two outstanding matters: One, underneath thriving, pulsating modernity, the German people possessed within them the *Ur* story of racial superiority and the right to conquest of the other. We might turn to the Swiss psychologist Carl Gustav Jung and his theory of the collective unconscious holding within it the archetypal experiences of an entire nation. Somewhat like an onion, layers of recall, both conscious and unconscious reside within us all. The deepest of these, to the very center of the onion, dwell unknown within us—until some passionate appeal to them awakens us to violent darkness. Two, current culture is neither the highest form of human relations nor the unalterable inheritance of a tribe.

Culture merely consists of behaviors shaped by beliefs—and beliefs have great malleability as well as ancient roots. A current popular manner of regarding things places culture at the top of a pyramid, with political, economic, and social matters descending down and determined by it. In reality, the relation of all these matters appears more as a circle than a skyscraper. A people's beliefs may change fairly radically in very short order, and in so doing change culture as well. A people's deepest beliefs, however—the *Ur* stories of a tribe—will prove the hardest to change.

Founding Myths

> Myth: A usually traditional story of ostensibly historical events that serves to unfold part of the worldview of a people or explain a practice, belief or natural phenomenon.
>
> A popular belief or tradition embodying the ideals and institutions of a society.
>
> *Merriam-Webster Dictionary*

> Mythos: A Greek word meaning "word" or "tale" or "true narrative", referring not only to the means by which it was transmitted but also to its being rooted in truth.
>
> Ancient Origins

Nothing holds a tribe or nation together quite like a *founding myth*, as has already been described above for Germany. Founding Hero stories abound as testimony to this, all possessing some element of myth regarding a founder. But what happens when one tribe gains control over another and seeks to adopt it? Then, something must be done to create a new, unifying founding myth, or continual conflict will disturb the two tribes' relations. Almost by definition, success in marrying two or more tribes or nations together involves the *metaphysical*—that which exists in a realm one order or two above the tales of a hero founder. As a rule of thumb: The new founding myth that integrates two or more tribes or nations must be at least one order of belief above any existing order. Furthermore, while the *hardware* aspect of uniting disparate tribes cannot be neglected, without the *software* founding myth a successful union will fail. The *hardware* of course, may best be described as *law and order*—the police function of any government, exemplified by the Qin. The solution to perennial warfare amongst tribes, then, must be the inculcation of a metaphysical universe atop a physical ordering of things.

Founding myths may take one of two forms: First, a conquering tribe or nation may simply absorb portions of a conquered people's own heroic myths. In the West, the Romans appear as the all-time great myth thieves; they adopted pretty much wholesale the entire mythic structure of gods and goddesses conceived by the Greeks. When a former enemy's myths become absorbed into a new entity, that gives the conquered peoples a sense of ownership within the new entity. The new, mythic confederation then possesses an even more powerful metaphysical basis. Otherwise, a founding myth must get stitched together entirely of new cloth. In reality, and until very recent times, a larger nation's founding myth always incorporated elements from defeated tribes.[9]

For the Chinese, that supernatural superstructure took the form of the Mandate from Heaven descending down from *Tao*—the impersonal, natural order of things. Ancient Chinese philosophers sought to engage the people, common and noble alike, in aligning with the harmony of the supernatural *Tao* in order to bring harmony on earth. Ancient Chinese stories, such as those encapsulated in *The Water Margin,* add to the overall myth and comprise the founding mythology of the East. The myth is very supernatural. The five Confucian pairs are very natural.

Perhaps the finest example of a metaphysical founding myth appears in the Hebrew Torah. Here, the founding myth begins with the creation story—a look into the sacred. Many tribal and national myths over time included creation stories, but none approach the brilliance of the first three chapters of *Genesis*—partly because *Genesis* appears to be the product of a cultured and literate court society, not the legend of a primitive tribe. It may well be that the *Genesis* writer lived some half-dozen centuries after the recounting of the actual founder's myth—the Abraham story. *Genesis* paints a picture with words of a supreme deity of both ineffable and intimate dimensions who holds the thread of all human history in his words. In any case, the book provides the sacred superstructure for Israel's tribal founding myth.

The Torah founding mythology is anything but a sanitization of what actually took place on the ground. Its writers never appear to flinch from some truly ugly truths about humanity: warts and all recounting. It begins with the Lord God calling one single human being, a man part of a seminomadic tribe of no great wealth or repute—a primitive clansman living on the edge of a great city-state. The writer then takes us through the trials and perils—the good, the bad, and the ugly—of that one man, Abraham, and his progeny. They appear to reach the end of the story when all 12 tribes of them, descended from their common father Israel, descended

[9]One should note here that only very recently, within the diversity movements of the West, have political movements sought to divest their nations of "appropriated" mythic elements from defeated subgroups—thereby eliminating one powerful source of national unity. The same political movements strive to create new, negative founding myths, myths that attack the pillars of the union. How this will play out remains to be seen.

from Isaac descended from Abraham, ultimately descended from Adam, find themselves laboring in slavery in ancient Egypt. Stripped of humanity and indeed of any founding story of themselves. The spoiled refuse of a brutal bondage.

Then, through a series of miraculous events, one of their members, Moses by name, stands in a desert transfixed before a fiery bush that cannot be consumed. And the Lord God recalls for Moses who He is and what He has promised a once and future people of His own choosing. Moses by the strong right hand of the Lord God leads his people out of bondage and eventually to a promised land. Moses before the Lord God on the mountain of the Lord receives the basis for all Jewish law. All in all, it stands as a most remarkable founding myth—a second or third order metaphysical creation standing above the secular story. It unites twelve pitiful, squabbling tribes, numbering perhaps in the hundreds of thousands, into one people with a powerful founding myth. And although the resulting nation Israel ultimately fails in antiquity, it rises again in our own time. And the figure of Moses leads us right into the last subject matter of this chapter.

Of Brave Reciprocators

> You have heard that it was said, "You shall love your neighbor and hate your enemy." But I say to you, love your enemies and pray for those who persecute you.
>
> *Matthew* 5:43-44, ESV

> What you do not wish for yourself, do not do to others.
>
> Confucius, *Lunyu* 12.2, 6.30

> These all died in faith, not having received the promises, but having seen them afar off, and were persuaded of them, and embraced them, and confessed that they were strangers and pilgrims on the earth.
>
> *Hebrews* 11:13, KJV

In the extended Prisoners' Dilemma game, playing simple tit-for-tat is the most successful common strategy—mirroring in our application of the game the reality that in primitive tribal relations, if one tribe got attacked, the best strategy was to attack back. Then, other tribes might learn to leave it alone. Maybe. The problem with tit-for-tat is that it can easily degenerate into continually repeated warfare. Some reversing incentive is needed to bring harmony or peace. In the game, only one other strategy could beat tit-for-tat: the Brave Reciprocator. The Brave Reciprocator always returns good for bad—the mirror-image of the nasty player who always gives his opponent a bad. Played over enough iterations, the brave-reciprocator strategy will beat all others. Whom might we regard from our studies so far as being a brave reciprocator? Confucius, who sought to bring harmony within a terrible period of warfare in China? Moses, who led his people out of captivity and made of many one nation? Socrates and Aristotle who sought to inculcate virtue into ancient Athens? Jesus who died by judicial murder in order that all men might be made free? Mahatma Gandhi who used a nonviolence developed out of the teachings of Jesus to free India from the British Raj? Surely, all of them.

Note that all of these six brave reciprocators received some form of rejection by their own people, except perhaps for Aristotle. Two died by judicial murder. Confucius was not murdered but did receive severe persecution. Together they define the meaning of *brave reciprocator*—men willing to die for their beliefs about the importance of peace and harmony. Should we mark them down as failures? By no means! Consider what these men accomplished: Confucius defined for China the way to harmony and taught a very pragmatic course for achieving it. In various forms, his way to harmony has remained with the Chinese for some 2,500 years—and still has force within Chinese culture to this day. Moses, by following the Lord God's plan for peace, created the underpinnings for one of the world's first emerging nation-states, founded upon law and justice, dedicated to helping the poorest and neediest—something Jews do to this day. Aristotle and Socrates defined for the West the nature of true virtue—and set the foundation for all modern science. Jesus, some would argue, fulfilled the Hebrew scriptures and laid the cornerstone for the peaceable kingdom to come: Righteousness and peace kiss.

The world of these men's times considered them failures. They suffered humiliation and persecution. Yet, how many of their warrior opponents changed the world? The warrior conquerors never remake human institutions for the better. The broken statue of the warrior Ozymandias, symbol of the conquering warrior, still remains broken and abandoned in the desert of time speaking mutely and without effect: "My name is Ozymandias. Look upon my works ye mighty and despair."

Whenever the world turns upside down, whenever something totally new and holding the promise that we shall live on the higher uplands of human peace, love and joy, look for one of the few—the band of brave reciprocators throughout time who have changed the hearts and minds of mankind for the better. They stand as the true men of valor.

Conclusions

Large and complex human governing organizations can never succeed long-term strictly upon the *hardware* application of raw force to conquered peoples, or even upon the application of *law and order* police power. Longer term, *peace and plenty* pointing toward the higher uplands of happiness and even joy must enter into the mix. *Plenty* may be partly material in nature, along with other hardware factors technological in nature. *Peace*, however, requires software factors—especially founding myth. Peace, then, requires as change agents the philosophers and brave reciprocators of human history. It may all add up to a place where "righteousness and peace kiss."

***

1. A nation's *hardware* devolves from the engineers and administrators and provides technology and power to create *plenty*.
2. A nation's *software* devolves from its philosophers and brave reciprocators who provide the fruitful beliefs that create cultures of *peace*.
3. Only when both *hardware* and *software* effects come together into place can a *common good* get created for everyone within a country.

***

Discoveries:

The past was far bloodier than the present. In percentage terms, far more people got starved or slaughtered in the ancient world than in our own time despite our world wars and mass extermination projects, because of the nature of the perpetual tribal warfare then omnipresent. Nothing then existed to counteract the cult of the conquering warrior. Harmony simply did not exist.

(*Continued*)

(*Continued*)

"Software" changes always precede "hardware." Before men's behavior with regard to violence and theft changes, their beliefs about the goodness of combat first has to change. Beliefs always come before behavior and shape it.

The classical philosophers were the greatest benefactors of mankind. The philosophers through a drawn-out process of discovery and debate determined the better ways of human relations to yield peace and harmony out of war and hatred.

Every race is first won or lost in the human mind. Beliefs determine conduct. Before the moral or immoral action comes a belief about that action. Change the belief and change the conduct.

Perception is always subjective. Perception determines our reactions to observed events, but perceptions are always filtered through each person's perception filter: To a large degree, we see not what we see, the objective reality, but what wish to see—what our beliefs desire us to see in an event. Perception tends to reinforce what we already believe, before any perceived event occurs.

Culture is neither fixed nor determinate of politics, economics or social relations. Culture consists of the sum total of all human beliefs and interactions within a social group. Culture shapes beliefs which largely determine conduct, but beliefs are malleable, and changing beliefs changes conduct which changes culture. Culture does not sit unmolested atop the social pyramid but rather joins hands with beliefs and conduct in a great circle of social being—a Three-Legged Stool.

Game theory can help us understand complex human behaviors. In a version of the Prisoners' Dilemma, the behavior of social groups toward one another can be modeled: Social groups may either cooperate with each other to enlarge the sum total of human happiness, or they can attack and steal from one another for personal gain. Only four pure strategies emerge from the extended play of this game: Three of them are aggression, tit-for-tat play, and passivity. Tit-for-tat almost always wins—which partly explains the ongoing

(*Continued*)

(*Continued*)

aggressiveness in clannish and tribal cultures. Only one strategy, the fourth, achieves peace and harmony in the long run—the brave reciprocator that uses nonviolence as a weapon to defeat aggressive conduct *in the long run.* In world history, the brave reciprocators include Confucius, Moses, Socrates and Aristotle, and Jesus. And India's Mahatma Gandhi.

Times of violence, chaos, and uncertainty frequently give birth to philosophers of peace. Chaos itself motivates some men to consider ways to bring order and peace. Because beliefs determine behavior, and perceptions influence beliefs, philosophers who see the appalling nature of violence will seek for ways for people to see things differently; they will seek to discover how to change common beliefs about conduct.

The Free Rider problem in social relations. Some people will always engage in bad behaviors, because they believe that no one—not the gods or the God, or the authorities, will notice. Free riders that go unpunished will unravel the intricate lace of civil discourse and conduct.

Blut und Boten. Blood and soil lay at the very heart of each person's being: *Blood*, or the affinity of those of one's own tribe, and *Soil,* or the locality of one's birth and living, have a buried but primeval influence even within sophisticated societies. Heroic warrior tales of the tribe still stimulate primal rage. Primitive blood and soil beliefs, every person's *Ur*-story, always threaten to bring violence and chaos out from the surface of civil conduct. Lurking in the cellars of humanity, they are very hard to extinguish.

Founding myths define the metaphysically-based solutions to organized violence. In order to unite tribes and destroy hero warrior codes of conduct, the classical philosophers created second and third order metaphysical understandings for human relations—meta-realities. Only a meta-reality founding myth has the power to unite hero-warrior tribal myths to form a stable great society in a larger political unit—a nation-state.

(*Continued*)

(*Continued*)

Founding myths absorb mythic elements from defeated rivals/enemies in order to give conquered peoples ownership in new and larger entities.

Brave reciprocators—the world's true heroes. Overcoming beliefs deeply entrenched in the human heart and continually reinforced by subjective perceptions requires "world turned upside down" cultural change. Only brave reciprocators—people with the courage to rise above tribal hatreds—can initiate progress toward peace and harmony. Only then can "righteousness and peace kiss."

Chapter Three

The Three-Legged Stool and the Quest for Harmony

Overview: We took up the fundamental issues of *hardware* and *software* components to human governance in the previous two chapters—both issues relating to the emergence of the nation-state. The last of three fundamental issues—the Rule of Three—gets developed in this chapter. In it, we argue that dyadic human organizations—essentially *command and control* in nature—are inherently flawed and unstable without third, mediating institutions as well. We regard the issue of mediating institutions as being necessary for peace and harmony within three areas of organizational life: *executive, judicial*, and *marketplace.*

If you do not change direction, you may end up where you are going.

Old Chinese aphorism

Introduction: The very first Three-Legged Stool

The Idea of the Numinous

And He said, "Draw not nigh hither: Put off thy shoes from off thy feet, for the place whereon thou [Moses] standeth is holy ground."

Exodus 3:5, KJV

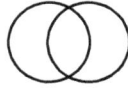

The first *physical* three-legged stools doubtless served as stable campfire seats for irregular ground; then presumably came milking stools. Here, however, we take up the subject of the first *metaphysical* three-legged stool—an institutional arrangement in which three countervailing forces bring about a balance between those forces, achieving a harmony, or at least a peace, within group relations. Once more, there are just a few stories, ones that reveal the existence and workings of this stool. The stories recount the existence and effects of three institutions that have perpetuated tribal organizations for perhaps 30,000 years, right into our present time. The three institutions? The sacred (or taboo), the sacrificial, and the shamanistic. From these seemingly unrelated primitive arrangements came an evolution that would contribute to the stability of the tribe, and eventually the nation-state.

In the beginning was the *idea of the numinous*.[1] It seems that from the earliest records of paleolithic humans, searches have been carried out in the quest to find some supernatural meanings to the *first-order questions of life*: Who am I? Where did I come from? What happens when I die? Modern anthropologists speculate that paleolithic caves with their vivid paintings found throughout the world had purposes, beyond security, related to the quest for the supernatural. The caves themselves generally feature paintings in vivid colors of powerful animals—bison, horses, antelope, cattle—and birds. No fish; nothing aquatic. Bone remains suggest that the caves were sites for shamanistic worship calling upon the invisible forces of the supernatural, including animal sacrifice—and sometimes human.

Two directions within this quest for the supernatural appear to have existed: One, the acquisition of power. Primitive humans believed that great power dwelt in these animals, power that might be acquired through the killing of them and the drinking of their blood. Similarly, the blood of a defeated and dead enemy tribesman might get drunk in order to acquire his strength, and to deprive his living tribesmen of the same. Blood had great significance within ancient beliefs of humans worldwide: There are just people, and all people believe the same few stories—blood obtained through sacrifice; blood drunk. Perhaps frenzy from the whole experience, then perhaps rampages: Blood drove aggression. Blood sacrificed to

[1]Rudolph Otto in *The Idea of the Holy* formulates the idea of the numinous that we rely upon here.

supernatural beings was thought to please those beings and to buy their favor—especially in warfare against other tribes. More aggression.

The other direction? The pursuit of the numinous—the all-powerful, all-consuming totally other, eventually perceived as the *holy.* The numinous drove submission. Probably through the shamans' trances, tribal elites came to believe that some actions and places were meant to be reserved without trespass for the supernatural powers, which in turn became identified with their earthly image counterparts, idols, made in the image of the powerful animals. The shamans were, and still are, the workers of both naturalistic healing and super-naturalistic communication with the numinous. They therefore dealt in revelations, portents, prophecies, curses, hexes, spells—the full panoply of witchery. They came to assume great power in all primitive tribes, because they very often proved to be right. Therefore, they drove both primitive taboo law and sacrifice. Law was what the numinous conveyed through the shamans to be wrong; law instituted taboo: the "thou shalt not." Taboo bound even the most powerful rulers. Do not go against that which is taboo. Shamans dictated what should be sacrificed to the numinous, the gods, as either payment for earthly power over others or for wrongs committed against others.

Although many anthropologists have observed these primitive institutions still working today in such places as Haiti, the manner in which the three work in sympathy with one another, like unto a Three-Legged Stool, seems to have been ignored. Perhaps we should begin a consideration of this matter by observing the significance of the three sympathetic institutions for a primitive tribes' ruling elites. We might first observe how frail is the picture painted by the peaceful savage philosophers such as Jean Jacques Rousseau, beginning in the 18th century. The peaceful primitives picture culminates in Dr. Harari's recent book *Sapiens.* Lolling about and eating fresh fruits and vegetables, and chatting one another up, the happy natives supposedly lived the most joyful of lives. In reality, as well documented in both current anthropological research and ancient texts, their lives were anything but carefree, or free, for that matter. Every member of every primitive tribe, even the tribal leader and elites, almost surely was shackled by the threefold institutions of taboo, sacrifice, and shamanism, which worked together to bind tightly all human initiative.

Consider the matter of going to war or to raid. While the tribal warlord would have a dyadic relation—leader/follower—to his warriors, the matter of launching a surprise attack could not be undertaken with impunity. If the spirits of the tribe were against such an action, it would doubtless become a bloody failure. No, the tribal chief would first have to consult the spirits—if for no other reason that his men, normally followers, might revolt without the assurances of the spirits. How might the chief, then, obtain a judgment about the matter? One of two ways: He might first offer sacrifices, to be "read" by a member of the priestly caste or by a shaman—a medium or witch doctor: What do the entails reveal? Or, he might first directly consult a witch doctor. The Israelite King Saul did this with the Witch of Endor, and the prophecy pointed to his doom.[2] This whole procedure was also meant to assure the tribal chief that he and his warriors would be breaking no taboos placed by the spirits. If the action passed these tests, and proper sacrifices were offered, then it could be undertaken with a high degree of certainty of success. In this manner, a rough and ready version of the Rule of Three worked out: The shaman and/or the priests mediated between the chief and the spirits and between the war chief and his warriors. The shaman may have mediated between priests and ruler also.

This was all fine for the elites of the tribe, but what about the commoners—the followers of the chief and the spirits? How did they tie in to all of this? Here once more, even at the lowliest level, taboo, sacrifice, and witchery mattered. If, as a lowly tribal member, I were to believe that another member had wronged me—let's say, stolen and eaten my chicken—then I might consider a confrontation, but never an act of outright violence. That would be taboo. Besides, I might be wrong about my accusation. And so, I would go in secret to the tribal witch doctor about the matter. The witch doctor would enter into a trance state—perhaps induced by a powerful herbal hallucinogen. If he received confirmation from the spirits while in this state, he would so inform his "patient." Then, the patient would pay the witch doctor to place a curse upon that man. The payment would take the form of a sacrifice made to the spirits, perhaps in the form of another chicken, but with the dead corpse handed over to the witch doctor. The curse might take a mild, or even a very violent form. If within the next several days all of the chickens of the tribal member doing the initial wrong up and died, no one would be surprised.

Of course, errors or great retaliatory anger could arise—at either the level of the tribal elites or that of the very humble. If the party on the receiving end of a curse felt wronged himself, or very angry, he might himself approach a witch doctor, maybe the same one or maybe not, and

[2] 1 *Samuel* 28.

ask that witch doctor to put a curse on the man who initiated that curse against him. And so, a game of tit-for-tat could materialize. This sort of game would be unlikely to occur, however, for fear of the consequences of committing taboo—placing false curses. In summation, the three aforementioned institutions operated together to bring a sort of peace and harmony within the physical, emotional, and supernatural realms of the whole tribe.

The Surprising Endurance of the Tribal

We know so much about these primitive matters, because this Three-Legged Stool still sits stable in many current primitive tribal Voodoo cultures. Its very existence troubles many elites of the West today; after all, this stuff *is* very primitive and therefore cannot really be true—they think. We are almost all at least quasi-Hegelians today, believing in the sole power of reason and rejecting all notions of tribal or familial spirits, or the supernatural generally. How, then, shall we reconcile observed realities with rational prejudices? We should begin by stating very clearly the truth: Voodoo stuff works. When someone gets a death curse placed upon him, he dies. Breaking taboo generally brings down disaster upon the interloper. Fear of the numinous is for these people very real. On the other hand, witch doctors also sometimes bring down remarkable healings from out of the spirit world.

Two possibilities exist as explanations: One, this is all a matter of psychology. People believe this Voodoo nonsense, and so they do become sick, or die, or have other bad things happen to them. It's in their minds. The problem with this facile explanation? Well-documented cases of deaths following curses exist where the unfortunate individuals clearly have no knowledge of those curses or of the people having curses placed upon them. Twentieth-century thinking then may turn to the paranormal, a quirky sideline to the psychology field. The other explanation appears even less palatable to the modern mind: The numinous really does exist. Mankind has since Paleolithic times actively sought out knowledge of the numinous and of the power existing in the numinous—something we wish to explore next.

Whatever the true explanation, the primitive Three-Legged Stool did, and still does, really exist, and it has worked to bring a perhaps very twisted measure of peace within primitive tribes otherwise known for extreme forms of violence and cruelty. See Dr. Pinker on this one.[3] We should not minimize the abominations practiced by primitive peoples—for they have included such things as extreme forms of torture and also human sacrifice excruciatingly painful to the victims—even going so far as to involve tribal rulers sacrificing their own children to the tribal spirits. It has been a peace based upon cruelty and upon the sheer, stark terror of the numinous.

One should note in summary that the sacred, sacrificial, shamanistic Three-Legged Stool does not appear to have ever had a well-defined administrative apparatus. Both priests and witch doctors seem to have arisen spontaneously from out of each tribe. No priestly or shamanistic schools seem to have existed. While sometimes passed down generationally, priests and witch doctors might also arise spontaneously. It might also change form radically as men sought to know more about the nature and identity of this mysterious matter—the numinous, the holy. After all, we are all learners.

The Evolution of the Tribal

> Before we had logic we had stories, ritual and symbols.
>
> Synopsis of *The Symbolic Species*, Terrence Deacon

East and West, the learners of the ancient world sought to know more about their own mysterious origins and about the mystical sense of the totally other, the numinous, whether personal or impersonal. In the East, the search led to the discoveries within Taoist and Buddhist beliefs. While pointing toward a penultimate, impersonal but totally other reality, in practice the East tended to see human experience as a dyadic struggle between light and darkness, war and peace, harmony and disharmony—a continual dyadic interplay of cosmic significance. In the West, the learners struggled on the way to discovering triadic structures. If tribal institutions about the numinous were disturbingly crude, that did not mean that the real nature of the numinous dwelt in that crudeness. All thought, certainly all science, has always begun at a level of a certain crudeness. Consider for instance widely held beliefs about humans existing on a racial superiority-inferiority scale. Very crude, indeed.

---

[3] Stephen Pinker, *The Better Angels of Our Nature*.

From the first, primitive Three-Legged Stool, something very different, but clearly related, gradually emerged—still in the shape of a triad: First, taboo changed from inchoate threat to mean beliefs about law coming down from the gods, or the One God. That meant rulers must use law to bring about order in the world of gods and men. Positive law followed, written first by the Greeks, by human lawmakers for men. In both cases, gods and men, the execution of order through the enforcement of law emerged from taboo. Ritual sacrifice vitiated its raw bloodiness to yield the concept of *justice*—at first divine, then of human nature, but always with a sense of keeping a balance in which the bad that men do gets repaid in some form of retribution. Thus, the image of the scales of justice appeared as a powerful symbolism—especially when personified and symbolized by a blindfolded Lady. The evolution of shamanism with its aura of evil influence hanging about it yielded to the prophet—particularly of Israel, most notably Isaiah, but also of Greece and Rome. The shaman becomes the forecaster of the future and the speaker for the achieving of the higher uplands of righteousness and peace—indeed, the conscience of the race of *homo sapiens*. All utopians and dreamers of tomorrow spring from the prophets' roots. The prophet confronts wrongdoing and corrupt lawmakers and executives. In ancient Israel, the prophet Nathan called out the powerful King David—"Thou art the man"—and brought about that potentate's humiliation.[4] From out of the bloody and primitive came the ideals of Western philosophy. The prophet stood as the mediating leg of this new Three-Legged Stool, demanding justice wherever there was none. *Law and order*, *justice*, and *mercy*. A new Rule of Three.

From the Visual to the Symbol: The Emergence of Conceptual Thinking

The movement from the primitive forebodings of Paleolithic man to the sublime conceptions of Hebrew scriptures and of the Taoist and Buddhist writers follows the developments of the human mind. The noted neuro-anthropologist Terrence Deacon speculates that primitive humans lacked the cognitive capacity for logic.[5] First, he speculates, came stories. Stories

---

[4]2 *Samuel* 12:7.

[5]Terrence Deacon, *The Symbolic Species: The Co-Evolution of Language and the Brain.*

were easy, and to this day they provide windows into human experience. The Hebrew writers always saw reality in terms of *relationships,* personal in nature—the essence of story; later on, the Greeks invented dispassionate categories of inquiry. Ritual symbols followed story. It is a true intellectual leap to go from stories about the great hunt for the bison to creating an image standing in for that great beast, a symbol to which belief attributed the same great powers as the beast itself. Symbols could then lead to logical thinking—and also ultimately to sacramental thinking, wherein the symbol could be seen to stand for some metaphysical and invisible category of existence—such as objective science and the idea of the *holy.*

The idea of the holy in turn led to the conception of third-level metaphysical thinking, which in turn yielded Taoist thought and the mandate of heaven for the East, and divine rights for kings in the West. Ultimately, the idea of the holy led to founders' myths far different from the inchoate dreads of Paleolithic mankind. Metaphysical founding myths, as laid out in Chapter Two, emerged from out of inchoate fears of the numinous and evolved through heroic warrior gods to sublime beliefs about heavenly origins.

Technology and Government

In what follows, we shall strive to discover the pathway leading to forms for the effective Rule of Three within the development of nations, a pathway that we maintain leads inexorably from the primitive tribe to the nation-state. A very good place to start is with a fundamental principle: *Technological revolutions drive structural changes in the governance of the affected tribes and nations*. As a corollary, technical *evolutions* downstream from *revolutions* then have been carried out through advanced national structures, eventually nation-state in form. Governance revolutions then make possible the advance of technical evolution. We have in our own times seen this pattern play out for the last 300 years or so. The Industrial Revolution in particular began with individual human creativity; that revolution's progression depended upon certain institutional changes within evolving particular nation-states—especially Great Britain. Intellectual property rights stand out as the most significant institutional change therein. The Chemical Revolution followed a similar pattern, this time centered in the emerging new German republic. The same pattern then appeared within the Second Agricultural Revolution that introduced nonorganic fertilizers—a technical offshoot of the Chemical Revolution but advanced by property rights liberties within Great Britain and the United States particularly. Nonorganic fertilizers broke the previous precarious link between cereal crop acreage and animal herd size. In our own times, authoritarian regimes in Russia and China drove rapid technological development, but only for basic industries. Governance evolutions did not follow technological revolutions.

With this as an introduction, what then drove the evolution of national forms of governance toward the triadic nation-state?

Which Came First—the Civil or the Military?

Today we quite rightly perceive the military as a somewhat necessary appendage to civil government and society. Many of us possess an inherent dislike for discipline and obedience, so we also dislike and distrust things military. Especially in the West, many see the military as the problem regarding peace, rather than a solution bringing peace. But was it always so? In reality, in terms of human organization, the military came first. We can readily see this today in some primitive intertribal relations that still center upon nearly continual, usually low-level, warfare. Above the level of the immediate family, the military—and the warrior ethic—dominated. Blood feuds at the clan level have persisted since the beginnings of recorded human history. Tribal feuds make up one of the few basic stories of human history. The reason is almost transparently clear: The presence of continual threats of violence, both from without and within each clan and tribe, necessitated command and control organizational structures. And these structures all have one thing in common: They are dyadic in nature. The leader and the led. Do what the leader demands, or die, or get raped, or serve as a slave. Only the primitive Rule of Three—sacred, sacrificial, shamanistic—prevented even bloodier outcomes.

Parenthetically, the military structure of human relations formed the resulting structure of productive enterprises shaping the Industrial Revolution. To this day, many private enterprises work in a military, top-down, manner—as do industrial and government labor structures. In the West, military organization shaped worker union responses to the corporation. This in turn accounts for why labor-management relations, in America at least, have so frequently been warlike as well. The East escaped the worst of these industrial struggles, having already created cultures favoring group over individual identities.

The matter of dyadic relations has great importance, for the social sciences have abundantly established that dyadic relations are inherently, and unavoidably, unstable. Yet, some nations have achieved a large measure of stability—and did so even in ancient times. A further look into the deep past will reveal the sources, and threats, to the stability that we find there—and also a key understanding for how to create stability in the present and future.

The Agricultural and Animal Husbandry Revolutions

The axle is easy; the wheel is hard.

Charles Krauthammer, *Things That Matter*

Back once more to that most pivotal of revolutions in all human history. The issues that the Agricultural Revolution raised for humankind have really not been fully appreciated from the point of view of the complexities in work, technology, skills, coordination, intercourse, and property rights it triggered. When paired with the related Animal Husbandry Revolution that closely followed, things became very much more complex and challenging indeed. Ultimately, these twin revolutions spelled trouble for dyadic tribal relations that brought so much cruelty to human existence.

One should never minimize the human skills required for hunter-gatherer living—especially those related to the arts of stalking and killing game. Nevertheless, these skills were far more primitive than what would be required for what followed, and they were dyadic: Every hunting and gathering party had its leaders and followers—and little in between. What little wealth a tribe possessed could easily be divided equally without contentious argument. Indeed, our present nonmetric counting system, based in equal divisions of a whole, descends from how tribes determined the shares of a hunt: A four-man hunting party cut up (literally) the whole of the capture into quarters—in half and then in half again. The share for the tribe's dependents got divided into halves several times. The system had great flexibility, as each category of member in the tribe, for instance children, could receive lesser or greater overall shares, still divided equally.[6]

[6] Well into modern times, the whaling industry paid its participants on the basis of shares or "lays" that could be valued differently by classes or workers: Captains and harpooners got much larger lays than the sailors who mainly provided muscle.

Practical carpentry and engineering advanced on the basic concept of dividing things in a similar manner: To put a timber in the center of two other timbers, fold a measuring string in half. Want four equal parts? Do the same again. That is how we still think.

The Agricultural Revolution introduced massive new requirements—largely driven by needs for new technical advances: soil conditioning, control of water resources, intercourse, accurate annual calendars, weather forecasting, willingness to make longer term investments, risk-reward calculations, incentives to industry, and protection of property rights. And of course, methods for controlling government corruption as well: *If there is anything to be stolen, a corrupt government official will try to do it.* A truly stunning array of industrial and social changes occurred in relatively short order—perhaps several thousand years. The beliefs that shape cultures can change dramatically fast: A thousand years is fast in Neolithic time.

Agriculture first drove human organization toward a feudal model, East and West, as tribal leaders quickly learned how to rent out their territories to the newly made farmers they relied upon for surpluses. None of these changes occurred through central planning; everything happened by spontaneous evolution. The changes took millennia to evolve completely. Nor did they happen peacefully. Ruling lords did see protecting their peasant farmers from marauding tribes as a worthwhile activity, in order to reap a larger part of a larger agricultural surplus. The Agricultural Revolution, then, birthed the institutions of feudalism and policing. Feudalism itself evolved out of a need for physical security from without and within, a security that could only be provided by a large, controlling entity—one that of course needed to be fed, through taxation in kind.

One should note the single thing it did not birth: agricultural collectivism—the bane of the modern world. The modern examples of collective farming on a large scale notably include slave cotton and sugar plantations, and the farming collectives of Russia and China. Brutality and starvation followed in their wakes. The exceptions appear within small, homogeneous countries such as modern Israel where kibbutz collectives meet the requirements of a singularly-purposed population. While the ancient records contain many, many instances of government officials forcing slave labor on massive public works projects such as those created by the Qin, farming rarely benefited from such efforts, aside from government-directed intercourse with farmers aimed at tax collection. The government carts could do that part of economic intercourse involving moving crops, either to market or to the lord's own storage barns. The difference is stunning; why one and not the other? This discrepancy should point us toward the inherently most important aspects to operating an agricultural economy: incentives to labor and inventiveness, soil management, and property rights. These three factors, in turn, will point us to the factors limiting the success of agriculture in bringing about peace and plenty.

Agriculture in the pre-mechanized equipment era meant very hard work indeed—backbreaking human labor. Unlike hunting, it had little flexibility in required work regimes, little time in season for resting and sauntering about. Without a generous return to it, labor would get withheld. Crucial activities such as manuring the soil or irrigating plants or pulling weeds would get stinted. Landlords always had incentives to increase rents and to practice *rent-racking*: Should a farmer with insecure land rights strive to improve the soil under his care, his landlord might very well auction off his improved land to another. Best then to do as little as possible to feed one's family amidst the choking weeds. It took immeasurably long time periods for landlords to learn the simple lesson: Long land leases bring greater crop yields. A basic principle driving human behavior: *People do what they know how to do, even when it no longer works*. We are all slow learners.

The land itself rarely was the property of the individual peasant and his family, given the feudal system of land control. And so, right up into the 19th century, the matter of land rents vexed economists in the West. It became so concerning that any attempts to obtain larger than normal profits, often through government corruption, got called *rent seeking*. Even today in the West, seeking extra-normal profits from government monopolies and other favors gets labelled *rent seeking*. Parenthetically, well into the 20th century, land in Great Britain was owned by the Crown and not by citizens who could only have a leasehold on it. Generally speaking, agriculture could only flourish when farmers had rights to the fruits of their own labor.

The soil itself makes for the most fascinating element for agricultural development—because its necessary conditioning led to the Animal Husbandry Revolution. Certainly, going back to Neolithic times, people had observed that plants grew very well indeed in dunged soil, which could occur naturally. On the other hand, soil not dunged produced increasingly poorer plant yields, year after year. Applying dung to soil quickly followed in-place agriculture itself: Rich soil yields rich crop yields. One ready source of dung, of course, was what used to be called, euphemistically, *night soil*—human excrement collected, usually at night when the better folks slept, for the purpose. In some traditional societies, in India for instance, the unfortunates of a particularly lower caste received the dubious honor of a monopoly on collecting other peoples' poop.[7] Determining the "rights" to poop would become a weighty matter in all agricultural societies—right up to the Second Agricultural Revolution and its embrace of chemical fertilizers, which in turn had come from the Chemical Revolution. The matter of animal manure becomes really quite fascinating, however, when one explores its relation to the Old Agriculture (before the advent of chemical fertilizers commenced the New Agriculture). Manually manuring crops is a weighty matter, and one requiring both physical and mental brawn.

While domesticated animals had some limited place in hunter-gatherer tribes, dogs for hunting and security, for instance, animal husbandry only really came into its own with the advent of in-place agriculture. In the beginning, keeping domesticated large animals had the triple purposes of supplying manure for crops, nutrient-rich plants for peasants, and also meat—and *horsepower* to ease the physical burdens imposed upon humans by such agriculture. However, these same large domestic creatures had to be fed themselves. Here the brainy part of agriculture grew: How should I as an individual farmer allocate my land between crops to feed my family and grazing for animal stock? Too much land devoted to people crops, and crop yields fall due to lack of adequate animal feed and manure. You can only spread the stuff so thin. Too many grazing cattle, and cereal food shortages develop for humans. The balance of things has to be gotten right—especially in more northern climates where feedstock requirements come into play for wintering over a herd.[8] Out of such knowledge came the incentives to change animals themselves.

Selective breeding goes back at least some 5,000 years. Cattle got bred for larger size and more meat, or for greater strength. And, bigger cows, more poop. Remember, it is always more costly to haul food to

[7]Recently in North Korea the people have been give minimum weights for collections of their own excrement. How a starving population can meet such requirements boggles the mind.

[8] One might add in that it is a tricky matter even to know when to plant and when to harvest. Some very wise men observing the heavens created in turn the Neolithic computers still seen marking the landscapes of places such as Stonehenge in southwestern England.

people than for people to walk to food—the amount we consume is related to our own weights. So, draft animals came of selective breeding. They performed specialized labor-enhancing tasks such as plowing and hauling crops. The same sheep and goats that provided wool for the cloth that largely replaced animal hides for clothing in agricultural communities also provided meat, milk, and manure. And then, oh rats! Rats and other rodents could quickly consume a quarter or more of an annual food crop if not deterred. So, selective breeding yielded domesticated cats and dogs who specialized in destroying rats. And water. Large animals eventually became harnessed to means for irrigating acreage in semi-arid lands—such as the Middle East where, to this day, the Israelis, one may readily see, develop advanced technologies for water collection, conservation, irrigation, and desalinization. Animals are great. The whole combined revolutions in agriculture and animals became a most complicated ecosystem. None of it came about by central planning. All of it introduced new modes of doing work—things that changed culture forever.

Lastly, the matter of property rights. One might begin by observing that agriculture and animal husbandry allowed for, indeed required, far greater population concentrations than those feasible under the old hunter-gatherer economy. The development of larger settlements and, eventually, of market towns and then city-states only became possible because of the dual effects of population concentration and division of labor. The world's first economist, Adam Smith, understood these factors very well, especially division of labor.[9] Property rights had little role to play in human affairs until the effects of the Agricultural Revolution became more apparent. Prior to that, certain hunting and fishing grounds constituted the sum total of concern. Then, things got complex., as we shall shortly see.

The Birth of Trust

The big twin revolutions—Agricultural and Animal Husbandry—worked another major change in work modes: needs for *trust* from former dependents. The new emerging existence of significant material wealth and of complicated intercourse in the means of producing that wealth created a need for dominant male members of family groups to entrust other members with significant responsibilities. This certainly applied to a

[9] Adam Smith, *The Wealth of Nations*—especially the beginning on division of labor.

farmer's sons. It also applied to farmers' women. The image of a farm couple as like unto a pair of yoked oxen began to appear. A radical redefinition of male-female relations within the broader social order began—most significantly amongst ruling elites. King David of ancient Israel (reigning roughly from 1000–960 BC) possessed many wives, although only eight got named; his successor King Solomon had gotten 1,000 wives and concubines—many of them pregnant. Whew! Hard work that, keeping all members of a huge harem happy. In a few hundred years' time, the kings of both Judah and Israel were monogamous—having only one consort—and some of them possessing significant political power of their own—such as Jezebel. By the time of Jesus of Nazareth, polygamy was severely frowned upon, though most women had no rights within marriage and could be divorced at will.

In general, the nature of male-female relations had serious implications for social stability. In hunter-gatherer and semi-nomadic arrangements, a major part of tribal conflicts the world over involved the theft of animals and of women. The theft of women only exacerbated the tendency for wealth inequality. Tribal leaders accumulated several, and even many, wives, while their dependent tribal males might never gain a woman at all. This inequity also promoted the formation of outlaw bands, groups of lawless men without women, unable to form stable family relations, who preyed upon the vulnerable. Once the twin revolutions began making emperors and then feudal lords wealthy, possessing a large harem at first became for Middle Eastern potentates a powerful means of conspicuous consumption, to adopt a phrase from Thorsten Veblen. Yet the standard of more wives and concubines for the wealthy than for the poor itself broke down—in favor of one wife for each man.

Why should such a movement occur at all? A thorny question. After all, women had no rights to pursue the issue. Why would not men simply continue in the age-old fashion, treating women like cattle or slaves? No great body of direct evidence seems to exist for why the change happened. One must suspect that the change had a relation to the twin revolutions that were causing the world of work to turn upside down. There is one fascinating clue contained within a famous passage in Hebrew scripture—*Proverbs* 31. It runs to 31 verses as well, far too long to quote at length here, but a small sample will indicate its content:

> An excellent wife who can find? She is far more precious than jewels

> The heart of her husband trusts in her, and he will have no lack of gain....
> She is like the ships of the merchant; she brings her food from afar....
> She considers a field and buys it; with the fruit of her hands she plants a vineyard.
> She dresses herself with strength and makes her arms strong.
> She perceives that her merchandise is profitable....
> She opens her hand to the poor and reaches out her hands to the needy.

While this Proverb surely has an idealized nature, it does point out several things regarding the wife's role in the new family of the twin revolutions. First, women were taking on new and responsible roles far beyond those of mere slaves. Second, women were being *trusted* by their husbands—trusted to undertake new and demanding actions. And men, in turn, apparently became trusted—somewhat—not to screw around with the female help, as Abraham had done. New roles and trust were being driven by the complex demands of a market-based social order. Husbands and wives now, to varying degrees, cooperated, coordinated with, and complemented each other—and not just in making the beast with two backs. It became important for the first time that a husband and wife should form a close bond and relate to one another humanely, even if not equally. Marriage as a formal institution offered both parties assurances of long-term commitment, of mutual trust. It would become a normative institution. It protected both parties, but women more so, from violations attempted by people outside that bond—from rapists and competitors. As a related evolution, polygamy began to lose favor, because it severed bonds of mutual trust—as the Hebrew story of Abraham's number-one-woman-scorned, Sarah, relates.[10] It easily created situations involving competition amongst multiple wives and concubines. There are only a few stories, and the seductive concubine versus the aggrieved wife was one of them.

One last piece of the puzzle now falls into place: The institution of monogamous marriage internalized a major dimension to the overall violence culture—the theft, seduction, rape, and general abuse of women. Violence directed by male gangs against the women in communities would nearly disappear. The individual conflicts between one man and

[10] See *Genesis* 16 for the story of Sarai (Sarah) and Hagar.

one woman replaced all of that macro-violence. The "war between the sexes", whilst nettlesome, stood as a great advancement over male gang violence toward women—and against the resulting vengeance-taking that marked earlier arrangements. Marriage must be regarded as a most amazing revolution in human social organization.

Marriage was also truly the revolution that mankind has failed to perceive. Perhaps this situation exists because of the near-universal assumption that men and women have always lived together in, perhaps, long-lasting relationships. This, however, modern anthropologists have called into question. Very likely, the male and female members of the human species called Neanderthal did not even live together at all—just as some great primates to this day. Men and women lived separate lives, with male raiding gangs preying upon female communal groups. Settled living for males began with semi-nomadic tribal life and eventually evolved into the institution of monogamous male-female pairings. The Agricultural Revolution and its needs for secure, individual farmer property rights consummated this institutional form's union with the emerging nation-state. The father needed to be known with certainty for the secure transmission of farmsteads to progeny.

Modern people also assume that marriage devolved out of individual passions for objects of affection and that marriage is meant to be companionate and romantic—a sexually-driven dyad. Romantic love as a prevalent institution is an economic extravagance requiring a level of community wealth reached only in the consumer societies of the modern Western world. This is all far from its original purposes which had social and economic roots. In this regard, one might consider the institution of the marriage banquet, and its long social history down to the present day. Current Israeli wedding banquets have roots that go back some 4,500 years in time. Such celebrations link a new couple to both family and local community—socially and economically—whether or not the underlying marriage was arranged or not. The critical understanding: Marriage vows could not be broken lightly, and social elites could and did enforce marriage covenants. So, for the world where the wedding banquet arose, marriage was not a *dyad* but a *triad*—where the mediating third leg of a Three-Legged Stool was local officialdom having the power to enforce marriage contracts.

Within the twin technological revolutions, then, a social revolution in relations between the sexes was occurring, not only within Judaism, but also within the Greco-Roman world—and very significantly, also within

Chinese culture. The manner of proceeding by which cultures adapted to such change, however, would be very different—East to West. In the East, Confucian thought with its five pairs created a system of dual relationships in which one party received authority over the other (except in friendships where the parties were equal). This meant that for the entire social order, relationship harmony through authority would be system-enforcing. When the members of one pair failed in maintaining harmony, founded in obedience by the lower to the higher member such as husband-wife, the next pair up the hierarchy of pairs would intervene to rule in favor of what they regarded as proper—forming a proper Three-Legged stool. As harmony, and property rights, between offspring and parents would be threatened and perhaps broken by half-relations, monogamous marriage would become normative—East and West.

Breeding a New Society

> In the great chess-board of human society, every single piece has a principle of motion of its own.
>
> Adam Smith, *Theory of Moral Sentiments*

With what institutional changes then did agricultural and animal husbandry impregnate government? First, shared gains in a surplus: Tribal and feudal governments learned over time that simply extracting a surplus from a peasant farmer by force did not end well. The farmer might simply, in return, withhold labor. Feudal lords learned that without the infrastructure necessary to move crops to market, or to the lord's storehouses, farming labor became useless to them. Ruling lords began a long tutorial in how not to kill the golden goose. In modern sociological terms, rulers needed to recognize that peasants had grown a reaction function to despotic behavior played out on the "chess-board of human society." Old style despotism no longer worked so well. The ruler had thought that peasants were like chess pieces in the great game of life; now, the chess pieces had a motive power of their own. And then there was the matter of providing protection against raiding intruders. That rang up heavy costs for defensive operations. In turn, defense required a taxing regime to pay for this element of the common good—which in turn required the development of an administrative capability within an executive government. Lastly, a means of adjudicating disagreements between the administrative state and the individual, and between individuals, became necessary, a subject taken up next. What needed to get built was an administrative state with three legs: executive, worker, and grievance adjudicator.[11]

The Quest for Equitable Justice

Beyond basic use-of-land rights, terms of tenure came to matter greatly in agricultural societies. For how many years does a peasant farmer's right to farm a piece of land extend? Here, we have truly superb Scottish Highland records from the 17th and 18th centuries to draw upon. While considerably later than our Iron Age story here, the Highlands had changed relatively little in over a thousand years, so their history is instructive. In a nutshell, the Scottish landed lairds had been keeping their tenants land tenures at only a year, very short indeed, in order to keep close checks upon their loyalties, and as a result, farmers invested little or no labor in soil management and improvement. Crop yields were abysmal. Under a progressive plan for Highland agriculture, tenancies got pushed out to five or 10 years, or even more. Yields increased dramatically. Prior to extended tenure, the situation reminds one of that which existed in Soviet Russia: "They pretend to pay us, and we pretend to work." The details of land tenure mattered, then and now. Both God and the devil are in the details.

Many other property rights issues grew with the agricultural economy. If my pigs or cows get into your field of oats and partake of a feast therein, who shall bear the burden of the cost? Whose responsibility is it to maintain walls—"dry stain dykes" in the Scottish Highland vernacular—and fences? If an animal gets in my fields, and I kill it, how should that event be adjudicated? And there's the rub: what kind of adjudicating should occur? And this brings us to the next basic issue: How shall rights be adjudicated in this newly complex ecosystem?

Rule of Thumb/Rule of Law

> Rule of Thumb: An English phrase that refers to a principle with broad application that is not intended to be strictly accurate or reliable for every situation. It refers to an easily learned and easily applied procedure or standard, based on practical experience rather than theory.
>
> *Wikipedia*

[11] See Appendix A for an extended description of Rule of Three governance in Anglo-Saxon England.

> ...to let the punishment fit the crime....
>
> Gilbert and Sullivan, *The Mikado*

> If the people are led by edicts...they will try to avoid punishment, but not have a sense of shame. If they be led by virtue...they will have a sense of shame and moreover will become good.
>
> Confucius, *Analects*

It seems that in the beginning of the Agricultural Revolution, farmers practiced give-and-take, argument, and violence in order to reach a rule of thumb for the most common situations involving property rights conflicts with their neighbors, and their landlords. Some of the rulings reached probably came from hunter-gatherer rules and simply got adopted into this new environment. For instance, take the case of a farmer who secretly moved a field boundary marker. Might that resemble moving a fishing weir or game marker? Well, then apply a similar punishment. At some point, the rule of thumb approach would fail in adjudicating complex property rights matters. Two rather fascinating developments arose from these complexities: First, because the rule of thumb evolution occurred so slowly (more change occurs in one year today than it did in a millennium 5,000 to 10,000 years ago), people developed the sense that their rules were not man-made but god-given. The role of feudal governments was not to make laws but to discern what laws had already been given. The idea of man-made law would seem revolutionary, when it came. From these earlier roots, the whole philosophy of natural law devolved. Second, because all law was given law, the role of a judge would be to interpret natural law to fit from an old case to a new case. A record could be kept for all such cases, thereby creating a paper trail for future interpretations. To this day, all Anglo-world rulings at law—common law—descend from this sensibility.

The world's first known compilation of such rulings occurred in the reign of the Babylonian emperor Hammurabi who ruled from 1792–1750 BC. His Code consisted of 282 case laws, or rulings, collected toward the end of his reign. The cases covered what we would call commercial law, family law, criminal law, and civil law. Penalties got assessed based upon the status of offenders and the circumstances of the offenses. The Code clearly had antecedents, some perhaps written, and united Semitic and Sumerian traditions as it sought to adjudicate cases from a large empire.

For its time in history, it showed significant advances from its more primitive roots, outlawing the blood feud and the law of vengeance—replacing these primitive notions with *lex talionis*, or the law of retribution.

The critical matter here is that the Code traces the progress in law away from the private, sometimes vigilante, form of justice to the institutional form wherein wrongs become adjudicated in a court. The law of vengeance was a rule of thumb that established the private right to wreak slaughter upon a person's whole family or clan for a perceived wrong done by him. One should note here that the law of vengeance certainly contributed to the tribal tit-for-tat behaviors that made primitive life so violent. Vengeance evolved into retaliation, which limited acts of vengeance to those immediately in the wrong. The law of retribution (sometimes referred to as "eye-for-an-eye" justice from Hebrew scripture) placed punishment in the hands of an adjudicating court and limited punishment to an action commensurate with the wrong committed. Gouge out my eye, and the court may order your eye gouged out in retribution. For some centuries, distinctions in punishment followed rank in social order, however. The elite got off lightly.

The Mosaic law code developed in Israel over a century after Hammurabi, and perhaps did not take on a written form until far later still. It, too, operationalized the law of retribution, and is the source for the "eye-for-an-eye" metaphor. And, of course, it came from the Lord God, the Supreme Lawgiver.[12] Mosaic law could be quite harsh and restrictive, especially in its dietary and holiness requirements and punishments; it also contained large areas of humaneness—honoring parents, providing for widows and children, and offering hospitality to strangers. It required periodic debt forgiveness—in years of Jubilee—so that it, in today's jargon, leveled the playing field and drew its citizens closer to wealth equality. Mosaic law appears to have largely eliminated favoritism for the elite.

Roman law that emerged in mid–fifth century BC has been very important for the shaping of modern European law; its basis was essentially administrative in nature. For modern Europeans, its most important element was man-made law, passed by an assembly within the republic and enforced by administrative law courts, ideally without prejudice to any citizen's personal status. Once more, law moved from rules of private

---

[12] *Exodus* 21:22–25.

revenge-taking to written strictures encompassed by *lex talionis.*[13] And, first for the Israelites, and then for others, social rank would cease yielding judgments automatically favoring the wealthy elites.

The formal Chinese coding of law happened during the Qin rule (221–206 BC), a time of severe *law and order* government action, but that certainly did not mean that the Chinese *fu* or model itself originated then. Chinese law almost certainly followed a course similar to that in the Middle East: Agriculture brought with it informal rules that eventually became formalized and administered by a bureaucracy. At the time of the Zhou, emperors issued proclamations indicating the form or model upon which China would be in harmony with something like *Tao*. Law became codified during the short rule of the Qin; law itself, however, was shaped by Confucian idealism and received interpretation from the famous Confucian pairs. And law descended from the *Tao* in the heavenlies. Even the emperor came under *Tao*, as Israelite kings came under the Lord God, in judgment. Humaneness became a prime Confucian virtue, as it did in Israel and then eventually in most of the West. While the evidence for this path is less certain in the East than in the West, we know Chinese developments walked the same path, for there are just people and just a few stories.

The Birth of Citizenship

The earliest Greek city-state law was based in traditional rulings and traceable to a time contemporaneous roughly to the Zhou in the East. Because ancient Greece never formed into a unified nation-state, much law developed in it could be categorized today as international law respecting the relations between city-states. When dealing with the *hoi polloi,* Greek law could be extremely cruel, Draco's law (7th century BC) being the root for the English word "draconian." Even here, law made a clear progression by replacing easily manipulated oral rules with written law: rule of law, not rule of men: adjudication, not revenge—ideally, of course. That may seem a small mercy within a legal code that prescribed the same penalty for all proscribed acts—death. Make the crime fit the punishment. One might say, a little tongue-in-cheek, that Draco pioneered

[13] The Law of Retaliation: that punishment for a crime should correspond in degree to the unlawful act of a perpetrator.

the modern Soviet justice system, wherein some wags said that for every illegal act, large or small—10 years in the gulags!

What makes ancient Greek law so significant, however, did not involve its roots in *natural law*—formed of traditional, harshly punitive rules. Its significance came out of its unique new direction in law-making—*positive law*. Put baldly, the Greeks invented *citizenship*. Hitherto, every member of species *homo sapiens* had lived as either within the rulers' party, or the party of the ruled. Citizenship introduced a third party to the institutional equation; it became archon or ruler, citizen, and wage-earner/slave—another Rule of Three. Citizenship evolved toward a greater role in the government for what we might today call the middle class citizen, who could advance into government roles previously held only by members of the ruling oligarchy and its professional supporters. A citizen, unlike an Athenian slave, possessed inherent rights protected under positive law—the foremost being a right to a new form of adjudication for accusations of wrongdoing. For the regular *hoi polloi*, it was a quick run-up to the local ruler and a swift sentence with little or no chance to make a case. [The judicial murder of Jesus of Nazareth gives sharp insight into just how such justice worked—everywhere.] But for a Greek citizen, the accusation would be brought before a jury of peers chosen by lot from a large jury pool. Sadly, one must note, the three-level social structure invented by the Greeks also permitted slavery to flourish in the West until the 19th century.

The Greeks appear to have also invented *freedom*. A citizen of Athens was free to think and to debate anything, and free to express even heretical beliefs—except under special circumstances, as we shall see. Along with freedom, the Athenians took long strides toward the development of the individual. He was free to vote his preferences in the assembly of citizens, and to participate in jury actions related to his fellow citizens. He could own land—a right denied noncitizens of the lower orders. And, he could own slaves—although it appears that slaves in ancient Athens more resembled wage workers than bondsmen. He could also by election become one of the city's magistrates. A citizen stood between a slave and a magistrate, and the totality of citizens possessed the power to mediate between the other two ranks in the social order—indicating a Three-Legged Stool. A citizen was nevertheless a privileged minority—perhaps some 20% of the total *hoi polloi*. Meanwhile, all ancient Israelites were given limited forms of liberty: Liberty is bounded freedom, while freedom is unbounded liberty. Freedom rarely works out well.

Along with citizenship, limited degrees of freedom, and individuation came growth in creativity. While other cultures, especially Chinese, experienced stunning developments in the arts, Greek creativity also blossomed in objective thinking and the birth of the sciences. Note: State-sponsored efforts in the liberal arts always restrict creativity with ideology—and frequently distort both science and technology. Consider the 20th century's Nazis and Russian Communists and their warped and perverted science.

A basic question remains: Why? Why did the Greeks of Athens invent democracy, citizenship, freedom, and individualism? Here we must turn to physical environmental factors. First, the Peloponnesus, unlike its neighboring Italian peninsula, had relatively poor land; the Agricultural Revolution never developed fully. The diet was not cereal grain heavy and more resembled today's Mediterranean diet than it did the bread-bowl diets of the Middle East. Then, we need to consider the matter of geography. The Peloponnesus has an extraordinarily convoluted shoreline—at one point nearly severing the peninsula roughly in half at Corinth. As a result, Greek life was wed to the sea and to the 1,400-some islands controlled by the Greeks—contributing to the manner of livelihood and the protein-rich and varied diet. Fishing, cottage gardening, and intercourse with Asia Minor dominated economic life. And the geography was and is still awesomely mountainous. Caught between the mountains and the convoluted shorelines, the Greeks found themselves isolated into rather small living spaces posing large difficulties regarding intercourse with neighboring tribes. These factors all mitigated against an evolution in social order toward empire and feudal forms leading to a nation-state. Because of these environmental hardware factors, founding myths for the many isolated tribes never reached a second order metaphysical level by creating a unifying founding myth above the tribal level; instead, each tribe, small or large, grew its own domestic gods and goddesses—and its own founding mythology that made uniting with other tribes so difficult.

It seems, then, that early developments in the adjudication of conflicts marked the beginning point for a necessary third leg for human institutions—a leg that would, together with ruler and ruled, or accuser and accused, eventually bring more stability and harmony along with it. The humble Three-Legged Stool serves very well as the symbol for the Rule of Three. After all, the Three-Legged Stool will always be stable—no matter how irregular the ground upon which it sits: In geometry, three points in space always define a plane, and a plane is by definition stable.

King, Priest, Prophet

The evolution of Western adjudicating courts gets brilliantly described in the narrative histories found in early Hebrew scripture. No other work of ancient writings about tribal affairs comes even close to that appearing in the *Book of Judges*. Judges begins in the aftermath of the ancient Israelite's escape from Egyptian bondage. This escape narrative has provided Israel and the Jews a third-order metaphysical founding myth that helps hold a Jewish nation together even to this date. Something, however, went terribly wrong in the aftermath of a partially completed conquest of a promised land. Simply put, after initial success occupying hill and mountain country east of the Mediterranean and its rich coastal plains, the 12 tribes of Israel lost their group coherence and began engaging in internecine conflict. The founding vision failed—partly due to geography, and mostly due to human unkindness.

The *Book of Judges* describes the horrors of those conflicts—even to the near extermination of one of the tribes. It also describes the structure, such as it was, of government for the tribes. Each tribe possessed general autonomy and little apparent local government control. Instead, the tribes adopted what may well be the general form for such human groups: They recognized men, and some women, called by a deity as their judges and warlords who could both adjudicate disputes and lead the tribe's fit adult males into war against other tribes. Violence was endemic; genocide of sorts occurred. Butchery became quite savage. While many modern secular scholars and activists point to this Hebrew horror show as something unique and disqualifying of respect for Jews and all of Jewish history, they miss the simple point: *All* ancient tribes behaved at least as badly, and what we have, warts and all, from the Hebrew experience and testimony gives us a shocking insight into the true nature of tribal animosities. Tribalism did not yield noble savages. It yielded savages. Above all else, the Hebrew narratives possess a brutal honesty.

Why did the Hebrew experiment in nation-forming fail so badly for its initial several hundred years? Just as in the case of the Greeks, geography played some role. The rugged hill and mountain country terrain presented significant difficulties for forming and maintaining a nation-state. So did skill sets. While the Philistines and other coastal plain tribes had advanced significantly in the arts related to agriculture, warfare, industrial skills, and seaborne intercourse with other Mediterranean areas, the Israeli former slaves had not. In modern economic terms, they lacked human capital. And, the occupiers of the land that the Hebrews contested for also had the advantage of a general, unifying founding myth of their own—one that had great power in its embrace of the sexualization of and from its gods. Fertility gods and goddesses reigned supreme, and their followers behaved accordingly. The Israeli God of holiness ran up against a plethora of gods and goddesses of sex. Sex won out—at least initially. Eventually, the ancient nation-state of Israel also encountered the allurement of domination—of control over, and enslavement, of other peoples. It ran on the rocks of human nature—which is by natural law neither humane nor good.

Within the framework of tribal leadership, judges for each tribe adjudicated the usual boundary, property damages, thefts, and murders and marriage issues common to tribal life. Each judge could hear evidence in a dispute, but each judge would also serve as jury in the adjudication. The potential for corruption, favoritism, and systematic abuse of the poorer individuals within a tribe always presented itself. Eventually, in places such as Zhou Dynasty China and medieval Europe, feudal courts would also place a heavy thumb on the scales of justice. Feudal abuses of justice would always become more severe than in the tribal form—for the feudal lords and retainers possessed the power inherent in the control of land, something lacking in tribal structures, and also more stuff to steal from the peasantry. What mediated tribal abuses in Hebrew culture appeared as admonitions for the humane treatment of strangers, widows, and children. And of course, the tradition of Jubilee—the returning of property to original family owners every 50 years—helped as well.

The reformation of Hebrew relations began when the burdens of defeat and occupation coming from the advanced economies of the plains became heavy enough for the Hebrews to go beyond periodic tribal-level revolts to a more organized form that helped create a new Israeli nation-state. Hebrew scripture always attributes their eventual success to divine intervention—first through their king of great renown, David (ruled 1010–970 BC), and then by Solomon the wise (ruled 970–931 BC). Solomon eventually created something more than a nation-state; he conquered others of those many short-lived empires of their time and place. But we only mention this by way of introduction to the form of governance in ancient Israel.

The Hebrew nation-state had three important figures within it: king, priest, and prophet. It would be a misunderstanding to regard the second and third of these roles as being the merely silly, primitive offspring of some crude spiritism. Fundamental Hebrew ideology held that the

Lord God Almighty had promised them a homeland and committed to intervening in their internal and military affairs so as to uphold His love and commitment to them—all this promised to Israel's founding father, Abraham. Each king should act so as to achieve God's promise, but how might he accomplish such a thing, being merely mortal and frequently blind to the Lord God's vision for his people? Two matters of importance come from the combination of God's promises and men's fallibility: First, a man appointed by God but independent of the king should offer daily sacrifices to the Lord God by way of obedience to His commandments and atonement for man's wrongdoing. A cynic might call this the buying of favor, a believer the due response to God's holiness. This figure was the Chief Priest. Second, while the Deity might speak directly to a king by way of guidance in decision-making, a counterbalance, a check, upon the king's right hearing of God's directions had to be appointed as well. The is figure was the prophet. King, priest, prophet—three key leaders of one government if you will, co-equal and designed to be checks upon one another—an early Three-Legged Stool. No man should hold more than one position, no king more than two. When King Solomon seized all three roles, his empire shortly broke in two. Divine retribution; holy justice? Destroy the Three-Legged Stool on which the nation sits, and you destroy the nation's balance—and shortly thereby its future.

The prophets constituted the wild cards in the deck for ancient kings—somewhat like the philosophers and advisors of our own time. Prophets, some of them, could be manipulated—bought and sold. Some of them could be completely transparent and truthful—and maybe lose their heads for it. Today, false diplomats get fired and false intelligence officers imprisoned, but none lose their heads—at least in the West.

Not only ancient Israel had this form of government. In Greek city-states and the Roman republic, kings ruled but minded what the priests saw for the future in the entrails of slaughtered animals. Prophets encouraged and admonished kings—and lied to them when bribed. On the whole, this three-part structure had some mollifying effects upon the rule of kings—especially as most kings lived in a deep fear of offending either the Lord God or one of many gods and goddesses. All in all, the three-part control structure of the primitive tribes lived on, in sublimated form. The structure could and did dominate feudal nations—Chinese, Middle Eastern, and European—for many centuries. By the medieval European period, prophets had degenerated into court fools—flea bites on the skin of kings, but sometimes the fools were wise, and wise men fools. And sometimes the fools lost their heads, too: "And my poor fool is hanged."[14]

All of these examples just mentioned—Hebrew or Greek—had elements of the Rule of Three present in what we would today call their triadic functions of government. While a Hebrew prophet might speak against a king or for a wrongly accused individual, a separation between the ruling of kings and the adjudicating of judges never took place. For a movement in this direction, one must look and Athens, and particularly to Solon.

The Jury Versus Socrates

> Socrates modeled his career after his midwife mother. She delivered babies, and for his part Socrates could always tell when a young man was in the throes of trying to give birth to a thought. Socrates considered his philosophical work as midwifery (maieutics). This method, later also called the Socratic method, consists in eliciting knowledge by a series of questions and answers.
>
> *Theaetetus* by Plato

In 399 BC, an Athenian philosopher and general gadfly named Socrates (470–399 BC) found himself on trial for impiety and corrupting the morals of the city's youth. *Freedom can only be stretched so far—and then the mob rules*. Within the Athenian democracy of the time, no formal prosecutors existed within the justice structure. Any citizen of the city-state could bring charges against another Athenian—citizen or slave. In the Socrates case at public law, a citizen named Meletus, backed by two other citizens, instigated charges claiming that the elderly man had engaged in impiety and in the corruption of the youth of the city—somewhat akin in notoriety to LSD-head Timothy Leary of the 20th century. The case became something of a notorious scandal of the time, its verdict never really pleasing either side—accusers nor defendants. That verdict, of course, became one of the few in world history to be known by every school child in the West, at least until recently. Socrates was condemned by a jury and sentenced to death by draught of hemlock. And he took it. Better than exile at age 71?[15]

---

[14] *King Lear* 5.3.369.

[15] The outcome echoes down through history to inform Winston Churchill's retort to Lady Astor when that stout female said to him, "Winston, if I were your wife, I'd give you

The case has bearing here because of two factors: one, the nature of the charges themselves, and two, the dynamics of the jury. To most modern ears, the charges seem crude and primitive—both impiety and corrupting youth hardly raising contemporary eyebrows, except amongst Muslim devotees. But cast into the ideology of fourth-century BC Athens, the charges were very serious indeed. Athenians believed that their city's prosperity, and even its continued survival, depended upon their making the right oblations to their pantheon of gods and goddesses. Any actions against the gods would have been far more serious than modern westerners debunking democracy in favor of dictatorship. And the Athenians generally at that time were very touchy about city-state security—having recently lost the Peloponnesian War to Sparta. Clearly, the gods had to be treated particularly delicately. Socrates was at best agnostic on the whole matter of the gods. And perhaps his agnosticism had been extended to youthful followers, setting them against the gods as well. All in all, a delicate matter.

Now, the city-state of Athens prided itself in its form of *democracy* (meaning roughly, in today's western jargon "Power to the people!") that sought to let rule by its citizens be the rule, but without any hanky-panky going on—like corruption within the elites. So, for this trial of the century, a jury, not of our customary 12, but of probably 501, or even 601, got drawn by lot from a citizens' annual jury pool of some 6,000. The drawn jury sat for the day for one trial, in which accuser(s) and defendant(s) gave speeches. And then the jury members voted and determined the punishment. The idea? The large, and odd-numbered, jury would inevitably reach a decision and would never become a hung jury. What the Athenians apparently had not reckoned with was the very real likelihood that, in some cases, the jury members might readily turn into a mob—and a mob demanding cruel and unusual treatment of an unfortunate defendant. What might have called into being something like a flash mob convicting Socrates?

Socrates, of course, was no mean thinker; he was perhaps the most brilliant of the large passel of earlier Greek philosophers. His fame, aside from the resulting trial, came from his most seminal contribution to scientific thought—the *Socratic method*. In it, the interlocutor asks a series of *why* questions of another, all aimed at helping the other understand something of which he may be only dimly aware. The result: new knowledge that had been previously unknown. It appears from the available evidence

---

poison. To which he replied, "Madam, if I were your husband, I'd take it."

that Socrates employed his method upon his accusers, who rapidly became furious at his importunity. Like the interlocutor in a minstrel show, his questions hit home and caused great laughter amongst the observers. And so, he drove the jurymen into convulsions of anger. The truth is that mankind cannot withstand very many *whys*—probably not more than six on the same subject. Just ask a mother dealing with a precocious two- or three-year-old. The jury was not a three-year-old, however, and enough members turned on Socrates to condemn him.

The trial of Socrates vividly points out the glaring weakness within the Athenian structure of democracy: its failure to assign separate roles for prosecutors, judges and juries, and also its failure to separate the executive and legislative functions. With these beginnings, pure democracy has evermore had a weakness for *passions* over *interests*—most crudely in the form of mob rule—which then generally leads to some form of oligarchy or rule by the elites.[16] Thus failed the Greek city-state of Athens, democracy's inventor.

The other danger to a nation-state comes from without rather from within: The Roman republic that grew out of the Greek model failed through its inability to protect itself from totalitarian impulses. We might point to leadership failures on the part of the republic's patrician oligarchy—extreme foreign adventuring and related civil disturbances—as root causes of failure. Once more, a failure for want of an effective three-legged stool for government. Nation-states must regard natural boundaries when doing foreign policy: The urge to conquest of other tribes and nations so often only means a nation-state's conquest by those others in return. Tit for tat.

In modern philosophical terms, rather than Plato's "opposing sides" terminology, the Greeks created something akin to the Hegelian dialectic—in which logical theses and antitheses yield a new synthesis.[17]

Property Rights and Boundaries

The failures of tribes, feudal nations, and nation-states alike had much to do with *boundaries*—and conflicting meanings for bounded property rights. Hunter-gatherer tribes certainly regarded property rights—but the

[16] See Albert Hirschman, *The Passions and the Interests.*

[17] Georg Wilhelm Friedrich Hegel, *Phenomenology of the Spirit.*

property rights that concerned them involved seasonal hunting, gathering and wintering locations. Violations of such rights certainly led to significant conflicts, although in just what proportion to overall violence we cannot know. The rise of the city-state and the nation-state demanded a fundamental change in rulers' thinking about property rights boundaries. Hunter-gatherer tribes saw boundaries as activity-based and seasonal; sedentary agricultural communities saw boundaries as permanent and based, of course, in control of agricultural land. Hunter-gatherer and nation-state sensibilities over this matter certainly produced running conflicts, right up into our own era in time. Doubtless nation-state boundaries partly got determined by geologic and topographic features of the land itself. Agricultural dominance meant that hunter-gatherer and nomadic tribes gradually migrated, under compulsion, into lands undesirable for agriculture—where some live to this day.

The second, and far greater, matter for boundary allocation arose after the feudal and nation-states had largely triumphed, and that matter involved how much suitable land should comprise a nation. We note in closing here that the feudal state tended to fail due to government-directed external overreach—attempting to extend boundaries beyond geographically and culturally related features. The Zhou in ancient China provide a good model in this regard, that of classic overreach. Nation-states ultimately fail due to internal forces, but those forces have external causes. The ancient nation-state of Israel ultimately failed due to inner corruption of a ruling elite, but its dalliance with acquiring empire had contributed to that corruption. The Roman republic played the empire game as well, causing civil unrest over the costs of empire and thereby permitting the Republic's overthrow by a tyrant named Julius Caesar.

Both Judge and Jury

The fundamental weakness in all ancient efforts at fair and just adjudication involved the temptations to collapse triadic forms of trial into a dyadic form. Ideally, a jury of an individual's peers should stand between a judge and the accused. Far too often, both then and today, the inherent roles of judge and jury become dominated by one or the other, and dyadic justice is no justice at all. For Socrates, the large jury became an angry mob that condemned an innocent man. For Jesus of Nazareth, corrupt judges ignored the negative evidence of some witnesses and the failure of tainted witnesses to agree on evidence amongst themselves in order to force an extralegal conviction. In general, ancient legal proceedings made it far too easy to overrule and suborn witnesses who stood between the accused and the judge. Only in fairly recent times has a true Three-Legged Stool of justice stood protecting both accused and accuser—and even in recent times this has only been the case within certain Western-style democracies. The Three-Legged Stool of justice has been, and will always be, under threat from corrupted human practices.

Intercourse and the Marketplace

It appears that the limited trading carried on by hunter-gatherer tribes had a distinctly different nature from what Adam Smith liked to call man's "propensity to truck, barter, and exchange one thing for another."[18] And this begins our delving into the good Dr. Smith's claim regarding propensities—one that has become hotly disputed within our own time. First, we might note that Adam Smith appears to have seen the "propensity to truck and barter" of which he writes as a fundamental truism, as something basic to all mankind—an underlying human behavioral trait. We just like to swap stuff. Smith, of course, was a conservative institutional political economist. The political left in the West has little respect for his views and sees things very differently; Marxists especially view all trading for personal gain to be greedy and immoral. Better for a whole community to share out goods as needed, as some tribes practiced until very recently. And so, the Left celebrates the gift-giving potlatch of the tribes native to the Pacific Northwest, in which opulent harvest feasts became an opportunity to give away or destroy possessions that may have taken several seasons to collect, all as a display of power and conspicuous consumption by a tribal chief. The Right, of course, clucks at the waste of it all. The potlatch cemented the social status of the chief. It also served as a way to save face for a high-status person who had suffered public embarrassment, and also a way of competing amongst tribal elites or between tribes. Establishing primacy in a pecking order by proving one could collect and destroy the most stuff surely beat open warfare.

On a serious note, though, what have we learned about organizational evolution that might cast some light on Dr. Smith's contention? First of

[18] Adam Smith, *The Wealth of Nations*, Book I, Chapter 2.

all, in one regard, the Marxists have got it quite right: Primitive tribesmen almost certainly did not truck and barter, or exchange, to any great degree. It would have been far too dangerous to attempt to do so. Most likely, an ambush would put paid to any such efforts. And of course, second, little by way of trade goods existed in the first place. Trade only got interesting with the growth of industry producing valuable stuff, like hoes and axes, axles and wheels and animals to pull them, and other such throw-offs from agriculture. Within the tribe, most goods got shared out more or less equally—something communistic that the Marxists would have approved of. If plenty existed, everybody feasted. If little, everybody tightened their belts. Some tribes did advance foodstuffs to others in need, but such altruism likely was very limited by the realities of tribal rivalries. Reciprocity in goods required trust, and trust was usually in short supply.

Intertribal trade as best we can determine did not involve face to face dickering at all; instead, a physical location got established, through the workings of tradition, at which trade goods would get deposited. Then, someone from another tribe might come to the place, find some goods, and take them, in return for some other goods. This might at first sight seem a bit dodgy as a marketing mechanism; why not just take the goods left at the trading site without leaving anything in return? Should we believe that trust in barter existed amongst tribes that continually engaged in at least low-level warfare? The answer to the conundrum appears in the form of taboo. Trading locations simply could not be violated, without incurring the wrath of the gods. Doubtless some barter thieves did take goods without a reciprocal. Doubtless also some got caught and hung, and their fates may have contributed to respect for the gods.

First problem solved. But what about the second problem: Without face-to-face exchanges, how could bartering occur over how much of one good would get given for how much of another? Here again, the answer comes from taboo as unwritten traditional ruling. The tribesmen believed that the gods had provided the exchange rate (just as they had the punishments for breaking taboos)—so many rabbit pelts for one deerskin, for example. Only when a tribesman found that inflexible, fixed rate attractive would he approach the trading site to make the exchange. The conclusions we may draw? Ancient tribal barter was not true barter at all, because the rate of exchange was inflexible: Needs for trading might vary, but the terms could not. Gains from trade, therefore, were practically nonexistent. And, it would appear, mankind was not, in the beginning, predisposed to trade. No propensity to "truck and barter"—at this time.

Does this mean that the good Dr. Smith got it wrong about basic propensities for trading? By no means. We maintain that the demands of the Agricultural Revolution taught men to bargain, and thereby called into being propensities to truck and barter. Eventually, such propensities became almost baked in to our collective DNA. Trading for a better buffalo-drawn plow in order to vastly increase crop yields could concentrate a man's mind wonderfully in regard to gains-making. Probably the big breakthroughs came in gains from trade involving longer term assets—plows and wagons and such. Almost certainly, these Neolithic men discovered the principle of gains from trade for both sides through a barter arrangement literally thousands of times, and far before the economists did. The stumbling block to furthering such gains took the form of cumbersomeness of trying to directly barter very different goods. At some point in time, the search for a common good by which to measure the relative values of all other goods began.

Monetizing Liberty

In the primitive hunter-gatherer tribe, so much of life got directed by taboo. Taboo set innumerable boundaries around all individual behaviors. Freedom as we now know it, particularly in the West, was for all practical purposes nonexistent. Non-freedom extended to bartering for goods: fixed exchange rates—determined forever by the gods. Forever clearly did not last, for multiple anthropological digs have turned up plenty of very old coins. The oldest have been dated back to about 700 BC. They originated in China, the Middle East, and India. Very likely, older ones may be found—for the Agricultural Revolution dates back far earlier. No hunter-gatherer coins have been found. The wampum of American eastern woodland natives did not serve as money, and very likely hunter-gatherers never created money. Wampum-like crafted strings of shells were not terribly durable and so would fail the test of time. Nobody yet has found 2,500-year-old wampum.[19]

Economists and bankers usually ascribe three purposes for money: medium of exchange, store of value, and unit of account. While money

[19]Footnote to history: British colonial administrators once tried imposing paper money upon some African subjects living in hot, humid conditions. Disaster struck almost overnight as the paper money quickly disintegrated.

surely possesses these traits, the money trinity misses what truly matters with regard to it. Money relates to human needs, passions, and yearnings to be set free. Here we maintain that the evolution of money truly begins with the quest for *liberty*. The interplay between demands for liberty and supplies of mediums for exchange drove the evolution. This focus immediately removes money from a descriptive collection of its traits to a relationship with human beings—an absolute and a relative. Indeed, money and liberty called one another into being. Without liberty, money had no individual human purpose; without money, liberty is forever stunted in its growth. Strange as it may seem at first, the people-money relationship begins with a matter we have just been discussing: boundaries.

Let us remember first that paleolithic people were not at all free, but rather bound by subsistence living requirements, taboos on behaviors, and extreme threats to their safety and security. These bounds only began to be eased when the Agricultural Revolution kicked in, turning mankind's world upside down. Second, let us like good Confucians define our terms so as to provide more clarity to the issue. Freedom in its pure sense does not exist at all—and never will. This is because freedom is *unbounded* liberty: It means that I can do anything I want. But this is patently impossible. Conversely, liberty is *bounded* freedom and, therefore, actually exists on a continuum from very little to much, depending upon the boundaries placed upon it. Indeed, much of the whole human condition may be evaluated on the basis of how much liberty individuals should be permitted, and no, maximum liberty is not an unalloyed good thing. Too much leads to conflicts, because the liberties of others then become violated. Boundaries, after all, have the overall purpose of reducing conflict. Too little liberty results also in conflict eventually, when people rebel against authoritarian rule. Little liberty creates short term stability. Greater liberty yields a blossoming of creativity itself. Had the constraints on liberty for Paleolithic man never been eased, we would all still be pathetic subsistence hunter-gatherers continually under threat from larger and stronger reptiles and primates. Cheese it Jack; here comes a saber-toothed tiger!

Money stands as one of mankind's greatest creative achievements, and greatest liberators. Once Neolithic men invented it, gains from trade simply exploded. Of course, in order for money to become effective, the barter taboo needed to become overthrown; the terms of exchange needed to become relative to supplies and demands, not fixed. This no doubt took hundreds, and even thousands, of years. Change moved slowly in the Neolithic age, but eventually the boundaries surrounding the terms of exchange got backed away. The new boundaries that appeared had to do with the thumb-on-the-scale sort of thing—the enforcement of moral conduct within a marketplace where price mediates between supply and demand. When get-rich schemes involving engrossing, forestalling, and regrating appeared, they would be stymied by the watchful eyes and ears of the officials charged with assuring a fair market. Market towns became incorporated for the purpose of assuring fair weights and measures, and truthful descriptions of products. Controls over conduct could not, of course, provide protection against individual losses. A law of markets states that some individuals will suffer strings of losses without having done anything to deserve such outcomes. Nevertheless, the overall law of markets greatly improved people's lives over the previous law of the jungle.

When this evolution worked its way through whole economies, a form of dynamic stability emerged—a Three-Legged Stool comprised of buyers, sellers and market-based price as an adjusting mechanism balancing the other two. The Three-Legged Stool of the marketplace produced something quite remarkable: the satisfaction of all buyers and sellers through the mediating influence of price. The price mechanism replaced most resorts to violence. Every buyer is then also a seller—provided, of course, that few leakages from within and without each local economy occur. Then, every little village becomes a commonwealth.[20] Not only that, the resulting prices took into account all of the upstream and downstream costs associated with each good. For the first time ever, unsatisfied demands and supplies disappeared, and the price of a good factored in its production and marketing costs. This humble Three-Legged Stool brings both market stability and dynamic growth to the entire capitalist enterprise that has in turn yielded the richest societies ever.

The Invention of Politics, Custom and the Common Good

> Good fences make good neighbors.
>
> Robert Frost

War and politics represent the two basic means of resolving conflicts, be the conflicts at national, local, or individual levels. War aims to crush opposition. Politics aims to mediate between opposing interests so as

---

[20] Jump forward to Chapter Nine for a proposal for a world of commonwealths.

to avoid conflict in the first place—in modern terms an example of the Hegelian at work. The Greeks, in truth, invented politics. The trial of Socrates was a political event, sadly one in which politics failed in the face of a passionate mob. But at its best, the Greek democratic assembly did work to mediate between the *polis* and the executive functionaries of the state. The political arena requires the existence of a Rule of Three: executive, *polis*, and parliament (of some form), where parliament mediates between the other two. Marriage also was meant to have a third leg, some form of arbitration between pairs. In this sense, marriage was political—frequently requiring arbitration between families of betrothed pairs and then between marriage partners. Property issues were perhaps the most common areas of friction, although extracurricular affairs threatening marriage bonds must have weighed heavily in the overall balance. Before monogamous marriage, male-female conflicts were endemic. Without marriage, trust, and politics, civil society cannot either become created in the first place, or long endure. When this civil triad becomes embedded within a social order, custom gets created, and custom creates stability and some measure of peace and harmony.

The propensities for trucking, bartering and exchanging in themselves created another stabilizing effect: a Three-Legged Stool comprised of beliefs about the good life, material goods that bring individuals happiness, and customs regarding behaviors within each local resulting culture. Culture arises out of customs. Customs once settled upon tend to yield regularity in behavior and stability of outcomes.

The evolution of interests from out of passions came about through the fertilization of the social order with liberty.[21] Passions were and are the hallmark of tribal relations—as told us by the *Ur* stories about heroic combat. To this day, one of the chief conflicts within successful nation-states involves the continual need to convert passions into interests. Then, interests under the influence of founding myths may become common goods.

Beyond custom, interests became definitions of the common good as a mediating higher-order belief shaping culture. Three basic human needs, a triad of deep emotions, in turn define common good: *love and affirmation, significance, and security.* Security makes possible the other two. Another Three-Legged Stool. Then, righteousness and peace kiss, and lovingkindness becomes the third leg. In the East, *Tao* shaped the

[21] Hirschman, Albert. *The Passions and the Interests: Political Arguments for Capitalism Before Its Triumph.*

common good. In the West, for the republic of Rome, Cicero defined the common good as *common interest.* For early Christianity, Augustine defined it as *common love*.

Conclusions

All advances humankind has made in forming peaceful, creative societies have come through the rough, trial-and-error process of discovering what works to overcome tyranny, either of the *strong man* variety, or of the chaos of the mob. Those forms of human governance that have dyadic structures always yield oppression, violence, and stunted growth and creativity. On the other hand, triadic structures—Rule of Three in form—for human governance offer the potential for liberty, peace, and creativity to blossom. It appears that the very first such triadic structure evolved in the Paleolithic, hunter-gatherer period during which humankind's fear of the nameless, shapeless, all-powerful *numinous* worked as a third leg mediating between the worst impulses of individuals and leaders alike. Over millennia, human efforts to comprehend, and often to control, the numinous led both to efforts to placate or bribe this mysterious, all-powerful force and efforts to comprehend it. From such efforts at comprehension, *thinking* as we think of it today, evolved as well. The power of conceiving of physical symbols standing for immaterial concepts would lead to theology, philosophy, and science. All aspects to modern civilization evolved from discoveries involving the Rule of Three. So, the Three-Legged Stool stands apart from all else as mankind's greatest invention.

Within civil societies, Three-Legged Stools may well number in the hundreds—certainly at least in the dozens. It appears, however, that the three most important of all Three-Legged Stools create harmonies within these areas:

- Executive administration and spontaneous technical change
- Fair and unbiased adjudication of wrongs
- Marketplace intercourse

Together, all three have the potential to lead human beings toward a common good—a commonwealth that achieves justice and peace on the high uplands of human love, creativity, and joy.

***

Discoveries:

The Rule of Three. All stable human institutions have a triadic structure where one of the three legs to the stool mediates the potential conflicts contained within the other two.

The role of the numinous. Humans have always searched for a metaphysical meaning for existence, pain and suffering, and death. When a search successfully enters higher-order metaphysics, such as the quest for a monotheistic God or a transcendent state of being, human societies can create founding myths that rise above material conflicts and create harmony out of inter-tribal conflicts.

The triad knitting tribal life together. The first Three-Legged Stool shaping a measure of peace and harmony grew out of the fear and awe of the numinous that in turned yielded taboo, sacrifice, and shamanistic beliefs and practices. Their continued existence in primitive tribal life today proves their effectiveness.

Stories, rituals, and symbols precede logic and rational thinking. Human choosing of a single thing over others did not begin with rational analysis; it began with story. Story presents a pattern for choosing: Reenact a story from the past for the present, or reject it? Rituals reinforce the lessons of story. Learn to communicate story and ritual in symbols and the gateway to logic and rational thinking opens. The gateway to metaphysical thinking also opens. Humankind did not possess logic from the beginning; it had to evolve out of the triad of story, ritual and symbol—another Three-Legged Stool.

Three fundamental functions must come into existence in order for a for a nation-state to work. The executive, judiciary, and markets. These comprise the most fundamental Three-Legged Stool for any great society. The executive comprehends the defense of the realm in addition to domestic duties. And markets comprehend politics.

The Pathway from tribe to nation-state. The tribal form of governance evolved into empire, the feudal, and the nation-state, driven by basic human concerns for *love and affirmation, significance*, and *security.* And also driven by the interplay between technology and governance.

(*Continued*)

(*Continued*)

The technology-government relation. Technological revolutions drive structural changes in the governance of the affected nations. As a corollary, technical *evolutions* downstream from *revolutions* then have been carried out through advanced national structures, which are mostly nation-state in form. Governance revolutions make possible the advance of technical evolution, then.

Military organization preceded civil organization. Dyadic command and control organization once dominated both civil organization and the orderliness of markets. Replacing command and control with triadic structures always has been, and probably always will be, the main challenge in creating peace and harmony.

A basic principle driving human behavior. People do what they know how to do, even when it no longer works. In Neolithic times, progress frequently took a thousand years, or even much more. We are all slow learners—even today.

The twin great revolutions: Agriculture and Animal Husbandry. Agriculture in turn demanded animal husbandry for its motive force and soil enriching capabilities. These two revolutions combined to cause a hither-unimagined cascade of change in how people lived. The impacts broadly affected three areas of peasant life: incentives to labor and inventiveness, soil management through animal husbandry, and property rights.

Brains and brawn. The Neolithic new agriculture required tedious and tremendously tiring physical exertion, with little rest from labor. It also required thinking things through in regard to the fine art of balancing plants and domesticated animals. Because of the need to balance brains and brawn, and to capture and retain a surplus, forced communal systems of agriculture have almost always caused starvation.

The birth of trust. Success in the new Neolithic agriculture demanded radical new ways of organizing labor. One of the biggest results was the birth of trust. Success demanded especially that couples work together and trust one another. Women, especially, could no longer

(*Continued*)

(*Continued*)

be treated like animals; women became full partners in a male peasant's enterprise. The result: monogamous marriage and the internalization within marriage of previously external tribal and intertribal conflicts. Trust, in turn, required that men no longer abuse women and that there be no screwing around with other women, or men, outside marriage. Trust was also necessary in order to preserve property. Marriage actually became a Rule of Three fundamental to civil society, not a dyad. In both China and the West, third-party arbiters worked out disagreements between each couple: Confucian pairings and Middle Eastern adjudicating within the marriage institution worked to vastly reduce violence and theft.

The Great chessboard of human society. Under the new agriculture, the peasantry for the first time ever escaped complete dominance by ruling chieftains and other elites. For a long time, rulers failed to see that they could no longer live like chess players moving peasants about willy-nilly on a chessboard. Now, each chess piece had a motive force all its own, and that needed to be reckoned with.

The Evolution of law. Law as we know it evolved from taboo first into negative law—"thou shalt not"—and then into positive law based in rights of citizens. Similarly, justice evolved from the law of vengeance to the law of retaliation and then the law of retribution—from the wholesale slaughter of whole communities and tribes for the wrong committed by one member to individual punishment commensurate with his or her crime.

The Hebrews invented the relational Three-Legged Stool. Law, justice, and mercy came to define the just relationship between ruler and people, and between people. The Hebrews invented the relational trinity.

The Greeks created individual freedom and citizenship, and objective thinking. These brilliant innovations set the foundations for advanced civil society and placed a formidable force between rulers and the *hoi polloi*—another example of the Rule of Three.

(*Continued*)

(*Continued*)

The Greeks also invented politics. Politics is the art of domesticating violence by creating a new Three-Legged Stool permitting competing goals to adjust themselves via compromise.

The Greeks also inadvertently created mob rule—the downfall of popular democracy. Rulers, the assembly, and the people comprised the Greeks' great Three-Legged Stool, but in weakening traditional sovereignty of a single ruler at the expense of a popular assembly, the Greeks also introduced the potential for mob rule—the Achilles heel of popular democracy itself.

Boundaries play a major role in the stability of any tribe or nation. What is taboo, or unlawful, versus what is permitted constitute one basic boundary. Private property rights constitute another, and a boundary critical to agricultural, and eventually industrial, civil life. Secure boundaries for the tribe or nation itself constitute a third. Without secure and stable boundaries, civil society cannot exist.

The marketplace—intercourse in goods—comprises the Three-Legged Stool balancing through the price mechanism the various supplies and demands of the people. The result is gains from trade that make everybody more well-off. Such intercourse did not exist within the domain of hunter-gatherer tribes, for the taboo that allowed permanently warring tribes to exchange goods also barred barter. Gift-giving somewhat ameliorated the severely restricted nature of trade. The Agricultural Revolution required that the ancient taboos be broken down. Then, mankind's general "propensity to truck and barter" could begin to work. Barter was a barrier to efficient trading.

Monetizing liberty. The ability to express price in terms of a common denominator made trading highly efficient and created a truly workable Three-Legged Stool of intercourse. While money itself had three properties—medium of exchange, store of value, and unit of accounts—the creation of money had a more fundamental purpose: It allowed people the liberty to pursue solutions to needs, fulfillments of yearnings and desires to have a measure of freedom

(*Continued*)

(*Continued*)

to do so. The sum-total of all peoples' monetized liberties in turn created the potency of the nation-state to achieve high plateaus of happiness.

Liberty yields interests displacing passions. Passions drove the violent behaviors of primitive tribes. Liberty and intercourse created interests to replace unruly passions. The most challenging issue for all nation-states to this day revolves around the need continually to convert primitive passions into civil interests.

The end goal for the nation-state. When the basic balancing mechanisms, the Rules of Three, within a nation-state function adequately, in their entirety they yield something we term *the common good.* Cicero defined common good for the Roman Republic as consisting of *common interest.* For the East, it took the form of the *Tao.* For the Christianity of Augustine of Hippo, it was and still is *common love.*

Part One Conclusions

The Three Foundations for Comity

And the cow and the bear shall feed; their young ones shall lie down together: and the lion shall eat straw like the ox.

Isaiah 11:7

We hold these truths to be self-evident, that all men are created equal, that they are endowed by their creator with certain unalienable Rights, that among these are Life, Liberty, and the Pursuit of Happiness. That to secure these rights, Governments are instituted among men, deriving their just powers from the consent of the governed....

Thomas Jefferson, Declaration of Independence

Life, Liberty, and Estate...[the three components of Property].

John Locke, *Two Treatises of Government,* 1689

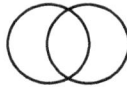

Near-perpetual human violence roiled the ancient world; endemic conflict represented the natural state of humankind. Comparatively speaking, the 20th century generated far fewer violent deaths than any other—despite its two horrific World Wars. This fundamental state of affairs has to astonish our present generation brought up to believe the opposite. The last 70 years have in fact been the most peaceful ever. This state of affairs begs two questions: Why has this been the case, and will this state of affairs continue? In an effort to provide some answers to these existential questions, we have examined the history of the ancient world, going back to the period prior to the world's first great technological leap, the Agricultural Revolution, with regard to war and peace.

Our findings about factors determining the evolution of governance—from clan to tribe to empire to feudal kingdom to city- and nation-state—run to several dozen. They all point, however, to only three basic principles:

- Founding mythology
- Boundaries
- The Rule of Three

Even the smallest units of governance, the clan, have always required some "glue" to hold them together against the centrifugal forces of people's propensities for rebellion. Within clannish and tribal governance, that glue takes the form of the Heroic Ancestor who founded the group. Founding mythologies for empires and feudal kingdoms always seek to create founding myths of metaphysical significance: Actual sovereigns reign under the auspices of either a glorious ancestor or some nonmaterial and sacred entity, so that the earthly ruler has some potency devolving from the founding ruler, the gods, or the inanimate forces controlling this world. The weakness within such founding myths appears in their inability to command the loyalties of conquered tribes who understandably feel themselves separated from the distant ruling class. City- and nation-states have long sought buy-in from all of their peoples from all tribes by creating higher-order metaphysical founders' mythology, such as *Tao* or God. Their founding myths necessarily possess complexities as the myths seek to incorporate within them the patriotic actions of the commoners. Without a strong founding myth, nations necessarily fall apart.

Successful human governance always requires the evolution of coherent boundaries, and not only of the geographic and communal kind. Legal, ethical, and moral boundaries must also get created—and seen to devolve from founding myth. One should remember that all law is moral, and law and its application must work against those who would destroy the mythic center and its boundaries. Lastly, for the effective application of individual human creativity and effort to evolve, property rights must come into being. According to England's John Locke, every human being has a right to his or her own property—which consists of "Life, Liberty and Estate" [a fundamental Rule of Three defining the people's condition within a civil society and employing liberty as the mediating institution].

Boundaries create the conditions for a civil society. Without boundaries, all attempts at comity will prove futile. The hallmark of a successful city- or nation-state, then, appears in the form of a flourishing civil society.

Underpinning these two fundamentals, the Rule of Three must evolve from experience to form the third leg of the stool of right governance, and that Rule's application must overcome natural human propensities toward the *strong man* and conversely toward the *mob*. The fundamental Three-Legged Stool for successful government allocates authority between an executive, a legislative, and an adjudicating leg—where the adjudicating leg mediates between the other two and between governance and the people. Adjudication itself forms a Three-Legged Stool where an impartial jury mediates between accuser and accused. Within an evolving civil society, liberty mediates between the individual's pursuit of happiness and the boundaries of law. Markets evolve to set free human creative energies; the price mechanism mediates between individual and corporate demands and supplies. In the Three-Legged Stool of markets, governance mediates between the behaviors of market participants with regard to quantities and prices and the laws upholding fair practices. Within individual relations, three institutions mediate between parties in conflict: the marriage institution, religious organizations, and voluntary organizations more generally. Labor organizations mediate between worker and management.

Every triadic relationship underpinning a great society will be under constant threat from forces desirous of destroying the triad and replacing it with a dyadic relationship giving one party power over another. Eternal watchfulness is the price of liberty.

Part Two

Anno 1500 to 2019

Our Present Age
Cowboys and Dragons: Applying the Deep Past to the Modern Era

The Second Great Technological Revolution and Its Consequences for Governance

Part One to this book—The Deep Past—examines the old Agricultural Revolution and the changes that this revolution brought in governance and human nature. Other and associated revolutions related to the primary agricultural dynamic also occurred: Animal Husbandry and Plant Genetics in particular. But agriculture drove everything. Our study of this remarkable revolution yielded many discoveries regarding how ancient peoples' changes in governance came about as responses to fundamental technological change, all of which we found to sum up to the big three principles for increasing human beings' general peace and plenty: *boundaries, founding mythologies,* and the *Rule of Three.*

For this our second part—Our Present Age—we asked ourselves two questions: One, was there an outstanding technological revolution triggering changes within governance occurring within our present age, something as significant for our time as was agriculture in the Deep Past? For our purposes, we defined the Present Age as comprising roughly

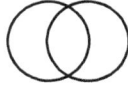

1500 to today. Two, did any such fundamental technological advance get followed by the working out of the same Big Three Principles for progress toward peace and plenty for our futures as human beings?

Yes—on both questions. The qualifying revolution took the form of movable type mass printing of documents—the Printing Revolution, originating with Herr Gutenberg. Of course, other major technological revolutions also have occurred within the present age: most notably the Industrial and Chemical Revolutions in the 19th century, and a plethora of additional revolutions within the 20th century—especially the Electrical Power Revolution. However, we make the case that every following technological revolution depended upon printing, and also upon the governance changes printing fostered.

Unlike in the Deep Past, the advances in technology and related governance changes largely occurred in the West, without similar changes simultaneously happening in the East. As a result, the world competitive posture East and West appears dramatically different, with the Chinese Dragons, until just recently, very far behind the Cowboys in both rodeos—the technological revolution rodeo and the adaptive governance for peace and plenty rodeo.

The three Principles for Progress Reshape the World

Within our present age, the significance of boundaries has stretched far beyond physical borders, separating such areas as property rights and patent protections upon innovations, basic human rights, and protections for the private realm over and against the public realm of governance. Also within our present age, we have witnessed the rise, and fall, of monumental attempts at subjugating the age-old founding mythologies of many tribes and nations through the imposition by mass-communicated propaganda of new ideologies, consisting of reified variables strengthened by the passions propaganda promotes—such as those of Karl Marx, Vladimir Lenin, and Mao Zedong.

One might well say that our first two principles work as much to promote stability in governance as to further technological and governance advances. The third principle, the Rule of Three, however, has truly made worldwide peace and plenty a reality for many—balancing as it does the dark forces of totalitarian rule on the one hand and mobocracy on the other.

The Land of Peace and Plenty

> You white folks got it so good, when you reach Heaven you'll scarcely know you've arrived.
>
> A black African to a Western white missionary

Let us observe that something over 90% of all the world's people lived in wretched poverty from *homo sapiens*' inception until our present age, which began around 1500. Today, according to a detailed Brookings Institution study, over one-half of the world's population now live middle class lives—or lives of the wealthy. People who live lives vulnerable to a fall into poverty comprise just over 40% of the human world population, and that leaves the actual poverty level at just 10% of all the world's people—a truly stunning finding, perhaps. Meanwhile, acts of war, as Dr. Pinker has told us, have fallen dramatically as well. We maintain that much of the gain in both peace and plenty have come about through the workings of the three principles we have discovered, and especially from and through the Rule of Three.

The Brookings study on its face seems far too good to be true; every day we Westerners get bombarded with news about horrendous poverty everywhere, including within the United States. How do we square Brookings with the news version of reality? It is very helpful here to recall the Confucian term *zhengming* or the *rectification of terms*. In ancient China that meant calling things what they truly are; in the modern West, the principle for propaganda says, *let me define the terms, and I will give you the desired result.* Brookings defines middle-class as being comprised of people who have some discretionary income above that needed for survival. On this basis, thanks largely to the Green Revolution beginning in the 1960s, billions of the peoples of Asia and Africa became enabled to escape the continual threat of starvation—and thereby gain the blessings of small money surpluses. Of course, for modern Westerners, such people—called the *vulnerable* by Brookings—do not qualify as middle class at all, but rather pitifully poor. Poverty is partly, or even largely, subjective.

We have devoted much of this part of our book on the Present Age to examining roughly the last 100 years of significant events within six countries: China, Russia, Iran, Israel, Great Britain, and the United States. The three authoritarian examples have failed by the measures of peace and plenty. The three democracies, under which the Rule of Three has prevailed, have generated stunning levels of plenty, and also large measures of peace.

We conclude that the West's high rates of very well-off middle-class folks got arrived at through the working out of the many applications of the Rule of Three stimulated by the Printing Revolution. For the East, not nearly so much so, for authoritarian regimes reduce the possibilities for peace and plenty very much. How this all worked out becomes the subject of our following three chapters.

Chapter Four

Revolutions in Intercourse/ New Schools of Thought

Overview: While the West languished in darkness for some 500 years, China passed through an evolution to become the world's preeminent large nation-state, one experiencing a Renaissance in the arts and sciences and displaying previously unimaginable wealth. Then, in a fairly short span of time (let's say 1200–1800), the West went through a similar evolution to China's own—beginning approximately 1,500 years later than did China's. Once more, technological change drove changes in governance and people's thinking about how to gain peace and prosperity came before evolution in governance. And Western change also included a Renaissance in arts and sciences. The Western evolution eventually led to the American Experiment.

Origin of the English word *intercourse*: Late Middle English: from Old French *entrecours* "exchange, commerce", from Latin *intercursus*, from *intercurrere* "intervene", from *inter-* "between" + *currere* "run".

Oxford English Dictionary

Introduction: What Could Possibly Go Wrong?

In Xanadu did Kubla Khan/a stately pleasure dome decree/Where Alph the sacred river ran/through caverns measureless to man/down to a sunless sea.

Samuel Taylor Coleridge, *Xanadu, or a Vision in a Dream*, 1798

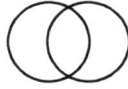

Fascination with China and things Chinese in Western wealthy circles held sway for some 700 years or so. Coleridge wrote his fantasy, opiate dream-induced poem *Xanadu* toward the tail end of this period. The period itself began shortly before the Venetian Marco Polo completed his famous 24-year journey to and from China (1271–95), during which he spent 17 years in China itself, as a favored representative of the fifth Great Khan—Kublai Khan. Polo's book (in a number of versions) *Il Millione* or *The Travels of Marco Polo* fed Westerners' fancy for all things strange and wonderful from the Far East. Along with Polo's accounts came word of great Chinese inventions, of which the Venetians found paper money to be the most amazing—along with rocks that burned (coal). The Venetians were great traders, of course, and had for several centuries been a Western terminus of the Great Silk Road trading routes from far East to the Mediterranean.[1] The Venetians were also great copiers, readily figuring out how to make "Chinese" silk, for which the East–West trading routes had become named. Word of another amazing invention, printing, may or may not have come back with him. We cannot be sure. Perhaps printing developed independently in the West. In any case, what was the nature of the domain Marco Polo lived in for so long a time?

Genghis Khan began life in 1162 as a peasant named Temuchin, born near Lake Baikal in Mongolia. By the time he died in 1227, he had risen to create the world's greatest empire ever, until the British sort of stumbled into an even larger one during Queen Victoria's reign. His horse soldiers conquered all of Mongolia and the Asian steppes, and breached the famous Great Wall of China, thereby coming to conquer all of that great nation-state as well. The Silk Road trade routes were made somewhat safe for travelers through the simple expedient of the Mongols achieving rule over nearly all of trade route geography. Even so, a hazardous trip along the Silk Road might take several years and generate incredible costs to merchants; so, only the rarest and most valuable Chinese craft goods could bear that cost. But this, of course, is all stuff that schoolboys used to learn. And the Great Khan created the most exotic "pleasure dome" ever known to man—apparently far exceeding the wonder of the ancient Hanging Gardens of Babylon.

---

[1]Many specific land routes, as well as sea-lanes, comprised the so-called Silk Road that brought China's marvelous luxury goods to the few wealthy amongst the benighted Westerners of the time.

What interests us here is not so much the conquest story as the Chinese Greatness/Western Crudeness story. Mongol-Chinese trade ran from Northern Mongolia to the East Indies and to India and then to the east coast of Africa, and from the Chinese Pacific coast to the Mediterranean. Chinese oceangoing junks sailed to and around India and eventually traded with east coast Africans. At this period in time, it appears likely that of the world's total GDP, China and India generated a bit over one-half. Africa generated some fifth or so more—a share that grew as the Portuguese helped develop the West African slave trade. All told, China under the Han through into the Mongolian rule created or stimulated close to three-quarters of world GDP. Of course, the various native empires and tribes of the Americas also generated vast wealth. That leaves the supposedly great Europeans of the time with very little indeed. Europe was something of a beggar's opera.[2]

The problem facing the Western traders beginning roughly in 100 BC at the beginning of the Han Dynasty can be simply put: Western elites craved the luxurious outpourings that China produced, and the Chinese court scorned cheap Western wares. Result: a trade imbalance—perhaps largely caused by some rather snooty elite Chinese attitudes and certainly by the astronomical costs of intercourse. A fundamental power imbalance existed as well: Individual Westerners seeking trade deals with China had to attempt negotiations with the ruling elite, perhaps even with the Great Khan and other emperors, if they were to gain access to Chinese trading cities. Nothing better illustrates the power imbalance than the matter of tribute.

The Chinese court had such power, and control over its vast domain, that the court could operate a "pay-to-play" scheme. And we know when the scheme began, because we can date when it was the Westerners first began paying tribute to the Chinese royal court—around 100 BC. We also know when the scheme began to fall apart—in the 1840s when Great Britain forced Indian opium into Chinese markets, pretty much at the point of a gun. Until then, the trade imbalance between the West and China assured, partly through tribute, a growing flow of gold from Europe to China. Of course, Europe's gold supply got fairly regularly refreshed by Spain's rape of South America. Indirectly, Spanish gold enabled intercourse with China—and also some unhealthy price inflation for all Europeans.

---

[2] See the work done by Enodo Economics directed by Diana Choyleva.

China by the time of Marco Polo, then, ruled supreme as the world's largest empire and dominated international trade. It generated some third of global GDP and supported the most sumptuous ruling cities ever known. What could possibly go wrong?

Technology Revolutions Yield Governance and Intercourse Revolutions

Three great new technological revolutions led to downstream changes in the related matters of governance and international intercourse—all in turn eventually leading to the dominance of the West. The technological discoveries involved: phonetic writing, movable-type printing, and long-distance ocean shipping. The governance evolution began with the polemic pamphleteers and reached forward to the American experience, the nation-state conceived in liberty. International trade intercourse relied upon new technology in ocean-going shipping and upon institutional developments such as the private trading corporation form for financing and implementing trading worldwide. We shall be dealing here with governance changes first and then intercourse.

They Spoke in Many Tongues—the Babel Effect

> "Come let us go down and there confuse their language so that they may not understand one another's speech." So the Lord disbursed them from there over the face of all the earth, and they left off building the city. Therefore, its name was called Babel, because there the Lord confused the language of all the earth. And from there the Lord disbursed them over the face of all the earth.
>
> *Genesis* 11:7-9

The Hebrew Babel story captures the best properties of grand myth-making: the attempt to recount in a narrative form an underlying sense, in this case, for how human languages devolved from out of a root beginning language. Those today who laugh at the Babel story for its presumed fundamentalistic primitiveness miss the point. We know today that many languages did indeed evolve from a common base, an Indo-European foundation for all subsequent Western languages. Underlying Babel is a core human sensibility for a once-common root for human intercourse.

As people spread out to populate land and land masses, speech evolved along various pathways until the language of one tribe or nation could not be understood by the others. Americans can observe something of this in the changing nature of Canadian French from its Parisian French parent. The Babel Effect.

Because of the Babel Effect, nation and empire building in the ancient world faced severe challenges regarding intercourse between ruling elites and the many different peasant groupings, each with its own language incomprehensible to others. Even today in China, some 120 dialects get spoken within five basic language groupings. Due partly to the limitations in speech intercourse, the early nations used brute force and mass relocations of whole peoples in order to maintain discipline amongst the peasantry—the cattle-herding approach to rulership. Then, somewhere along the story line of history, a new and better approach sprang into being—partly at least driven by the radically different requirements upon government posed by the Agricultural Revolution: Some group came up with the idea of physically recording spoken words in the form of picture symbols. The Babel Effect indirectly drove mankind to evolve into the symbol-using species.

The first known writing form—cuneiform—developed amongst the Sumerians of Mesopotamia, circa 3500 BC. Cuneiform constituted the first use of line-drawing pictures for the representation of spoken words. Brilliant! Now, word meanings could be communicated to peoples speaking radically different languages. The Chinese began using word-picture writing during the Shang Dynasty (circa 1600 BC), and within 500 or so years, the Chinese bureaucrats of that emerging nation-state could carry out intercourse within a growing feudal empire composed of different groups with different languages. Cuneiform writing made possible a nation-state that no longer had to rely solely upon brute force or face-to-face intercourse for compliance. By the time of the Westerner Marco Polo, the Chinese government ran an exquisite and sophisticated bureaucratic state based upon advanced training in written language, Confucian principles for harmony, and communication upon (sometimes) printed paper. The Chinese government even stimulated inventive individuals to develop separate word-symbol woodcut blocks that could be selected and laid out in the desired order to compose a page—in effect movable print. However, the bureaucracy apparently saw no great advantage to this system over simply carving out onto wood a whole page of picture symbols when a great number of copies were required. The reason? Movable type using word symbols required too many word-characters to cut or cast for all the words in use. A "picture letter" for each word in use! The total word count for ancient languages certainly ran in the thousands—perhaps 5,000; that would be a lot of carving or casting—especially as commonly used picture-words would require many multiples for words which got repeated within a message. So, cuneiform printing worked well for a bureaucracy communicating in picture-letter form, frequently with people speaking in different tongues—but not so well for mass communication.

Sound-Symbol Writing

In the beginning…God said, "Let there be light…."

Genesis 1: 1 & 3

In the beginning was the Word….

John 1:1

A competing writing form emerged amongst the Semitic peoples, perhaps from Egyptian influences, around 1000 BC. Rather than being based upon pictures for words, it became based upon the sounds of syllables within words. The concept was quite revolutionary, for it meant that anyone who had learned the sounds of some 20–30 letters could both decipher and cypher the words in any message. Not only that, any spoken language could be also cyphered and deciphered—and then translated into anyone else's own spoken language. And all such words could be phonetically pronounced, although not with an accent that people such as the French would approve. People could thus speak, and sing, perfectly in a language unknown to them.[3]

One may say, with some caution, that the Hebrews invented consonants, and the Greeks invented vowels. That means that reading the earliest Hebrew texts can be quite challenging—as neither vowels nor spaces

[3] In around 1985, an American choir performed the sacred music of Russia in the Moscow Hall of Columns. None of the choir members knew Russian, but they could still "speak" to Russian audiences—performing great choral music banned by the Soviet government for some 70 years. Some Russians got upset with choir members who would not speak to them individually in Russian. Choir members could pronounce words that they did not know the meanings of.

betwixt words had come into use. Perhaps it was so to conserve valuable, costly paper? It also means that the great religious, philosophical, scientific, and dramatic creations of the ancient West all must date from after roughly 1000 BC—in written form. Previous to that, only oral composition and the memories of the great bards and storytellers existed—along with some rather sterile cuneiform writing. *Genesis* took written form after 1000 BC then, and probably within the courts of King David or Solomon. Homer's great Greek epics could finally get captured upon paper. The Western world was the richer for all of this.

The two systems of writing down words—sight versus sounds—yielded an anomaly for world history: Regarding writing, the Chinese were the first movers in the East, and picture-symbol writing helped make possible the bureaucratic control of the world's largest empire—even though the empire's people spoke in many tongues. First mover rewards. The fast follower West, by inventing phonetic alphabets, however, laid the groundwork for the West's eventual triumph in terms of world power and peace and prosperity for the common people—as we shall see.

A Movable Feast

> It is a press certainly, but a press from which shall flow inexhaustible streams.... Through it, God will spread His Word. A spring of truth shall flow from it: like a new star it shall scatter the darkness of ignorance and cause a light heretofore unknown to shine amongst men.
>
> Johannes Gutenberg

The intellectuals East and West who love to point out that the Chinese invented movable type first miss the whole point about the invention itself. Rather like using gunpowder for fireworks, which we know the Chinese also invented, movable type could be used as a toy, or as a serious weapon. Due to the technological/cultural anomaly of the West developing writing later chronologically and therefore with sound symbols rather than picture symbols, movable type became, not a toy as it was for ancient China, but one of the world's greatest weapons for transforming violence into peace. The pen can be mightier than the sword.

Johann Gensfleisch zur Laden zum Gutenberg spent roughly 20 years, beginning around 1435, in developing not only cast metal movable type for alphabetical letters and for numbers, but also in developing related technology: the printing press, oil-based inks, papers of the correct absorption rates. His represented the labor of perfection, a manual art, not the quick work for a profit that his over-the-years investors appeared to desire. The first fruit of this remarkable man's drive for perfection appeared in 1455 in the form of the world's first volume printing of an entire book, a great work of art in itself—the famous Gutenberg Bible.

Sadly for Johannes, 15th-century German fiefdoms and the French nation alike provided no property rights to inventions; no patent office existed anywhere, and no such office had even been conceived. So, it appears that Herr Gutenberg's inventions were stolen, largely through legal actions brought against him by his investors—who were not so much "angel capitalists" as doers of the devil's work.[4] Herr Gutenberg had little likelihood of gaining economic rents from his own genius.

The unintended consequence of Gutenberg's loss of monopoly rights readily became apparent: Almost anyone with a little capital and the guts to pursue the profession could become a publisher! Unlike, say, an ocean-going galleon, a printing press was a simple device, and cheap to procure, being merely an adaptation of the age-old winepress—as was technology for metal for type casting. The combination of willing printers and eager pamphleteers soon brought upon authoritarian governments something worse than a plague of locusts. Local and state governments tried mightily, and largely unsuccessfully, to limit the content of private printing establishments. What made the league of printers and pamphleteers so dangerously explosive, and even downright seditious, was the reality that a print shop could gin out 1,000 or so copies of a heretical piece of writing about either religious beliefs or political satire in a matter of a few days. The pamphlet could be distributed surreptitiously, and no sign of the nasty work would long remain in the offending print shop. It was the mass communication of seditious material against authority that made a pamphlet like unto fireflies in a bottle. All in all, this sort of intercourse was far more dangerous to the authorities than the sexual kind ever could be.

[4]Even with patent protections in place, men such as Orville and Wilbur Wright in our own era had to fight decades-long court battles, and still lost the licensing-monopoly power they sought—in order to profit from their innovative genius.

Asymmetries: Intercourse by Land or by Sea

Considering the matter of the intercourse revolution, a geographic asymmetry for centuries penalized Western traders seeking opportunities for gain in the Far East. Something eliminating that imbalance needed to occur for the West to challenge Chinese power in international trade. China's richest trading opportunities existed in Southeast Asia and India, followed by eastern Africa. While the sea routes around the Malay Peninsula could be very treacherous indeed (more from pirates than weather), sea distances—let us say from Shanghai to Calcutta—ran only about 4,000 miles for sailing craft hugging the coasts. The large, magnificent Chinese seagoing junks beginning with the Song Dynasty could make these voyages with relative ease—and did so until a Ming Emperor gave commands that such extended voyaging should cease, due to the dangers. The time period: roughly 900–1250. These trading voyages helped generate the wealth giving Kublai Khan the wherewithal to build his "stately pleasure dome."

Now consider the voyage faced by the West's first great navigators of Portugal, about the time that China's trading voyages ceased. The sea distance from Lisbon to Shanghai by the Cape of Good Hope (better described by its original Portuguese name as the Cape of Storms) ran some 13,000 to 14,000 miles. The journey could easily consume a year or more, but that was considerably faster than three-some years via the overland Silk Road routes. Until Western shipbuilders could design and construct sailing ships capable of making that long trip around the Horn through truly brutal sea conditions with relative security, trade would always be asymmetrically against the Westerners. Chinese junks might be seagoing craft, but they were designed more for coastal navigation than for blue water voyaging. The Western traders would require real blue water craft capable of weathering unrelenting winds and high waves—deep keel ships. Those ships would get developed only at roughly the beginning of the 18th century. Until then, China's position as top dog in the world trading contest would remain secure.

There were, moreover, difficulties needing surmounting in addition to the physical hardware—the ships. Who would have the financial means to fund such voyages, and bear the huge risks? Earlier Chinese emperors could do so, but Western feudal kingdoms lacked the resources, and perhaps the will to assume risk as well. England particularly, had forced financial limitations upon its kings, and queens: Only Parliament by long tradition could levy new taxes, and Parliament was also risk-averse.[5] The solution would eventually come in the form of an extension of medieval-period monopoly grants bought by wealthy aristocrats: Parliament could pass bills giving legal status to joint stock companies receiving monopoly powers in defined areas. The East India Company of London merchants and bankers received such a joint stock monopoly to trade in the East Indies, by grant of Parliament in 1600. The combination of blue water sailing vessels and the institution of the joint stock company in turn created the impetus for the English to develop complex risk-sharing strategies: Individuals' risks could be mitigated through the sale of shares in an investment to many shareholders. Risk-reward calculations could be made, and marine insurance could further mitigate risk. The famous Lloyd's of London firm began business in a London coffee house in 1688, insuring against marine losses.

What could possibly go wrong? This is the question we began with: What could possibly undermine China's world dominance that existed from roughly 200 BC to 1700 AD? It was, after all, a period bringing relatively great peace and plenty to China, largely due to its efficient bureaucratic machinery driven by written information exchanges and orders from on top amongst bureaucrats not knowing each other's spoken languages, and some reciprocal benefits to its trading partners. That left the West as the poor man out. Three essential matters of intercourse eventually undermined China's international trade dominance. The first two—alphabetic writing and movable type printing—led eventually to the changes in Western nation-state governance that would make the West dominant. The third—long-distance trading capabilities (and warfare capacities as well)—would allow Western nations to export dominance to China, just as China had earlier exported trade-based dominance to Southeast Asia and India. Tit for tat.

Polemical Pamphleteers

Returning to our overall thesis for this chapter, we had opined that similar processes of institutional development occurred in China first, and then in

[5]Parenthetically, the King could raise "ship money" without Parliament's approval, and such money was meant for seaborne defense of the realm. When King Charles I (1625–1649) used ship money to finance conflicts with Scotland, he was well on his way to creating the civil war over which he lost his head.

the West some 1,500 years later. In each case, technological revolutions also created needs for philosophical endeavors regarding how best to govern nations to achieve peace and plenty by taking advantage of new technology. In China, you may recall, the aftermath of the Agricultural Revolution with its feudalistic governance drove the Hundred Schools of Thought movement whose members began searching for that better way—eventually yielding the largest nation-state ever known and the Confucian ordering of a new society based upon a hierarchy of pairs, with each level's conflicts mediated by a higher third—a Rule of Three. One should recognize that, lacking mass communication technology, the itinerant philosophers of China needed to travel the country in order to disseminate their thought—a distinct burden.

It turns out that a similar process did occur in the West, beginning with triple technological advances—writing, mass communication, and seagoing vessels. The changes wrought especially by movable print led directly to a new outburst of thinking in the West, overwhelming the Dark Ages period of some 800 years (roughly 500–1300). This outburst of thinking disseminated by intercourse through mass communication eventually yielded the American Experiment in nation-state founding. The Western nation-state in turn would muster the advantages of human liberty and creativity very effectively indeed.

The Worshipful Company of Stationers versus Areopagitica

> Give me the liberty to know, to utter, and to argue freely according to conscience, above all liberties.
>
> John Milton, *Areopagitica*

> The mind is its own place, and in its own make a heaven of hell, a hell of heaven.
>
> John Milton, *Paradise Lost*

The Worshipful Company of Stationers was neither. Instead, from its origin in 1403, stemming from its successful petition for guild status from the Lord Mayor of London, it operated as one of many rent-seeking trade associations in London using monopoly guild power to benefit its members. It was only "worshipful" in that it aimed to keep its members out of hot water with both the Roman Church and English civil government.

Its goals resembled all trade associations' purposes of the time: Keep quality respectable amongst all tradesmen involved in any aspect of, in this case, producing books—and prices high by eliminating independent competition. And for God's sake, keep out of trouble with the law!

And so, its members began their long ride down the slippery slope to punishing speech disliked by ruling elites. This in turn meant acting as the religious and civil establishments' guard dogs, performing some acts of censorship. One word in its name did indeed measure up to its promise—"stationers." That meant that the guild members all had permanent physical premises from which to operate—they were stationary—rather than producing their wares on the streets as itinerants.

By the 1470s, with the growing international expansion of the Gutenberg Revolution in printing, the guild began claiming authority to regulate the import of foreign books, many from the radicals of the Netherlands who displeased the King of England mightily. In 1557, the Stationers reached a form of nirvana—a royal charter granted by the Tudor Queen Mary granting them real monopoly power over all aspects of publishing, backed up by the power to search private premises for any materials regarded as heretical or seditious. In short order, some printers found themselves run up before a secretive Star Chamber court to answer for their sins, without recourse to such judicial niceties as representation by lawyers or trial by jury. Rule of Three? Fie upon it. Down the black hole you go, miscreant. The government had no need to run its own watchdog institution when it could simply reward private guild members for doing its job for it—and do it far more effectively and cheaply. Part of the cheapness and effectiveness came from holding individual printers to account, rather than those slippery writers who were itinerants and who could easily elude the authorities. Being stationers had all sorts of ramifications for printers.

The next step along the pathway to publishing perdition came as the Company in 1565 established *de facto* property rights for printers in the books that they approved, licensed, and published—a cheeky way of relieving authors of their own intellectual property. Printers could now gain *copyright* (literally the right to forbid others to copy) to a title by simply registering a claim with the Master or Wardens of the Company. Not until the English Parliament's passing of the Copyright Act of 1709 under Queen Anne, as a logical extension of English common law, could authors gain some of the rewards for the mass communication of their own ideas. But by then, the Stationers' corporate power had largely evaporated. The Copyright Act restored to authors a property right in their own published thinking. The Chinese philosophers in the age before possessed no such rights.

Between roughly 1625 and 1709, however, a revolution in thinking about governance of the people had worked its way up through English Civil War's bloody fields of conflict. The most important figure during the run-up and through that conflict—let us say from 1625 to 1660, from the beginning of the reign of Charles I to the Restoration under James II—appeared in the form of a commoner only known for centuries as one of England's greatest poets.

John Milton lived a double life. Most people today, if they know of him at all, associate him with one of those pesky Great Books of Western Civilization that they know so well and have never read—*Paradise Lost*, a monumentally long poem, written in blank verse—leaving modern readers with a blank stare. Or, modern intellectuals may simply dismiss John Milton as a shameful member of the "white patriarchy." But this is John Milton the poet. The other is John Milton the polemical pamphleteer and sometime revolutionary government official, the man who wrote *Areopagitica*. And here lies our interest in him. The two worlds John Milton inhabited simultaneously get linked together by this one word—*liberty*. "Better to reign in hell than serve in heaven."[6]

The name for Milton's polemic derived from the ancient Greek *Areopagus* or "hill of Ares"—the location of the high court of Athens, an institution that regularly imposed censorship upon the distribution of writings against the state. Milton echoed the prose style of ancient Athens as a way, during the English Renaissance, for claiming authority for his work. He relates ancient appeals for liberty to his current argument against the Roman papacy that restricted and licensed only works that the ruling churchmen approved. He then argues that the free circulation of ideas has a direct relationship to mankind's moral and intellectual gains, and to the search for truth. As a good member of the Puritan party, Milton of course saw liberty of expression and religious practices as a necessary matter if mankind were to overcome the ravages of men's sin nature. Only liberty could shine light into human darkness.

Because of the basic reality that all individuals possess imperfect information and knowledge, only the unrestricted search through many experiments in either or both thought and action can possibly yield the

---

[6]See *Paradise Lost*, Satan's opening monologue, 263.

best outcomes, or the truth.[7] This reality underlies what we have called the Discovery Principle. Whether he realized it or not, Milton in his polemical life had placed himself squarely within the ongoing philosophers' debate seeking answers to the Big Three existential questions for life together in civil society. Those questions concerned right authority and governance: the issue of sovereignty; the issue of the peoples' relation to authority; the nature of the rules and boundaries that should limit human actions. By the following century, the American colonists would reduce the expression of these issues down to just three words: *sovereignty, representation, constitution*.[8] The answers that the polemical philosophers arrived at by then would yield the American experiment in individual and corporate governance—entirely based upon the Rule of Three.

Who Then Won?

John Milton's greatest polemical pamphlet, *Areopagitica,* got published surreptitiously without license right at the height of the English Civil War. He escaped any punishment for his actions, because the Parliamentary forces controlled London, disabling the power of the king's minions in that great city. So, Milton lived to become eventually a member of the Puritan regime under first the army and then the Lord Protector, Oliver Cromwell. Safe again. We might say that Milton versus the Worshipful Company ended in victory for him and for liberty. Then with the 1660 restoration of the English crown, Milton became a fugitive—old, sick, and blind. His Royalist brother Christopher may have intervened in the Court of Charles II to prevent his execution. By the time of the Glorious Revolution in 1688, the forces of liberty began to overcome government censorship—but by then both John Miltons—poet and pamphleteer—had entered together into Paradise. Who then won? Depends upon the evaluative timeframe.

The Great Triad of Western Thinkers

Not only John Milton, but also two other men of the post-printing revolution West fundamentally reshaped the direction of thinking about the

[7] See Friedrich Hayek, *The Fatal Conceit: The Errors of Socialism.*

[8] See Bernard Bailyn, *The Ideological Origins of the American Revolution.*

existential questions for a great society: Martin Luther and John Locke. We today regard Dr. Luther simply as an early Church reformer. We miss the point, perhaps because we possess so little awareness of Luther the polemical pamphleteer. Luther's polemical writings against the Roman Church unsurprisingly commenced only some 60 years after the Gutenberg revolution in printing. Pre-printing era revolutionaries went up in fire at the stake. Before printed mass communication, Luther's challenge to Church authority would probably have backfired, and placed him amongst the faggots in a bonfire, too. But instead, Luther could successfully argue for human liberty in the spiritual realm. Coming some 125 years after Luther's victory for liberty in spirit, John Milton successfully debated the issue of human liberty in the realm of the individual's freedom both of inner thought and outer speech—what we today call *freedom of conscience*.

Lastly, John Locke, exiled at one point to the Netherlands for fear of his life, successfully debated the issue of liberty for the outer man, the individual in the material world. Bedrock reality for Locke took the form of liberty in property, based in a property right in a man's own body. By extension, that meant a right to the fruits of his, or her, own labor.[9] Locke's significant writings followed by some 40 years those of John Milton. He would live and write long enough to influence significantly the ideological origins of the American Revolution.

Notice the pattern presented by this triad of great men: Their writings all followed, and to a major degree became public, after the Printing Revolution. Their respective writings all came before the idea of religious and political toleration achieved respect and political approval: Changes in British governance followed a revolution in philosophy. Philosophy overcame overt physical persecution, and not the other way round. "The pen is mightier...." The ordering of their three great breakthroughs regarding human governance began at the innermost circle: the human spirit. Free the human spirit and all else becomes possible. Then came the freedom of the individual person to think and to speak his or her own thoughts, without retribution from Bishop or King. Last to appear came liberty within the material world, beginning with a person's own physical body and capabilities. Spirit, soul, body—the Great Triad for God and Man found within Judeo-Christian philosophy and a primary example of a Rule of Three, where spirit mediates between soul and body.

---

[9]See John Locke, *Two Treatises of Government.*

Why the English Revolution Failed

No bishop, no king.

James I upon the necessity for Church authority and discipline

We mistook the word of man for the word of God.

An after-the-fact statement of truth by a
Puritan participant in the Civil War

The history books tell us something of the what, where, when, how, and *why,* of the English Civil War (1642–1651 by commonly accepted dating), and indeed, two sides—Royalist and Parliamentarian—did clash in this conflict. Taking a broader view, and looking back farther for beginnings, we see that the Civil War did not represent a successful step toward liberal governance so much as a failed revolution against authoritarian governance. Indeed, some called the conflict the Great Rebellion. Successful civil war versus failed revolution. Given that this revolution followed the Printing Revolution giving birth to England's own "hundred schools of thought" about human nature and its governance, one should ask the simple *why* question: Why did the English Revolution fail?

Of Diggers, Levelers, Ranters, and More: The Dissenters

No King but Jesus.

Motto of the fifth Monarchy Men

A dissenter (from the Latin *dissentire* "to disagree") is one who disagrees in opinion, belief and other matters.

Wikipedia

High-level Western thinking about humankind and our spiritual and secular governance came from men such as the triad we have mentioned, but much more went on besides their efforts. While not literally adding up to "a hundred schools" in the Chinese tradition, the Printing Revolution did set loose upon the English political landscape a very numerous, and truly unruly, batch of secondary polemical pamphleteers—each with his own take on what the English nation should become. The sheer range of their collective imagination beggars imagination.

By no means a complete survey, here are some of the contenders for the crown of outrage. The Diggers were a group of Protestant agrarian (hence the name "Diggers") communal living folks whose polemical pamphleteer, Gerrard Winstanley, presented their beliefs for the ages to wonder at: They desired to reform the country by converting it into a collection of small, rural agrarian village-communes scattered about the land—groups all holding possessions in common and thereby leveling the wellbeing of all. Then there were the Levelers themselves, who argued for a country based upon the will of the people, expanded if not universal suffrage, equality before the law, and religious tolerance—believing these all to be natural rights of man descending from the laws of God broken by the Royals. The Ranters were quite a fascinating little sect whose polemicists raved on about the pantheistic nature of humankind, claiming each person to have a bit of the Godhead within him. They encouraged general amoralism and had no truck with obedience to any authority. This particular belief-set would not take them far, but they did have a presence in the marketplace of ideas.

The full range of dissenters did not end with this outrageous triad. Some would seem to us today as more mainline: Baptists, Anabaptists, Puritans, Quakers, and also Congregationalists and Presbyterians. The Ranters made this lot seem pretty normal. Then there were the Familists, the Fifth Monarchists, the Grindletonians, the Muggletonians, the Sabbatarians, the Seekers, and the Socinians. And there were more—but one gets the idea after a while. Understandably, the good god fearing moderate folk of England could become quite put off by all this—and might worry about who would be running the asylum if any of these folks got control. If the ancient Chinese had been faced with such a lot making up their own hundred schools of thought, they should have had some misgivings as well.

Following the pamphleteering mania of these unbounded thinkers, and the loss of the king's head and with it the Royalists' cause for a time, a series of failed attempts at new forms of government took place—instigated by the three main actors on the stage: Parliament, the New Model Army, and the Army's leader—the man destined to become the Lord Protector of England, Oliver Cromwell. The Army leaders had the captured king executed, and then declared the monarchy at an end and England to be a Commonwealth. The Army's leadership expected the existing Parliament to carry out the legislation necessary for a working republic and for democratic elections. Parliament failed in this mission and was soon purged of its most rebellious members, its reduced numbers being then nicknamed the "Rump Parliament." So, the promise of a democracy produced instead a confusing rule by unelected army leaders. The common soldiers' riotous demands for radical political, religious and social changes first proposed by the even more radical polemical pamphleteers caused chaos in the land. Army rule, too, failed to unify the country. Oliver Cromwell dismissed Parliament and became, in effect, a dictator—a new monarch in all but title.

Cromwell's words dismissing Parliament ring down through English history: "You have sat too long here for any good you have been doing. Depart, I say, and let us have done with you. In the name of God, go!"[10] When Oliver Crowell died, no good succession plan existed—other than to appoint his weak-willed son as the next Lord Protector. That smacked far too much of monarchy for leaders supporting a republic. By 1660, the general lot of people in Britain saw to it that the old monarchy got reestablished, under the son of Charles I. A revolution came around full circle. Nevertheless, the country did evolve toward what would become known as a liberal form of constitutional monarchy. Much may be said for Charles II, who did not do the following: He did not carry out a bloody putsch but came to power by the request of Parliament. He did not take general revenge upon the Parliamentary faction that executed his father. He did not act against the will of the people expressed through Parliament. He contented himself with a private life of indulgence denied him during his lean years in exile—particularly with regard to whores. Presumably he even received from his ennobled paramour, Lady Castlemain, a *Poor Whores' Petition*—a satire penned by whore house owners in the aftermath of the 1668 Bawdy House Riots. All in all, he was a good King.

Conclusions

The first Western replay of ancient Chinese events eventually leading to a nation-state form of governance failed in its first instance: The English

[10] Some 180 years later, during the initial crisis period early in World War II, MP Leo Amery quoted Cromwell's words to Prime Minister Chamberlain—who went. Winston Churchill then became Britain's new wartime PM.

Civil War hung fire. At a very general level, all of the thinking and debate amongst the philosophers and pamphleteers of the time failed to stumble upon the Rule of Three, without which, failure would eventually result.

Some conclusions, both truths and fallacies:

Truths:

- *Changes in both governance and intercourse follow revolutions in technology* making possible new approaches to peace and prosperity. Returning to subsistence living will never do what technology can do to lead us on a pathway to joy.
- *Thinking things through*: The philosophers will use debate and discovery as the tools to craft new approaches—many of which will hang fire. If the search for truth leads to the Rule of Three, healthy changes will eventually come into being. Otherwise, things will merely revolve back to where they began, probably at a more brutish level.
- Many things may go wrong during the search for peace and plenty, things sufficient to delay healthy changes for a long time, maybe forever. What may go wrong comes from three fallacies.

Fallacies:

- *The Unitary Sovereign*. What we colloquially call the strongman continually threatens the pursuit of happiness and joy in human relations. No more pernicious fallacy exists than the belief that one man needs to rule over all others.
- *The "will of the people"*—popular mob democracy—always ends in conflict that returns governance to a strongman.
- *Micromanaged liberty*: Those partisans who would impose their own political, social and religious preferences upon others—in effect, micromanaging liberty—will destroy liberty for everyone. Those who desire both liberty and equality shall receive neither.

Chapter Five

The American Experiment

Overview: The discontented amongst the British population—before, during, and after the English Civil War—flocked to the newly established plantations in North America. Composed of four major groups—Puritan, Royalist, Quaker, and Scots/Irish—they comprised in total an out-migration to the colonies of some 350,000 mainly unhappy souls, over a period of roughly 150 years. These four groups agreed with each other over practically nothing, except their dissatisfactions with the British government—and hated each other thoroughly. How this contentious rabble ever formed a nation at all, let alone the most successful nation-state ever, forms our topic here. We consider, in turn, the very curious *basis for America's founding*, the *ideological and founding mythic proportions* for the new nation, and lastly its *structure based broadly and deeply in the Rule of Three.*

Introduction: "The World Turned Upside Down"

Full forty years this royal crown/Hath been his father's and his own
And is there anyone but he/That in the same should sharer be?
For better may/The scepter sway
Than he that hath such right to reign?
Then let's hope for a peace/For the wars will not cease
Till the king enjoys his own again/Yes, this I can tell
That all will be well/When the King enjoys his own again

from *The King Enjoys his Own Again*,
a royalist anthem sung early in the English Civil War

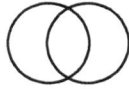

Every American schoolboy and schoolgirl used to know the story of how the British soldiers surrendered to George Washington and his Continentals and French supporting army outside of Yorktown in 1781. The Americans formed one line and across from them, the French formed another. The defeated British marched between the victors, their band reportedly playing a popular British song of the time called *The World Turned Upside Down*. For many generations, Americans carried in their memories the patriotic picture of the noble scene as portrayed by John Trumbull in his 1820 painting *Surrender of Lord Cornwallis*. Many also eventually had cheap reproductions of the heroic scene hanging on their living room walls. Americans of all ages thrilled to see their Revolution as the ultimate story about an underdog winning. Perhaps this is why Americans love to cheer for the underdog in sporting events—because we all sense that we were once underdogs, too. But was it true—that "world upside down" story?

First, let us stipulate that the "upside down" story has formed an important part of the overall founding mythology behind the American nation. Traditionally, it has been nearly as important as, for instance: the stories of the battles of Lexington and Concord, Valley Forge, the Liberty Tree—and even Parson Weems' cherry tree story about the youthful George Washington. Because it occurred in our modern era and after the Printing Revolution, the Americans can get a firsthand look back at how an overarching founding myth actually developed through such stories, as a curious mix of the factual and the fabulous (originally meaning "mythical" or "legendary"). There are just a few stories.

With regard to the Yorktown legend, on-the-scene commentators mentioned that the surrendering British and Hessian troops were granted the "full honors of war"—to march out with "drums beating and colors flying." Onlookers report that the British drummers played in a "slow, melancholy, and careless" manner—notice, no singing.[1]

The surrender parade itself covered some two miles of open ground. The difficulties with the legend now begin to appear: Over that length of march, it appears highly unlikely that the drummers would beat out the same, monotonous simple melody again and again and again. Rather, they would beat out a number of different tunes—perhaps even *Yankee Doodle*?

[1] See "'The World Turned Upside Down': Did the British Really Play the Sardonic Melody During the Yorktown Surrender" by Josh Provan in *MilitaryHistoryNow.com*, 29 May 2018.

Furthermore, and this is the clincher, the very same tune had at least two completely different sets of words. The first song, quoted in part above, was sort of a royalist fight song early in the Civil War. Named *When the King Enjoys His Own Again*, it gave support to the king's cause—in the manner of *The Battle Hymn of the Republic* and *Dixie* during the American Civil War. The second version was the one entitled *The World Turned Upside Down*. This song was a humorous little ditty mocking the banning of traditional Christmas frivolities under the stern Lord Protector Oliver Cromwell during the Puritan interregnum between Charles I (the one who lost his head) and his son Charles II. Which song did they play?

Of course, no one could know—then or now, for the British drummers (and probably fifers, too) could only have played the tune, not sung the words as well. The tune was the same. Which song did they mean to communicate—if either, or both? And so we have a real example of how fact and fiction comingle within in the birth of a myth. Yes, the British musicians could very well have played the tune, as well as a number of others, and they could have meant one, or both, of the songs sung to that tune, but we can never know which. Or, more likely, they just beat methodically on their drums: After all, they had just been thoroughly whipped by some country bumpkins, by their way of thinking. The uncertainty over the historical basis for the claim, however, does not diminish the overall truth of what the surrender meant for the British, and for the Americans. For the British, it was an unabashed defeat by the American rabble. For the Americans, it sealed their success in overturning British hegemony and autocratic rule.

What might each song have meant at that moment pregnant with historical significance? *The World Turned Upside Down* had the clearer sensibility: The mightiest contemporary power on earth had just lost, finally and irrecoverably, to a ragtag bunch of colonial country bumpkins (but only because the number two power on earth, the French, had helped out). No matter the details about the French, the Americans had won decisively, after a nearly seven-year struggle. This after England in all its military might, and its diplomatic skill at forming alliances with former enemies, had just 10 years previously fought and won the Seven Years' War against France and that country's allies—a war that became global in nature and could arguably get named the First World War. The news was stunning for the British, for all of Europe, and for the Americans as well. "World turned upside down" events do have great downstream significance as time marches on, as we shall see.

Of course, too, this song could be taken as quite sardonic: The Brits mocking the Yankee Puritans and their sober disregard for all Christmas frivolities. The mockery may have been quite pointed, as the general to whom the British surrendered was a New Englander and a son of Harvard College—a true descendant of the Puritans.

But what about the other song: *When the King Enjoys His Own Again*? Did the Brits mean to cock a snook[2] at the Americans? Did the Brits, then, mean to imply that the King would enjoy a future repossession of his now-former colonies? "We'll get even with you…?" That leads us into our discussion of a most unique happening following the American Revolution: the founding itself of the American nation-state. And no matter the literal truth behind the song, it did become part of the new American founders' myth, a mythology that would eventually unite a new nation. Founding myths frequently become composed of both true facts and falsehoods—and lose no power for their mixed patrimony.

The Smart Money

Imagine that you live in 1783, and the treaty between Britain and its former North American colonies has just been signed. Put yourself in the person of a middle-class Londoner, a man loyal to king and country, or of a member of the British elite, or of an ex-patriot Londoner—a tory Bostonian who fled the city of his birth after the end of its British occupation. For that matter, put yourself in the person of a wealthy, conservative Bostonian, Philadelphian, or New Yorker. Also, imagine that a market for betting on political outcomes existed at that time, just like on horse races—perhaps with the daily odds being posted in *Lloyd's Evening Post* or *The London Chronicle*. Would you have put money on the Americans succeeding in building a new nation? Or, would you have bet on their failure—on their breakup into several small, struggling states, or even upon their begging the British King for readmittance as colonies once more? Remember *When the King Enjoys His Own Again*. If failure seems like a flight of fancy to us today, think again. The smart money would have gone for failure—overwhelmingly.

In regarding the odds behind your bet, we can begin with the Common Heritage myth: that Americans and Brits were all pretty

[2]*Cock a snook* was an English slang expression of derision toward another, of unknown derivation, in which the first person mocks the other by sticking a thumb on the end of one's nose, sticking the other four fingers in the air, and then waving them about.

much alike. Not so, it turns out. Let's look at some common present misperceptions about America following the revolution: First, that the American people shared a common ancestry. Second, that they shared a common culture with their former mother country. Third, that the Americans possessed a common linguistic dialect and vocabulary. While some eight-tenths of all Americans indeed came from Great Britain (exceptions being African slaves, German quietists, and Dutch traders—with a smattering of Swedes—comprising nearly all of the rest), the British themselves were of mixed ancestry—Lowland and Highland Scots, Scots-Irish, Irish, and Nordic elements, as well as English and Welsh. One should not expect this hodge-podge in the parent country to yield unity when transported to a new land. Politically, the British had fought a protracted, violent civil war—over divisive issues still not resolved fully, and those differences involved how the nation should be governed—exactly the challenge that the Americans would face after the revolution. The mother country had also faced two threatening insurrections in Scotland, urged on by its constant enemy, the French. Indeed, the British comprised a wildly culturally diverse nation—regarding everything from politics and religion to dress, architecture, food preparation, and even language. This last item should make modern believers in the Common Heritage myth sit up and take notice: The British shared no common dialect or vocabulary. Henry Higgins in *My Fair Lady* got that right. "Why can't the English learn to speak?" Remember, BBC English did not yet exist. Now we can put some flesh on these matters.

Consider the various out-migrations from Great Britain to the colonies. They did not consist of a steady, homogeneous flow from decade to decade; instead, great gobs of people came in four great gushes from four different parts of the mother country over four different time periods.[3] Let's follow their trail.

A City upon a Hill

> We shall be as a city upon a hill, the eyes of all people are upon us.
>
> From *A Model of Christian Charity* by
> John Winthrop on board the Arbella, 1630

[3] We owe a great debt here to David Hackett Fischer for his book *Albion's Seed: Four British Folkways in America.*

It all began with the Great Puritan out-migration to Massachusetts Bay of some 25,000–30,000 people, largely in family groups, arriving between 1620 and 1640. Many left over religious scruples; some—such as the Pilgrims of Plymouth—had fled the cruel injustices inflicted upon them by Archbishop Laud and his brutal minions of the official state Anglican Church. In 1600, the government through the auspices of its established Church still exercised a heavy hand of discipline over its people—a condition not to change until the upcoming civil war. Not all who arrived in New England espoused Puritanism, but certainly well over half did. As the noted American author Perry Miller wrote, they were on an "errand into the wilderness"—a positively purposed venture in the founding of a new Christian nation, indeed not just a new nation, but the founding of a New Jerusalem on New England's rugged shores.[4] The American Puritan founding fathers perceived themselves to be nothing less than the next great stage in the History of Redemption by which the Lord God would bring about the final union of all his saints, to live forever in the *Book of Revelation's* New Jerusalem come down out of heaven. But, even the saints have to do earthly things in order to keep body and soul together.

The earliest arrivals, the offshoot-of-Puritan sect called the Pilgrims, desired a complete separation from English churches and the English state. They also read some particular passages in the Bible more literally than the other dissenting sects—a habit not uncommon in a time when specific Bible verses could become fighting words. For the Pilgrims, the particular passages came from the *the Acts of the Apostles* in the second chapter. Here the author, the physician Luke, describes how the earliest Christians in Jerusalem sold their possessions and used the money to give to any members in need—seemingly an early form of communism. When the Pilgrims put into what would become Plymouth in North America, they had already decided to raise their own food by a system of communal labor, where no one either owned land privately or worked it for his or her own benefit, but all for all. The result? They nearly all starved, and would have, had not some local natives rescued them and taught them how to raise crops in the good old-fashioned local way, using fish as fertilizer. The Pilgrims gave thanks, and so came our present Thanksgiving holiday. The urge to produce and share goods in common still springs up phoenix-like in America today.

---

[4] See Perry Miller, *Errand into the Wilderness*.

The Puritans emigrated mainly from one part of England only—East Anglia on the North Sea, where they had become accustomed to crafting goods for trade with the somewhat like-minded Protestants of the Netherlands on the other side of that narrow body of water. Theirs was an economic order built upon the stages of agricultural-industrial production mostly of woolen and linen goods carried out in small villages, each a free-standing natural community of local, family-based liberty ordered and bounded by strict religious and work-related limits to individual freedom of action. Theirs, then, was a relational liberty—the liberty of coming to the aid of a neighbor, of considering the effects of one's actions upon the natural community giving life and liberty. One might call them the progenitors of the Protestant work ethic.[5] Seemingly from time immemorial, they had lived in an ordered liberty shaped by their localized forms of oversight—of minimal government employing local worthies as volunteer civil servants, of magistrates limited by traditional deference to the people represented by their duly elected selectmen. Each such town, of which there were many, sat upon its own Three-Legged Stool: people, selectmen, and magistrate.

When the Puritan people followed the Pilgrims to America, they took their polity and economy with them, creating a little East Anglia where they went, right down to the various place names. The leaders of the party settling Massachusetts Bay also took something else with them of a precious nature—their Great Charter issued them by King James. Somehow, by accident or design (who knows which), their charter did not specify London as the headquarters from which they would operate—or any other place for that matter. So, the Puritan lawyer-leaders simply took ship with the Charter—and gained many degrees of freedom from a tight oversight by the Crown office of colonial affairs in the process.

There must have been in the early days of Massachusetts Colony a continual tension between religious calling and economic endeavor. Something, however, radically changed the nature of the tension, eventually converting the tension into a conflict between Colony and mother country. That thing was what also drew the second great grouping of British to America—the English Civil War. In the process, extending over some 50 years or so, the Puritans became Yankees. What happened went something like this: The New England Puritans by about 1640 sensed that they had gotten something very basic very wrong: The coming Kingdom

---

[5] See Max Weber, *The Protestant Work Ethic and the Spirit of Capitalism.*

of God looked more and more unlikely to be built where they had run to, and more likely to be built where they had run from: England. Some New England Puritans even did a reverse-migration and returned to the mother country to fight in the Parliamentarian cause, a number dying there in battle—or hung after the failure to achieve the Civil War's radical goals. The great discouragement over the defeat of their whole purpose for their "errand into the wilderness" made them into Yankees—people of a new land but not completely a part of it, as the American poet Robert Frost was wont to declare: "The land was ours before we were the lands."[6] They became a people pursuing economic advantage rather than a spiritual victory for Christ. In this manner, they also established a uniquely American pattern for failed utopias.

One more enduring element to the American story that originated in New England: A member of the last of the Puritan generations, a learned man named Samuel Sewall, published in 1700 the first anti-slavery tract ever written in New England, or anywhere else on earth for that matter: *The Selling of Joseph.* In this, Judge Sewall followed in the footsteps of the great English pamphleteers of an earlier time. Technological leaps yield ethical advances, sometimes. Of course, the slavery problem lives on with us even to this day, and slavery as a cruel institution still functions worldwide to steal life, liberty, and the pursuit of happiness from millions.

Judge Sewall, we may add parenthetically, stands out amongst New Englanders of his time for another reason: He had been amongst the sitting judges during the Salem Village witchcraft trials of 1692–93, and the only judge out of nine to repent of his judgments that brought 19 men and women to death by hanging or crushing—men and women almost certainly entirely innocent of any crimes. One Sunday five years later, during a service of fasting and prayer, Samuel Sewall handed Samuel Willard of the Third Church of Boston a note as his pastor strode down the center aisle. Willard read the note to himself, stunned at its contents. Then, as requested by Sewall, he read the note out loud to the entire congregation. While Sewall rose and stood before the congregation, Willard read out a confession by Sewall regarding the witchcraft trials, to the effect that he "desires to take the blame and shame of it…, desiring prayers that God would pardon that sin."[7] Public confession and humiliation; the asking

[6] Robert Frost, *The Gift Outright.*

[7] The full passage from which this quotation famously has gotten extracted apparently first occurs within Sewall's private papers.

for forgiveness. One assumes that Judge Sewall died a man at peace with himself; confession is good for the soul. Another witch trial judge, John Hathorne, appears to have been a terribly cruel man who had pushed his fellow judges toward convictions. John Hathorne never repented him of his central role in the trial outcomes. Some 100 years later, one of the judge's great-great-grandsons changed the spelling of the family name from Hathorne to Hawthorne. Nathaniel Hawthorne lived a fruitful life as a leading author of the American Renaissance in literature. He also remained haunted by his family's past for his entire life.

For King and Country

> "I thank God, we have not free schools nor printing; and I hope we shall not have these hundred years. For learning has brought disobedience, and heresy and sects into the world; and printing has divulged them and libels against the government. God keep us from both!"
>
> Sir William Berkeley, Governor, Virginia Colony

> How is it that we hear the loudest yelps for liberty among the drivers of negroes.
>
> Dr. Samuel Johnson

Even though the Virginia colony at Jamestown had been founded earlier than Plymouth, in 1607, that community barely survived—until the onset of that inglorious decade of the 1640s. Then, as wartime events began working against the Crown, discouraged royalists made their own out-migration, and not to New England where their sworn enemies resided. They naturally took up residence in the Virginia Colony that already had a royal governor amenable to their cause. From the period roughly 1640–1660, some 30,000 or so royalists, predominantly from the English southwest, made the dangerous crossing to Virginia.

Virginia Colony matters here because of its very different political-religious-social-cultural roots compared to New England. The early fortunes of Virginia Colony appeared dismal, from its founding until Charles I appointed the youngest son of a British baron, one William Berkeley, recently graduated from Oxford, sequentially to the privy chamber, the colonial office, knighthood in 1638, and lastly to the governorship of Virginia Colony in 1639. One might term this appointment prescient, as the timing set in motion two forces driving the out-migration to Virginia instead of only one: First, the usual demands made by younger sons of aristocrats for adult positions of some power. Under British primogeniture property rights, the eldest son inherited a father's estate, leaving some very nobly born younger sons with nothing. Perhaps not sheer genius, but the idea of setting these younger sons of aristocrats up as planters running large estates in the New World had a certain slick cleverness about it. Second, the crisis building up to the English Civil War encouraged the more faint-of-heart to flee to Virginia, thereby escaping the coming fight. This second force, too, had that quality of prescience about it, or dumb luck if you will.

Sir William Berkeley nearly single-handedly built the Virginia Colony. Because he controlled the land grants, he also controlled who would join the Virginia planters' elite: the right sort with pretensions toward social/economic/political continuity with their homeland where the common people lived closest to a slave's condition. And so, a landed aristocracy grew up in Virginia, living off the toil and sweat of indentured servants bound for labor to their masters for years. Eventually, black slaves from western Africa proved more amenable to their masters' discipline. They had first tried native Americans, but found them, unfortunately, more willing to die than obey their masters. In sum, Berkeley and his chosen planters recreated the social order of southwest England in hot, humid tidelands Virginia—right down to building their manor houses in the basic style of their English forbears. In England, their elite families had run the closest thing to a feudal state possible at the time. Their workers had few rights beyond those of medieval-era serfs. In Virginia, the elite families' younger sons duplicated that structure. While American historians have for many years denied the reality of what we might call the Royalist model for the Virginia settlement, claiming that these younger sons went to Virginia for any reason but the obvious one, the truth remains as follows. The truth goes to the peculiar economics of the Colony.

Nobody in the Tidewater area got rich raising and exporting tobacco. In fact, most Virginia planters remained endemically in debt to their London bankers—just like their relatives back home. No, agriculture alone would not prosper a man. But some Virginians did become very rich.[8] Those who became rich largely did so through direct wealth accumulation, rather than through the niggling numbers on profit and loss

---

[8] Several generations later, George Washington became perhaps the richest man in the Colonies; he traded for wealth, and he married it.

statements over the years. And wealth accumulation for the aristocracy in Virginia did, once more, follow the pattern of southwest England: Marry for it. Something else, however, had to come first—for at first, there was little wealth in the Colony to marry for.

That something else brings us to matter of playing favorites—of *crony capitalism* in our own vernacular. Some of the sons of the English aristocracy initially got rich in Virginia through taking marketplace advantage of free or subsidized government grants—in the form of large blocks of land given by the King to Governor Berkeley to distribute, to the right sort of people of course. In the process, wholesale land grants got broken up into many much smaller retailed plots. Those who gained small plots usually paid them off over time, through laborious sweat equity in the tobacco fields. The holders of the initial large grants paid relatively little for them, perhaps even nothing. The economy of Virginia, thus, got a jump start through crony capitalism. Anyone calling the elite Virginians "proto-capitalists" has got it wrong. Proto nothing; crony everything.

The royalist Virginians, one should note, believed very strongly in individual liberty—for them. Theirs became a scheme for hierarchical liberty wherein social status determined the degree of freedom allowed a person. Only in this regard did the masters of Virginia and the tradesmen of New England share something in common: a love of liberty. But even here, they disagreed more than agreed, for they possessed two very different notions of liberty itself. In Virginia Colony it was "liberty for me but not for thee." New England ordered liberty versus Virginian hierarchical liberty.

One last matter here about the Virginia elite and their propensity for following their English forebears in borrowing the labor of others without repayment or liberty—and this goes to back our basic model for technological innovation driving social and political changes downstream. After the revolution, most of the Founding Fathers—driven by the former Puritan, evangelical Yankees and our next out-migration group, the Quakers—decried the practice of depriving others of life and liberty. They also believed that slavery would "wither on the vine", so to speak, because the slave economy was almost totally based upon tobacco planting, and tobacco was exhausting the Tidewater's soil. So, the new nation got founded upon a Constitution that failed to explicitly outlaw the practice of selling Joseph—and perhaps working him to death. The "wither on the vine" proposition that seemed so reasonable itself died on the vine when Eli Whitney invented the technological wizardry of the cotton gin. King Cotton then made slavery pay, on the western slave factory-plantations.

The sad lesson to the tale: Technological revolutions always do yield social and political changes, just not always for the betterment of humankind. The Southern states made laws so restrictive that freeing slaves became nearly impossible, as Mr. Jefferson was later to discover.

No Cross, No Crown

> Right is right, even if everyone is against it, and wrong is wrong, even if everyone is for it.
>
> William Penn

> A Lord Proprietor is a person granted a royal charter for the establishment of an English colony in the seventeenth century.
>
> *Wikipedia*

> Quaker, byname of a Friend, a member of a Christian group (the Society of Friends, or Friends Church) that stresses the guidance of the Holy Spirit, that rejects outward rites and an ordained ministry, and that has a long history of working for peace and opposing war.
>
> *Encyclopedia Britannica*

William Penn entered into this world in 1644 at a time of crisis, being born in London but of parents from the English Midlands—both locations the scenes of great crisis in the English Civil War. He was raised and educated in Essex, a then-hotbed of Puritan thinking, where his family had retreated after his father Admiral Sir William Penn had lost a sea battle in 1655 and fallen out of favor with Cromwell's government. He reached adulthood during the earlier years of the monarchy's restoration. As a Lord Proprietor, he would create the colony of Pennsylvania, and form it to become both a refuge for persecuted Quakers and a utopian ideal—a peaceable kingdom free of religious persecution, a new Christian commonwealth. In this regard, he echoed the purposes of the Puritan John Winthrop's "city on a hill." In doing this, he would call into being the third great American out-migration—from roughly 1660–1725 and involving once more some 25,000–30,000 people—this time largely of the English Midlands, as well as significant numbers of German Quietists.[9]

---

[9]The Quietists would settle within Penn's new colony and eventually become the "Pennsylvania Dutch."

Notice the timeline: Puritans 1620–1640; Royalists 1640–1660; Quakers 1660–1725. Each out-migration brought roughly the same-sized population out of England but separated in time and by place of origin, and in each case the different burning issue of that different time accompanied the migrants—and remained with them long after its urgency had passed by in the mother country. To some degree, each group, cut off and isolated from its English vine of ever-evolving regional cultural inheritances, lived in a sort of time warp: The colonies became in time a living museum for various grievances and antique practices. As a trivial example, after the revolution, the American Tories who fled to London, and who saw themselves as quite sophisticated, got laughed at for being country bumpkins: The English language had moved on, but the New Englanders' speech hadn't. We would today easily understand Georgian London English; we would find the Boston Tories' high, frantic Norfolk whinny incomprehensible. Common language?

Continuing with the Quaker, or Society of Friends, story, William Penn of Pennsylvania offers a fascinating comparison with another *William*—Berkeley of Virginia Colony. To begin with, both men descended from successful families, Berkeley's the more so. As a favorite of the king, Berkeley had become a *de facto* Lord Proprietor in Virginia Colony by 1640, controlling vast lands to be doled out thanks to his family's connections with King Charles I. Penn received a huge land grant west of the Delaware River in 1681 related to the settlement of a large debt owed his deceased father by then-king Charles II—making him a Lord Proprietor as well. Berkeley intended to create a refuge for young royalists during hard times; Penn intended to create a refuge for persecuted Quakers during hard times. In some sense, both men tried to live out utopian fantasies. Neither truly succeeded, but Berkeley's elite cultural descendants became Revolutionary War leaders, founding fathers of the new American nation-state, and eventually Southern leaders in the American Civil War. In the 1830s–1840s, some engaged in efforts to create a vast, feudal New World slave empire by merging the American South with Central and South American nations and with Cuba. Potential treason? Yes. But what about Penn? He would create the exact antithesis to Berkeley's long-term influence.

After his father's failed naval battle, the young lad William Penn moved with his parents to Ireland where the family owned an estate. Then, the Admiral made a blunder greater than losing a battle at sea: He invited an itinerant Quaker named Thomas Loe to preach at the family manse. Just what moved the Admiral to do so we cannot say with certainty, but the outcome crushed his father's hope for William, Jr. who already had strong spiritual leanings from his brushes with the Essex Puritans. From his encounter with Loe, William Jr. eventually became a Quaker himself. But not before his father's remedies for his ill-judged invitation to Loe led to William, Jr. getting expelled from Oxford University for religious nonconformity. Parents beware of your efforts to direct your young sons' souls.

His father then sent the boy on a tour of the European continent, and to school at a Protestant college in France, hoping that this would cure the young lad of the religious enthusiasm that Oxford had not. He returned to London to read law at Lincoln's Inn for a year, and that was that for his formal education. His father then sent him to the family Irish estates once more, this time as estate manager. Pound some practicality into the young lad, eh? There, he heard Mr. Loe preach some more, and became a member of the Society of Friends—the Quakers.

Here we should mention very briefly the basic tenets of 17th-century English Quakerism and the origin of their disparagement through that name, before going on to outline how William Penn shaped and furthered these beliefs. According to the denomination's founder George Fox, in 1650 "Justice Benent of Derby first called us Quakers because we bid them tremble at the Word of God."[10] While this may well be so, it appears at least as likely that they received the appellation due to the manner in which some Friends would shake physically whilst under the influence of the Holy Spirit—a phenomenon observable even today amongst charismatic Christians. Whatever the case, their enemies meant the term derisively, and the Quakers accepted it as an exercise in humility.

It appears that their beliefs took shape amongst a group of people calling themselves seekers during the English Civil War, when members of this group, despairing of spiritual help from Anglicans, Puritans, Baptists, or any other, were waiting upon the Lord for guidance—and they believed that they received it from the Holy Spirit, or what they would come to call "the inner light." Experience shaped belief: the Quakers came to believe that all men and women possessed within them the inner light. One had merely to wait upon the Holy Spirit, the inner light, to speak truth—and then follow the Spirit's leadings. The Spirit led them to renounce the outward trappings of Christian worship, professional ministers, and church discipline. It also led some to become itinerant preachers—like Thomas Loe.

[10] See *Encyclopedia Britannica* website entry for Quakers.

Where this led we can see when we pick up the thread that is William Penn's legacy. He, too, began speaking in public, in open fields—being barred from polite, indoor venues. Eventually, he found himself arrested many times, imprisoned four times, and, largely whilst imprisoned, writing some 42 books and pamphlets, including the prison-writings genre classic *No Cross, No Glory*. He railed against the profligacy of Restoration England. He stood for the self-denial virtues of the Puritans and the Quaker appeals for transforming society. Above all else, he stood for religious tolerance, for freedom of conscience. Along the way, he won acquittal in the famous Bushell's case that established the limits to a judge's prerogative to influence juries—a crass violation of the Rule of Three at law. Penn had been arrested for inciting a riot after speaking in the street because the local authorities had padlocked him out of a Quaker meeting house. When the jury refused to find him guilty of a demonstrably false charge, Judge Bushell ordered the jury imprisoned until they changed their minds. They remained adamant. Upon appeal, the Lord Chief Justice Sir John Vaughan found that a judge "may try to open the eyes of the jurors, but not to lead them by the nose." Case dismissed, and the Rule of Three strengthened in the English system of justice.

In 1681, William Penn received that vast land grant from Charles II. He had earlier with fellow Quakers acquired land grants in east and west New Jersey. William Penn thus became a Lord Proprietor over the second-largest land grant given an Englishman by the crown. Whilst his later life turned very badly for him, his legacy stands out as clearly as that of William Berkeley. The early movement for the abolition of slavery came from the Quakers. Evangelical Christians descended from Samuel Sewall would support the Quakers in this grand endeavor—eventually resulting in the freeing of American slaves. Every American reformer since the Civil War to today's progressives owes a debt to William Penn. Henry David Thoreau and Mahatma Gandhi owe their concept of passive resistance to the Quakers as well. The Penn is mightier than the sword.

Born Fighting

> It is the foot-loose, those who have nothing to lose and much to gain, and (quite naturally) those who have not scrupulously kept all the laws—or who have felt the heavy hand of church discipline—who are most attracted to a new frontier.
>
> James G. Leyburn, *The Scots-Irish: A Social History*

The fourth and last great out-migration from Great Britain began roughly when the Quaker migration had run its course. This last group would become the largest of all; in the period 1715–1775, over 250,000 Scots-Irish, Lowland Scots, and Northern Britons (collectively called "Borderers") arrived in America—landing chiefly in Quaker Philadelphia. They constituted a scary prospect for the decorous and prosperous Quaker families living there—being, by contemporary bourgeois standards, quite dirty, smelly, unkempt, and scandalously dressed. Their women wore low-cut bodices and short skirts—and were quite forward with themselves. The Quakers encouraged the newcomers to leave the City of Brotherly Love and go west to where there was free land—and into what was then Indian country. The Borderers complied eagerly, desirous of the land.

The native Americans never really stood a chance against this lot, for they had all been born fighting, fighting the English King and his troops—and before that the Normans, Vikings and Romans.[11] They hated all ruling authority, and would eventually come to hate the new American government as well, rising up in the only real challenge to it in the misunderstood Whisky Rebellion.[12] Before they finished their migrations, they defeated the native Americans, settled the Appalachians, and moved westward all the way to Southern California. It would surprise no one who knew them that one of their own, eventually-to-be President Andrew Jackson, became the American Indian fighter *par excellence* and as president would force the Cherokee onto the long trail of tears to Oklahoma from Georgia, and earlier the British from New Orleans during the War of 1812.

The Borderers became the backbone of the American Continental Army during the revolution; some of them became quite famous—the Kentucky riflemen, and Daniel Boone in particular. They also became the backbone of the Americans fighting for Texan independence and of the Confederate Armies of the American Civil War, even though they kept no slaves and hated the Southern aristocracy that began, and lost, that war. They fought against the Union soldiers because, as one such Borderer put it: "… you're down here." They didn't cotton to being invaded, no matter the cause.

---

[11] See Jim Webb, *Born Fighting: How the Scots-Irish Shaped America.*

[12] There was nothing quaint about the Whisky Rebellion. Had not President Washington called out a large army to put the Rebellion down, and hung a few of the leaders, the United States might have separated in their infancy.

On a lighter note, the Borderers became the source of generations of big screen and TV entertainment for generations of modern Americans; they were the original source for the all-American cowboy. They invented cattle herding and driving, and rustling, whilst still in Lowland Scotland particularly. They also carried with them to America the music that would eventually become country western, music "discovered" in the back reaches of the Appalachian Mountains by record producer Ralph Peer in the 1920s. The Borderers possessed a fierce sense of pride and for liberty, defined as "doing what I want." They fought duels, and violent wrestling matches in which opponents' eyes were not infrequently gouged out by fingernails grown very long and hardened by scorching over open flames.

They also practiced a form of child-rearing that encouraged belligerent behavior upon the parts of their male children, whereas the Puritans practiced child rearing aimed at the unsparing use of the rod to discipline their children into the way that they should go as adults within an ordered liberty. The Virginia aristocrats practiced a form of child-raising that varied with social status: Children of the lower orders were dealt with ever so severely for any disobedience, but children of the elite were taught to Lord it over lesser children, and adults. Slaves, of course, had no rights any Southerner was wont to obey. Quaker children learned to practice passivity and humility in the face of insults and attacks. Unsurprisingly, the children of each migration learned to emulate the behaviors of their elders.

Harried out of the Land

The population density of Great Britain at the time of the American revolution had reached about 74 people per square mile. The colonies had about one-third the population, and nearly six times the land area, of the mother country. Population density was a little over five people per square mile. Two interesting tendencies appear from these facts on the ground: First, the four major population groups in the colonies chose largely to self-isolate, and they had plenty of land to do it in. Second, even though labor in colonial America was everywhere in short supply, each group had a history of "harrying out" of their lands any would-be interlopers. The Puritans harried out of New England the early Quakers who tried to bring their own form of Christianity there—going so far as to execute two, by stretching their necks. The Southerners harried out of their lands those people who were not of the Anglican persuasion. The Borderers had no truck with Anglican missionaries whom they abused and drove out as well. Even the Quakers shamed and shunned some of those not of their own religious and cultural practices. Plenty of space but hard borders. No shared founding mythologies. Often-times, autocratic justice that violated all pretense for the Rule of Three. What could possibly go right?

The smart money was on the failure of these four disparate groups ever to form one union. Why did the smart money lose?

Do-Overs: Ideologies, Founding Myths, and Three-Legged Stools

We rarely get the chance at a do-over—except perhaps in today's American schools and universities. Yet, in the case of Great Britain, the people got a do-over—in the American colonies. The issues that provoked a great civil war in England had gotten transported to the colonies. The institutional glue that held Great Britain together as a nation even through that civil war did not, however, get packed up to join all of the divisive issues in the New World. Strong dislikes/weak institutions: Centrifugal forces overbalanced centripetal forces. What transpired over the 1660–1788 restoration of the monarchy to ratification of the U.S. Constitution, really was a fantastic do-over. And not only that, the American situation created the closest thing to a controlled experiment in nationhood creation ever seen. What happens when you plant people of all practices and beliefs into an open space, and then let them sort out their differences by themselves? The *Lord of the Flies* outcome, or the Declaration of Independence?

Consider this: every other nation ever formed on the face of the earth began with the beliefs—the founding mythologies—of but one tribe. That tribe created a new thing, a nation, out of its strength in overcoming resistance by other tribes, sometimes through the harnessing of new technological forces, sometimes by the mere force of invasion.[13] The nations all grew through tribal conquests—except for the 13 colonies. Each colony's populists hated the other colonists, but not as much as each hated and feared British "tyranny." One should add here that the American "patriots" probably never comprised more than one-third the total population of the Colonies, the other two-thirds being made up about equally of Tories and the uninvolved. But one-third is plenty sufficient to start a

[13] See Appendix A for a description of this running outcome—in Anglo-Saxon Britain.

revolution. The sheer adversarial forces faced by and between the colonists drove them to a peaceful, happy outcome—a first-order paradox. How might this thing have come about?

Win-Lose: The Zero-Sum Game Trap Defeated

The Four Horsemen: War, Famine, Pestilence, and Disease.

From Thomas Malthus

Puritanism—The haunting fear that someone, somewhere might be happy.

H.L. Mencken

...peace, easy taxes, and a tolerable administration of justice.

Adam Smith

For nearly all of human history, as best we can tell, people held to strong beliefs about the nature of gains and losses in life: the *I win-you lose* trap. This holds true, because for nearly all of human history, economic growth hardly existed at all; very ironically, the potential for economic growth only emerged at the time when early political economists such as Dr. Malthus argued for its impossibility. Gains in one year might be wiped out, and then some, in succeeding years. Going back to this book's Introduction, we described the very different behaviors of the Cowboy American Ray Marks and his Dragon Chinese counterpart Chairman Ma. The American executive held strong *win-win* beliefs; his Chinese counterpart held the opposite *win-lose* belief, backed up by his perception of how 19th-century China lost out to the Westerners. As evidenced by Chairman Ma's emotional outburst, we know that the Zero-Sum Game Trap operates on both the material and psychological levels of human beliefs. At its very core, the Zero-Sum Game Trap goes from the physical to the psychological—*outer space* to *inner space*. For example, while the material effects of British "tyranny" against the Americans wore off quickly, the exaggerated memory of them became enshrined in the American's founding mythology and shaped its corporate soul. For the Americans, unlike the for Chinese, corporate experience included a great escape from the trap. How did the Americans, subconsciously, pulled this one off?

Humankind generally suffers from the delusion that beliefs conflicting with our own somehow both threaten and subtract from our own happiness. For instance, during the Commonwealth period in Great Britain (1649–1660), the Puritan ruling class outlawed such social niceties as theatrical performances and Christmas celebrations, and May Day romps. Now, at that time, nobody forced anybody to go to the theater or to celebrate holidays, but the Puritan overlords felt that these practices constituted a grave offense to Almighty God—and should be suppressed. Thus, the zero-sum game Happiness Fallacy: I can only get the happiness what I want by forcing you to give up what you want.

The flip side of desiring to repress the happiness of others took the form of refusing to cease repressing those whom one already had in one's power. King James I famously said, "No bishop, no king"—implicitly arguing that any leniency granted an out-of-favor group would cause that group to react against another authority holding power: Give up the disciplinary power of bishops and lose power as king: Yield on one point, and lose in the future on all points. Such zero-sum power positions, of course, become self-fulfilling: When a repressed people learn that nothing will ameliorate their condition, they feel that they have no option other than revolt. Nothing better illustrates this principle than ancient Israel's King Rehoboam who destroyed forever the ancient Hebrew empire when he refused to promise to lighten the northern tribes' load in return for their loyalty. The pattern repeated itself regarding the British government's rule in the American Colonies after 1765. Both of these illustrations constitute supreme acts of folly upon the parts of sovereigns toward some of their people.[14]

During the great pamphleteering debate in the period around the English Civil War, the many schools of thought coming into being argued for zero-sum positions that would infuriate opponents, such as: the destruction of the monarchy in favor of a republic (which then turned into a despotic regime), the creation of a Christian commonwealth with "no king but Jesus", the outlawing of wealth holdings by anyone—especially ruling class members, mandated agricultural communes, outlawing all church discipline, and so forth. None of these harebrained happiness schemes could possibly have succeeded—in the end creating nothing but unhappiness all around. Indeed, the Puritan commonwealth succeeded only in returning a monarch to power.

[14] See Barbara Tuchman, *The March of Folly.*

The English pamphleteers' panderings to their philosophical bedmates eventually died of an overdose. What took their place?

Three deep thinkers during this period—John Locke, Charles-Louis Montesquieu, and Adam Smith—provided the ideological underpinnings for escape from the zero-sum trap. First, John Locke's argument for workers having property rights in the fruits of their own labor undercut the monarchists' arguments for a sovereign having all rights over his subjects in order to protect them from potential rebellion: a circular firing squad argument if there ever was one. Second, Baron Montesquieu after delving deeply into the failures of ancient regimes such as the Roman Republic and the Greek city-states, discovered the principle of the separation of powers, whereby the integrity of government could be protected by stripping some powers from a sovereign and giving them to a legislature and a judiciary—and then setting them up to cross-check one another—a most fundamental Three-Legged Stool proposition. The American intellectuals of the time studied both men's thinking, eventually working them into the founding of the American nation-state.

The third thinker in our list, Adam Smith, wrote *The Wealth of Nations* too late—published in 1776—to affect the ideological underpinnings of the American Revolution, but his book did become revolutionary in itself in that revolting year. *The Wealth of Nations* promised an escape from no-growth, grinding, Malthusian poverty in the outer space for human conduct. Americans and Englishmen alike struggled to understand the felicitous nature of what Smith wrote, an inner space matter, and either absorbed something of it, or stumbled upon parts of it as they went along their merry ways to national liberty. In a little understood passage from *The Wealth of Nations*, Adam Smith had described the policy factors determining national economic growth and stability, and human happiness. Most readers today, if they notice the passage at all, take it as a short list of policy recommendations: peace, easy taxes, and "a tolerable administration of justice." It appears, however, that Smith did not regard it as a list, but rather as a relationship between the three chief policy factors determining outcomes for a nation's economy—another perfect Three-Legged Stool.

Each leg of the stool checked the others, as follows: *Easy taxes* limit the sovereign's resources expendable upon foreign adventures, or upon corrupting the judiciary. Limiting the corrupting of a judiciary in turn protects the property rights of citizens regarding their own labor and creativity and discourages monopolistic rent seeking by a sovereign's favorites—thereby yielding internal peace, plenty, and happiness. A tolerable administration of justice also discourages a sovereign's raising of taxes against the peoples' will, coming right around to peace. Also, ensuring individual property rights generally greatly increases the productivity of the people, leading to peace and prosperity. Even a cursory look at the behavior of the Stuart Kings of England reveals the radical significance of this Smithian Three-Legged Stool. And even a cursory look at the record of the first American administration under its new Constitution shows how President Washington and his cabinet discovered in practice the Three-Legged Stool: avoidance of foreign entanglements, no discrimination against particular groups regarding taxation, and a president of limited powers unable to corrupt the judiciary. Outer space shapes inner space.

Founding Myths and The Great Awakening

> If the spirit that is at work among a people operates as a spirit of love to God and man, it is a sure sign that it is the Spirit of God.
>
> Jonathan Edwards

> For he himself [Jesus] is our peace; who has made us both [Jew and Gentile] one and has broken down in his flesh the dividing wall of hostility…that he might create in himself one new man in place of two, so making peace.
>
> St. Paul, *Ephesians* 2:14–15

Picture for a moment in your mind the American colonies as being 13 offshore islands in an ocean, separated each from the other, and also from the mainland. Desiring few bridges between them, for each island's inhabitants generally disliked the other islanders, they found cold pleasure, *schadenfreude*, in the misfortunes befalling the other islands' peoples and disappointments at the other islanders' successes. Nothing caused them more grievous displeasure than the various religious beliefs of the others, beliefs that provided varying answers to the first-order questions of life, and death. The islanders did share some common beliefs and social customs and carried out limited intercourse with neighboring islands. Indeed, participation in the slave trade constituted most of their economic intercourse—a dark blot upon them all. What hope had they of reaching comity between them, or mutual protection from deprivations from the mainland? Perhaps they might form three, or even four, small, break-away nation-states; but could even those small unions survive? Then, something truly remarkable occurred: They began, seemingly spontaneously, to fall under the influence of the God that they had come to regard largely as an intellectual curiosity celebrated with religious cant and pomp, rather than a real person of power, the Lord of heaven and earth. Then, so to speak, all hell broke loose, and religious revivals flared up brightly throughout the colonies, the Holy Spirit doing battle with the forces of sin and darkness in the land—and winning. They listened, spellbound, to preachers such as the American Jonathan Edwards and England's George Whitefield of the thunderous voice who could preach to as many as 10,000 people in the open air—and be heard. They gathered from hundreds of miles around for evangelical "camp meetings"—an institution brought to America by the borderers of lowland Scotland. They fell (literally) under the spell of the Holy Spirit.

It is, of course, not our place here to describe the history of the Great Awakening, or to present an argument for why what happened did happen. Our interest lies in the effects that it had upon the deeply divided colonists who had been quite nasty, one to another. Each colony resembled a pyramid of power, with a ruling elite at the top. Each pyramid of power stood opposed to the others. Then, the Great Awakening came along and stripped the power pyramids of much of their force. How? The Awakening built what might be termed *bridges of loving kindness* amongst the "middling" people generally of all the colonies. The result, as prophesized in Paul's *letter to the Ephesians*, was to make a singular "new man" from many disagreeable folks.[15] In effect, the Awakening took a huge, horizontal slice out of the middle of the 13 tall pyramids of power, and then united that horizontal slice into a transformed single body—changing the 13 bodies into two factions, a dichotomy called by contemporary observers *the new lights* and *the old lights*. The new radicals and the old conservatives. Have you seen the light, brother? The revival in its full power lasted only a short time, from roughly 1730–1750, but it transformed the conduct of the nation, and even reached the slave population described as hitherto living in darkness without hope.

The great common focus that fell upon the Great Awakening's participants came from a single phrase contained within the Hebrew book

[15] See *Ephesians* 2:11–22.

of *Leviticus*: "Proclaim liberty throughout the land to all the inhabitants thereof."[16] Liberty became the glue that bonded together a strange collection of bedfellows—from Quakers to the few atheists who were at the time called *free thinkers*. The verse appeared on the famous Liberty Bell originally cast and hung within the steeple of the Pennsylvania state house, now named Independence Hall. It cracked and got recast several times—before cracking for the final time whilst tolling for the death of America's first great Supreme Court Chief Justice, John Marshall—symbolic meaning, coming just before the rising movement for liberty for the slaves and the great Civil War. The Liberty Bell, of course, long ago became part of one of the founding myths for the American nation.

The Great Awakening radically changed the odds for both the success of the coming revolution and of the forging of one nation out of many: *E pluribus unum*. It infused new power into the Puritan doctrines regarding a covenant between God and His people—nationalizing its scope. By so doing, it operationalized John Locke's contract theory of government, and the notion that a government that violated its contract with the people could be rejected or overturned. In doing so, it cleared the way for the Declaration of Independence, America's sacred-secular statement of belief. The revolutionary-era pamphleteers that shaped public opinion in favor of a new nation largely came from the New Light body of preachers.

They created the sense of the Lord God marching with his soldiers, as in the Old Testament, to victory on the revolutionary fields of battle—and long afterwards marching to perfect the union and free the slaves: "Mine eyes have seen the glory of the coming of the Lord…."[17] Every American army unit during the Revolutionary War had its own minister, usually a New Light preacher. Indeed, many of the campground revival meetings during and following the Great Awakening got held in the mountain regions populated by the very Scots-Irish who would form the hard, fighting core of that army. What was regarded as the Lord's army marched into a certain destiny, creating as it moved the growing force for a founders' myth for a new nation. That founders' myth—comprised of both fact and fiction as all such greats myths are wont to be—radically changed the odds for a new nation succeeding.

---

[16] *Leviticus* 25:10.

[17] Julia Ward Howe, *Battle Hymn of the Republic*, first published in *The Atlantic Monthly*, February 1862.

The New Lights filled many of the seats in the Continental Congresses, sitting right up until the new Constitution in 1788. They dominated as signers of the Declaration of Independence and the participants within the Constitutional Convention that created the new Constitution. As a whole, they truly did forge *e pluribus unum*.

Do you see now why the smart money would have lost?

The Rule of Three and the Governance of a New Nation

> The ideas that the colonists put forward, rather than creating a new condition of fact, expressed one that has long existed; they articulated and in so doing generalized, systematized, gave moral sanction to what had emerged haphazardly, incompletely and insensibly, from the chaotic factionalism of colonial politics.
>
> Bernard Bailyn, *Ideological Origins of the American Revolution*

> In a free nation, it matters not whether individuals reason well or ill; it is sufficient that they do reason. Truth arises from the collision and from hence springs liberty, which is a security from the effects of reasoning.
>
> Thomas Erskine, quoted at the trial of Thomas Paine, 1792

The American revolutionaries feared but three things on earth: the arbitrary power of a sovereign, the abuses of a parliament bought and paid for by that sovereign, and a corrupt and lawless judiciary. Their pamphleteers expressed these fears; they brought heat to the table—the heat of human passion. American intellectual leaders sought for answers as to how to control what they saw as tyrannical power over them; they brought light unto the threats. They searched both classical antiquity and current thinkers as to how to preserve liberty in the face of these dangers. In so doing, they set in motion a spontaneously evolutionary process of discovery and debate in print and in congresses that eventually yielded the American experiment in government of, by, and for the people. Right on, Thomas Erskine, as quoted above! The results of their discovery process took the form of an intricate pattern of Rules of Three—beginning with the discoveries of Baron Montesquieu, whose seminal work Americans of any intellectual credibility knew quite well.

Power Checks Power

> There is as yet no liberty if the power of judging be not separated from legislative power and the executive power.
>
> Baron Montesquieu

> Give all the power to the many, they will oppress the few. Give all the power to the few, they will oppress the many.
>
> Alexander Hamilton, *Federalist Papers*

Montesquieu possessed both the leisure and the brain power to delve deeply into the histories particularly of ancient Greece and Rome. From his explorations, he identified what we might call a three-part feedback loop critical to any fruitful understanding of why governments work well or, at the other extreme, transition to another form—or collapse into chaos. The ancients, of both Greece and Rome, had classified governments into a triad of forms: monarchy, aristocracy, and democracy. Each of these forms receives definition through its locus of power. If a city- or nation-state initially formed around its nobility or elite, then they might hold power indefinitely, for they ruled by decree and served as both lawmakers and judges. Should the people become restive under their harsh rules and biased findings at law, power would shift toward representatives of the people. Eventually, a democracy would emerge, and when it began to behave like a mob, the demand for a strong leader would emerge. Eventually, that ruler would set up shop and become a tyrant—who then might eventually get overthrown by challengers to him, who would reestablish an aristocracy. And so it would go—like a chronological merry-go-round.

Montesquieu had the brilliant insight: First, let the monarch become an executive, a personage charged with executing the laws passed by a legislature—not a mean distinction. Then, let the executive execute, the legislators legislate, and the judiciary judge—and let each be king in its own domain. This, of course, became the most basic Rule of Three informing the new American Republic. Montesquieu also redefined the three ancient forms of government into his own, based not upon power but upon the driving moral principles behind them: the republic based upon virtue, monarchy based upon honor, and despotism based upon fear. In each case, his classification devolved out of the central, animating emotion behind that form of government. He strongly favored the republic, and the American thinkers followed suit. The Americans would come to admire Washington for his Cincinnatus-like conduct; as did Cincinnatus in his Roman Republic model, Washington retired after the revolution rather than allow himself to become a sovereign or dictator, and he retired permanently after serving just two terms as president under the new Constitution. King George III of England expressed flabbergasted astonishment: The man could have had anything, but he just walked away!

While adopting Montesquieu's basic Three-Legged Stool for a republic—executive, legislative, judicial—the Americans had reason, from out of their experience with the British Crown, to regard the problems in governance that they faced somewhat differently. For their analytical purposes, they chose to define an issues triad consisting of sovereignty, representation, and constitution.[18] The sovereignty matter was perhaps paramount for them, for they had perceived the English king to be a tyrant—as Mr. Jefferson wrote in his Declaration. An effective answer to the 17th-century's Thomas Hobbes had to get made: Hobbes in *Leviathan* had argued for the necessity of an all-powerful sovereign in whom the people generally, as a form of social contract, vested power. The sovereign appeared to Hobbes as the only means of assuring collective security against rebellious factions that could run amuck. Now, the Americans argued that the all-powerful sovereign *was* the very danger to collective security in a great society that Hobbes sought general protection from. The absolute power of the sovereign could be checked by power given to the representatives of the people—and preserved through the oversight of an incorruptible judiciary. Replace the people's physical violence with speech in a congress—a act of coming together for discussion and debate. Make absolute monarch into limited executive.

The Americans, in Virginia and New England, had working governmental institutions pointing both away from and toward a limited executive. In Virginia, the people's popularly elected representatives comprising the House of Burgesses had sat since 1642, where they had the power to raise revenues and originate laws. In addition—very much like the English government—a Governor and his Council, both appointed by the king, sat with veto power over the Burgesses. The council also sat as a supreme court reviewing the findings of county

[18] See Bernard Bailyn, *Ideological Origins of the American Revolution.*

courts on appeal. In regard to the separation of powers principle, clearly the governor possessed executive, legislative and judicial power. The Virginia Colony under William Berkeley had simply recreated English government in Virginia.

The New Englanders had brought with them from East Anglia a form of town government that came close to pure democracy: The qualified men in the town voted upon all policy, legal, and revenue-based proposals brought before an annual town meeting—as some New England towns do to this day. They also elected virtuous selectmen to carry out, voluntarily, the various town government activities, such as fence viewer and surveyor, and they elected a chief magistrate to oversee those activities. They elected representatives to county and colony governments—representatives expected to do the townspeople's bidding. In sum, the frugal New Englanders made government into very thin gruel indeed for those wishing to feed at the public trough. The Virginia form could conduce to a form of sovereignty of the Governor, whilst the New England form could run to the abuses of democracy that might include mob rule.[19] Under Montesquieu's tutelage, the Americans would eventually reach the happy medium of the executive limited to powers only within the execution of the laws.

The matter of the people's representation also touched a raw nerve for many colonists. The English Parliament comprised of *commoners* (who were in actuality not so commonplace, being decidedly upper-middle class) and Lords did not truly represent the common folks; rather, it took the form of "virtual representation"—in a phrase coined by Edmund Burke—that over-represented some constituencies and failed to represent the newly-emerging major cities at all. It even had representatives from "rotten boroughs" with only handfuls of constituents. The argument that such a parliament could somehow average out the various interests so as to encapsulate a single will of the people rang hollow to the colonists. The colonists eventually settled upon a halfway covenant between virtual representation and pure democracy for their new national government: Townspeople elected representatives to a House of Representatives to represent them and their views. States elected two men each to an upper house to represent the interests of their states. All this aimed partly to thwart any rise of tyranny.

---

[19]In the run-up to the American Revolution, the British rightly regarded the American revolutionary Sam Adams' "Sons of Liberty" as a brawling mob.

Lastly, the Americans sought protection from the twin extremes of tyranny and mob rule through the third element of the triad—the concept of a written constitution. The term itself derived from the definition of one's physical constitution—particularly with regard to health, strength and appearance. The unwritten traditions comprising the English constitution regarded statute and common law, parliamentary conventions, and authoritative authors on the subject. The Americans feared that such an understanding would compromise the will of the people, and so they moved toward the idea of a written constitution as a locus of inviolable basic principles that would limit the actions of all three branches built upon it:

> We the People of the United States, in Order to form a more perfect Union, establish Justice, insure domestic Tranquility, provide for the common Defence, promote the general Welfare, and secure the Blessings of Liberty to ourselves and our Posterity, do ordain and establish this Constitution for the United States of America.
>
> Preamble, *The Constitution of the United States*

The Hierarchy of the Stools

> Civil power properly organized and exerted, is capable of diffusing its force to a very great extent; and can, in a manner, reproduce itself in every part of a great empire, by a judicious arrangement of subordinate institutions.
>
> Alexander Hamilton, *Federalist,* No. 13

The Americans employed, eventually, the Three-Legged Stool of limited government to every level from the federal to the state to the county to the town, and to the western territories that would become states—each level made stable and orderly by the basic Rule of Three. By the 1830s, Tocqueville writing in *Democracy in America* actually saw the county as the most basic level of American government—not the state. That was the level where most issues dear to American communities worked themselves out. The new constitution did guarantee every state within the union a republican form of government—thus assuring the replication of the federal government's basic Three-Legged Stool throughout all lower government. The Three-Legged Stool principle also permeated to all levels through the Three-Legged Stool of justice—prosecutor-defendant-jury—with a jury of one's peers mediating between accuser and accused before a judge. In European Roman-based administrative law, juries consisted of panels of other judges; juries of a defendant's peers constituted quite a remarkable innovation.

The Constitution and its attached Bill of Rights contained other Rule of Three conditions. A separation of powers principle lay behind each. The limited powers doctrine contained in the Constitution defined specific areas of federal power; all other powers devolved to the states or to individuals as residual rights. The federal judiciary formed a third, mediating, leg in federal-state disputes. Another Three-Legged Stool placed the basic elements within the nation's political economy under the federal government's power: free interstate commerce, uniform taxation, and enforceable property rights and other protections for liberty. As a cookie-cutter clause, the Constitution allowed for the country's expansion into virgin territory via the formation of new states, which had to follow the republican form that the Constitution mandated—in effect, the basic Three-Legged Stool for all states, including a state constitution. New statehood admissions would come to fall under the purview of the congress, where the various existing states could exercise a measure of control via voting for or against admission terms but could not write a territory's statehood constitution for it, even as one administration tried to do so in the run-up to the Civil War. It failed. The nation's supreme court could, and would, mediate issues arising related to new state admissions—thus forming another Three-Legged Stool. In this manner, the constitution provided the means for a single federal government to provide governance over a huge and expanding geographic area—a feat simply impossible for a single sovereign to execute faithfully.[20] The anti-federalists had warned that a single nation as large as 18th-century America could not get governed by a single entity. They got proven wrong.

The 1787 Constitutional Convention, whereby the actual document got debated and formed, itself modeled for the nation the manner in which the new representative congress would work to encapsulate disagreements and encourage compromise resolutions to problems that in more primitive

---

[20]As the Spanish found out in South America, where good governance was made impossible by the need to have every niggling administrative decision approved by the King in Madrid.

forms of debate would have been fought out on the field of combat, rather than on the floor of a house and senate. Something of genius lay behind placing many disputants within the same body for a thorough hashing out—the genius of compromise. Many points of view diminish the likelihood of a few factions engaging in win-at-all-cost behaviors. More about the matter of compromise follows in the next section.

Amongst the several basic compromises hammered out in debate, the big state/small state issue ranked right at the top. States with larger, or in some cases potentially future larger, populations wanted a unicameral congress with representation based upon head counts by state; smaller states desired protection from a tyranny of population. The final constitutional compromise coming from the Connecticut Plan created a bicameral congress with the popular vote electing a lower house and state legislatures electing a senate composed of two members from each state. The electoral college compromise also slanted power toward smaller states. In a sense, the entire package comprised a structure opposing any tyranny of the majority for the new nation. In another compromise, slavery favored by southern states received some short-term protections, on the naïve assumption that this peculiar institution would wither on the vine.

The states issue itself has, however been somewhat misunderstood, and the big state/small state dichotomy misses a key matter: Some states wished to assure that their own peculiar institutions received protection.[21] The issue went more to political and religious culture than to voting power in the new congress, and the divisions between the four major in-migration groups drove the debates—state establishments of religion dominating. The Massachusetts and Connecticut congregational church establishments—state-supported and partly financed, New Hampshire Baptists, and Virginia Anglicans/Episcopalians all wanted assurances that their peculiar institutions would not get suppressed in a popularly elected congress. The superheated issues around the matter derived their differences from the original four-part in-migration to America, and the resolution took the form of the Bill of Rights—which erected boundaries between federal, state, and individual interests—where federal interests constituted the most general and free from cultural taint.

[21] See David Hacker Fischer, *Albion's Seed.*

The Art of Compromise

> Classic [political] folly: ...mindless persistence in conduct clearly counter-productive to one's own self-interest.
>
> Barbara Tuchman, *The March of Folly*

> Do unto others as you would have them do unto you.
>
> The Golden Rule, *Matthew* 7:12

> This enormous catastrophe [the American Civil War] erupted because we failed to do the thing we really have a genius for which is compromise.
>
> Shelby Foote, quoted in PBS *Civil War* series

We have already mentioned the all-important role that compromise played in the founding of America's new political order. One should not, however, regard compromise as a commonplace occurrence in the 18th century—or at any time for that matter. In the run-up to the American Revolution, the British government's leadership in Parliament and administrative cabinet could never reach a mutually agreeable arrangement amongst themselves for power sharing with their North American cousins. In its failure to see the colonists' side of the argument, they created the great divorce between the two, engaging in a supreme act of political folly.[22] In fact, the Americans created compromise as we now understand it. Parliament under the existing British system tended toward winner-take-all solutions to complex, multi-factional disputes.

The American Constitutional Convention gave birth to a wholly new being on earth sometime over the torrid summer of 1787 in Philadelphia, that creature christened *compromise*. Prior to this date, compromise referred to a mutual assent to submit a disagreement to an arbitrator (from the Old French *compromis,* literally "together promise.") Traditionally, in tribal and feudal societies, that meant bringing the matter to the chieftain or sovereign for decision, a man unlikely to exercise objective judgement or to reach an allocation meeting the self-interests of each party. (The story of Solomon ordering a baby cut in two and each half given to one of

---

[22] See Barbara Tuchman, *The March of Folly.*

the female claimants really constitutes no example of compromise as we understand it today.) In its traditional sense, then, compromise required a ruling between two inferiors from a superior: a judicial relation. The Americans had no such ruling authority to appeal to—even if they had wished to, which they did not. The likelihood of reaching a detailed accord for how the government should be shaped must have, to many observers, seemed remote. Once more, the smart money would have been on failure.

Consider the conditions under which the 55 delegates from 12 of the 13 states labored (Rhode Island sent no delegates): To begin with, the weather that summer in Philadelphia probably set records for persistent heat and humidity—so unbearable that one southern delegate's wife reportedly departed for home where she reckoned life would be more bearable. The delegates themselves early on abandoned all hope of creating a stable government structure from out of the existing Articles of Confederation which was their charge from the earlier Annapolis Convention—opting instead to start over from scratch, an action for which they had no governing authority. Doing the thing surreptitiously, they kept all the windows and doors in the State House tightly barred so that no word might get out. They were all, of course, dressed in heavy woolen, formal 18th-century garb. How in blazes they ever kept their tempers in such an overheated bandbox escapes modern comprehension. And then there were the issues demanding resolution: relative federal power allocated to the various states, competing religious settlements, and slavery being the triple elephants in the room. Yes, the smart money would have been on failure.

Yet the Americans shaped a means of bounded argument under rules that avoided the twin pitfalls of autocracy and anarchy. It certainly helped that General Washington presided over the debates and kept order even when matters became as heated as the building. In effect, the Americans invented another Rule of Three institution, consisting of disagreeing factions, rules or boundaries of debate and a mutually acceptable third-party umpire to see that the rules got followed. By extending reasoned, deliberate debate under firm rules of conduct, the delegates could engage in what might well be called horse-trading. In effect, the delegates created a policy marketplace where proposals for good governance could be "bought" from or "sold" amongst factions. Implicit in the policy marketplace, of course, was respect for outcomes: Winners win and losers accept the outcomes. The acceptance of outcomes shall become a large issue in the next chapter. As the compromise system developed, it evolved into a futures market as well—infamously known as "log-rolling"—whereby one faction's present gain might be balanced by another faction's future gain—rolling the whole deal downhill into the future, so to speak. While later generations of Americans have found log-rolling reprehensible, the practice was far cheaper than the contemporary British system that involved buying off the nobility on the losing side with outrageous personal side payments—a corrupted barrel of worms if there ever was one.

To protect its compromise engine from getting disabled, the Americans put in place a remarkably effective set of blocking strategies, so clever that they might almost have seemed to be the work of the devil. Consider them today: One man, the executive, can block the wishes of 535 people—unless two-thirds of them override the presidential veto. Fifty-one senators can block the will of 435 representatives, and the president. And 538 electors can override the popular votes of some 130 million citizens. To top it all off, the blocking strategies require the votes of two-thirds of both houses of Congress and three-quarters of the states in order to amend them. Clever little compromise box they've got there.

The View from Thirty Thousand Feet

Looking at the American hierarchy of Rules of Three from the ground, one might describe it as appearing like unto a large cone—or perhaps, like one of those wire cages that gardeners use for raising tomatoes: a series of wire hoops connected vertically by other wires. When viewed from above, however, the whole structure resembles a series of concentric circles, the lowest and outermost circle representing the tradition of English common law underpinning the Constitution. The next level up and in represents the Constitution with its general rules and federal structure. Then come more and smaller circles for state, county, and local governments—and then married couples and the individual. Each circle stands for a boundary, a wall against intrusion from either side. The common law Three-Legged Stool bounds civil conduct on the inside from violence and from chaos without. The Constitutional Three-Legged Stool further bounds right conduct; extra-constitutional conduct gets limited by common law as protected by a judiciary. State Three-Legged Stools may further limit lawful conduct, and so forth right to the local level. At each level of the concentric circles, individual human liberty works as the prime mover at the top of the pyramid—limited by the structure's boundaries. At this point, it helps to remember the fundamental distinction: Liberty is bounded freedom; freedom is unbounded liberty. The American system grants its people generous liberty, not unlimited freedom. In the system, cultural differences get dealt with at the most local level; general issues—such as interstate commerce, foreign policy, and national taxation get dealt with at the national level: that is, through the Three-Legged Stool of federal government.

The whole thing, to adopt another metaphor, resembles one of those huge cone-shaped concrete cooling towers present at nuclear power plants—the ones with the tops of the cones cut off and open and curls of steam rising from them. The cooling towers possess immense stability, deeply grounded in bedrock as they are, and open to let off any pressures building within them. Those billowing clouds of emitted steam stand for the passions of people rising up and out of the whole structure—at the top—the various local levels. Stability and a safety system kiss.

Moral Inversions

> So far, about morals, I know only that what is moral is what you feel good after and what is immoral is what you feel bad after.
>
> Ernest Hemingway, *Death in the Afternoon*

> "*The terror*" was merely 1789 with a higher body count; violence ... was not just an unfortunate side effect ... it was the Revolution's source of collective energy. It was what made the Revolution revolutionary.
>
> Simon Schama, *Citizens*

During the heady days of student unrest in the American 1960s and 1970s, one of the cries frequently emitted from the belly of the beast was: "You cannot legislate morality." This was patently false, because all law is moral—in that law separates some conduct deemed permissible and moral from other conduct deemed impermissible, or immoral—even at the level of parking tickets. What angered the student radicals was not the attempt to "legislate morality" but the kind of morality that had been legislated; what they desired to be legislated was a different kind of morality—particularly in the area of sexual arrangements. We term this situation a *moral inversion*. Moral inversions threaten whenever a substantial minority of a larger population deem that the dominant group is actually the immoral one. The most significant moral inversion in the Western world, of course, occurred in the shape of the American Revolution. The threat of a moral inversion is the sure sign that a nation's stability will come under increasing attack.

In 1789, immediately following the approval of the American Constitution, a revolution broke out in monarchical France. In both America and France, rebel factions desired the overthrow of monarchical government. We already know the result of the American experiment—the birthing of the most stable nation-state ever formed—through, all in all, a most civil revolutionary war. What about the French experiment? As documented very recently by Simon Schama, the French Jacobins created the very antithesis: a running reign of terror fueled by terroristic violence itself—as though France had become a forest fire that consumes itself for fuel.[23] The American experiment ran on a triad: life, liberty, and the pursuit of happiness—a triad that comprised a control upon itself: Liberty did not grant license to terror and murder. The French experiment also ran on a triad: liberty, equality, and fraternity—a triad without a controller. The inherent difficulty in the French formulation? Liberty and equality are, and forever must be, incompatible. Uncontrolled by life and happiness, liberty tied to equality ran amuck. Period.

The moral inversion that drove the French experiment involved forcing particular viewpoints upon a resistant general public. The Jacobins desired to outlaw all and any vestiges of traditional French institutions—to the point of creating a new calendar and outlawing saints' days and the Catholic faith of most of the French. All traditional moral limits upon individual conduct at local levels got swept away. The moral became immoral, and vice versa.

Since the Terror, the French have run through five constitutions and still lack a stable democratic form of government—with "tractor democracy" standing in its stead: When the people outside of Paris get angry enough, the farmers surround Paris with their tractors and blockade the government until it yields to some particular demand. A hell of a way to run a country.

Today in America, one large group wants to impose upon everyone 63 pronouns where traditionally there have only been three: male, female, and neuter. This moral inversion cannot end well. Gender is for nouns.

---

[23] See Simon Schama, *Citizens: A Chronicle of the French Revolution.*

CONCLUSIONS

The American experiment can indeed get regarded as something approaching a controlled sociological study—in that the colonists were substantially isolated from their distant British government, a government consistently getting its thumb on the scale: Put four radically differing populations in a land archipelago, and see what happens.

We submit that the American experiment has succeeded because it met the three conditions for a stable and peaceful nation that we discovered in our 30,000-some year perusal of ancient institutions:

- Stable boundaries—both physical and legal and moral/spiritual in nature.
- A robust and generally accepted founders' myth.
- A governance built upon the Rule of Three.

In addition, from American and British writings, we have identified these three other factors working against stability, peace and plenty:

- The zero-sum-game Happiness Fallacy that says that I have a right to bar you from any happiness that I dislike.
- The Governance Fallacy that says any challenge to a part of overall ruling authority is a threat to all authority, together with its corollary: Oppression does not destroy revolt; it creates it.
- Moral inversions that attempt to replace what is generally accepted with a particular alternative demanded by a subgroup.

Strengthening peace and plenty, we have, lastly, identified three properties inherent in governance by the Rule of Three:

- Limited sovereignty, representative government, and a constitutional order, all shaped and ordered through and by compromise.
- Power checking power—also triadic.
- The interrelation of triads, so that each level has some control over the others.

Finally, we leave our readers with Adam Smith's overall formulation for a happy state: "peace, easy taxes, and a tolerable administration of justice."

Chapter Six

1979: The Great Inflection Point

Time past and time present
Are perhaps both present in time future,
And time future contained in time past.
If all time is eternally present
All time is unredeemable.
What might have been is an abstraction
Remaining a perpetual possibility
Only in a world of speculation.

T.S. Eliot, *Burnt Norton*

Overview: Six countries played major roles in making 1979 a landmark year for both international and internal political trends: America, China, the USSR, Britain, Iran, and Israel. Forty years on now, the same six nations still dominate news coverage. Even though these six nations' roots and experiences differ widely, they also display fascinating similarities—beginning with all six reaching grand inflection points in their histories—in the very same year of 1979. We will be utilizing the three fundamental principles driving political economy that we discovered earlier—boundaries, founding mythologies, and the Rule of Three—to discover what lies beneath this more than coincidental relating of three democratic institutions and three authoritarian states. The three sections to this chapter relate to: *updating the tools for good governance, the run-up to 1979, and the great inflexion point and beyond.*

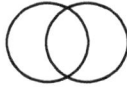

Introduction: Letting a Hundred Flowers Bloom

> The policy of letting a hundred flowers bloom and a hundred schools of thought contend is designed to promote the flourishing of the arts and the progress of science.
>
> Chairman Mao

Propaganda consists of the art and science of creating replacement founding mythologies—with the direct purpose of strengthening the legitimacy of a governing authority. Revolutionary propaganda may seek to instill the sense that the new mythology harkens back to an original: the new Nazis from out of the old Teutonic kings, for instance. Following victory over the Nationalist Kuomintang in 1949, the Chinese Communist Party under Chairman Mao desired to create such a replacement myth to buttress and legitimize the Long March and conquest myths. When he sensed that his regime had sufficient physical control over people and country, he wished to cement in place the idea that his was a new dynasty—in the traditions of the Chinese dynasties of old. The Chairman appears also to have believed that his thoughts both philosophical and political constituted the right thoughts, and so in 1956 he proclaimed a time for a full blooming of communist culture once more. Surely this would yield another Hundred Schools of Thought period in Chinese history like its progenitor some 2,000 years earlier—leading to a once-and-future flourishing of Chinese culture. And so, he let loose the creativity of the Chinese people, some of whom strayed very far indeed from Mao Thought. Repression followed. A pattern of forced socio-economic changes then set in: the Great Leap Forward of 1961 that devastated an already anemic Chinese economy and the 1966–1976 Cultural Revolution that tore the social fabric of the country apart. The period 1961–1979 saw the Chinese economy basically flat line like a failing patient in an ER bed at under $500 per capita annually, with significant dips during the Great Leap Forward and Cultural Revolution periods. By 1979, the country staggered under the weight of the Cultural Revolution's failed attempt at a grand moral inversion. Total GDP in 1979 perhaps reached $200 billion; by 2018, it would exceed $414 trillion. Why did this transformation happen? Why this inflection point in modern history?

Propaganda always has the task of creating moral inversions—making what has been seen as moral to be immoral, and vice versa. The great task of Communist Chinese propaganda following World War II involved destroying the peoples' faith in the warlord feudalism that had existed within the various dynasties for thousands of years and had taken firm hold again after the stillborn Chinese Republic's failure in the 1920s. Warlord feudalism had placed Chinese peasants in the unenviable position of both needing the protection of a strong warlord against the depredations of other warlord armies and needing to avoid the deprivations of their own warlord's confiscatory bureaucracy. Chairman Mao founded the Peoples' Republic of China (PRC) as being both something very new and yet very Chinese. It would promise to be the *peoples'*, not the warlords, or the hated Westerners. PRC art would glorify the worker, not the ruling class. PRC thought would develop the philosophy of the people and reject immoral Western capitalism. Of course, the government would intervene when necessary to assure the right outcomes.

Perhaps the failure of all this was inevitable. For the Chinese peasant, the *yin* and *yang* of all life had been far too deeply ingrained into his or her soul for shallow propaganda ever to reach. Always there would be the ebb and flow of the two vital life-and-death forces; always *yin-yang* would combine into a whole balance creating at each moment the necessary raw energy to preserve the overall harmony of the universe. Emperors might come and go; conflict between the dual forces would carry on forever. Peace and prosperity with economic growth, everything getting better—these represent the illusions of the West which will be swept away at some point. The Chinese people lacked even the word-meaning for utopia. Utopia? A Western illusion.

Section One: Updating The Tools For Good Governance: Boundaries, Founding Myths, The Rule of Three

Good fences make good neighbors.

Robert Frost, *Mending Wall*

Part One of this book led us to conclude that all human organization expressing itself in political economics evolved from boundaries, founding mythologies, and examples of the Three-Legged Stool structure for order. So far in Part Two, we have concluded that the interplay between technological revolutions and human organizational adaptations to those revolutions together created the modern administrative state and modern understandings of individual liberty. Our grand example here involves the manner in which the Western revolution in movable type casting/setting created freedom of expression and subsequently individual human liberty of conscience. The progenitor for such a liberal state, of course, came about through the spontaneous evolutionary process that we rightly call the American experiment, a process that yielded up 19th-century Western liberalism right along with the new-under-the-sun uniquely American form of government "of, by, and for the people."[1]

The question now before us asks what form this ongoing spontaneous process might be taking beyond the end of the 20th century—and on into the 21st where we all now dwell.

One should note right at the beginning that, like unto Adam Smith's famous good government relationship between "peace, easy taxes and a tolerable administration of justice," ours is not a mere listing, either: Boundaries, founding mythologies and Three-Legged Stools stand as one single, interrelated whole. Once the idea of boundaries became unshackled from physical fencing, words could evolve to signify rights—both negative and, eventually, positive in nature. Founding mythology communicates intergenerationally the emotional and spiritual energies that a people believe themselves to possess; as such founding mythology comes to stand for the moral foundations for a nation. A people seeing themselves as disciplined will in turn define their boundaries for conduct far more strictly than a warrior nation will. A people willing to develop the Rules of Three necessary for a civil society that protects the individual and foreign minorities within its boundaries will reach toward the high and sunny uplands of peace and plenty—toward harmony with other peoples and with nature itself. Perhaps the greatest example of the warrior nation/free labor nation divide in recent history involves the American Southerners and Northerners during its Civil War. The peace and plenty Northerners eventually defeated the warrior-nation Southerners—and eventually defeated the Southern national myth supporting chattel slavery as well, replacing it with the Statue of Liberty.

[1] Apparently, Mr. Lincoln discovered this phrase within Tyndale's translation of the Bible.

One should note that without overt outside interference, a fundamental congruence between boundaries, mythology, and the application of the Rule of Three will naturally evolve toward a balance over time.[2] However, such a spontaneous evolutionary process internal to a nation may be fundamentally upset by an exogenous factor imposed upon a people from without. The general question we tackle next here asks how changes in the nature and balance amongst these three factors played out in the 20th century. Also, which mattered more—the internal forces for spontaneous evolutionary change, or the exogenous changes imposed from without? In this last regard, one should search particularly for attempts to change moral foundations through impositions from outside a nation's core beliefs. Such efforts, truly audacious in scope and effort, we call attempts at moral inversions—the efforts to make what had formerly been regarded as good into bad, and vice versa.

Section Two: The Run-Up to Nineteen Seventy-Nine

Nineteen seventy-nine saw the histories of six countries critical to the world's future all reach growth inflection points simultaneously—points at which the slopes of their trajectories would change dramatically. China, America, the USSR, Great Britain, Israel, and Iran—three democratic institutions and three authoritarian states—would set the second post–World War II settlement's future into motion. This happening in itself stands as a most peculiar occurrence—one that reinforces the notion that underlying principles in some manner repeat themselves in world affairs—and tend to do so over a roughly 70-year cycle—a cycle that the English economist William Jevons (1835–1882) appears to have been trying to link to sunspot activity creating short-cycle climate patterns that in turn created economic cycles as well. We would most especially like to know if and how our three fundamental findings—boundaries, founding mythologies, and the Rule of Three—bring new light to the six stories of the six nations. Remember, there are just a few stories, and this holds true as much for the histories of nations as of tribes, clans and individuals.

---

[2] See Appendix A for a case study in such an evolutionary process.

The China Story

> Young man, there is a great deal of ruin in a nation.
>
> Adam Smith to Mr. John Sinclair after the British defeat at Saratoga, 1777

> The fault, dear Brutus, is not in our stars but in ourselves that we are underlings.
>
> William Shakespeare, *Julius Caesar* I.ii.140–141

The China story has its roots in the Manchu takeover of the Ming Dynasty beginning in the mid–17th century. It is a most curious tale, indeed, because it differs radically from most conquest stories—stories in which the invader defeats a less warrior-like people by sheer force of arms, and then pretty much obliterates their material and moral manners of living. The women get raped and forced into sexual slavery; the men get marched along a road of shame before being slowly and most cruelly executed—or worked to death in the salt mines. Exquisitely crafted works of art get carelessly tossed aside or taken as tokens verifying the defeat of an unworthy opponent. Much emphasis falls upon the shaming of a defeated people. But this pattern did not display itself in 17th-century China. Instead, in the Manchu takeover we appear to encounter the human analogue to brood parasitism in the avian world. Like an aggressive cuckoo bird, the Manchu warrior-leaders simply moved into the Ming administrative nest, raising their succeeding generations there, without making any changes to an already failing, overly bureaucratized administrative state. The best indicator of bureaucratic failure took the form of falling tax revenues, even while private GDP grew dramatically. If anything, the Manchu leaders who had moved into the Ming nest made matters progressively worse for the public fisc.

Under the later Ming, private entrepreneurship flourished—creating one of the world's earlier periods of great capitalistic expansion, in some regards resembling that of Venice at roughly the same time. Entrepreneurs created new markets, innovative products, and financial instruments permitting widespread international trading. Half a world apart, the city-state of Venice could trade with China via the various connector routes collectively called the Silk Road. Private sector demands for workers replaced the heavy hand of state-controlled slavery with wage labor. The wealth of the nation, defined by Adam Smith as the goods afforded the common people for their consumption, surged. China became middle class. Bureaucrats, creatures of the Confucian philosophical system, proved incapable of running enterprises within the fast-moving world of private enterprise. Entrepreneurs simply practiced privatization by default as state-owned and run enterprises lost their chattel labor to the lure of a real paycheck. The conundrum of the period for China: Why did the private, capitalist economy thrive whilst the public sector shrank in power and influence?

The Scotsman Adam Smith some hundred years later in 1776 captured the essence of China's entrepreneurial success: "peace, easy taxes and a tolerable administration of justice." The absence of an honest and forceful policing and judicial power of the state over commercial transactions, however, indicates that Chinese entrepreneurs through a spontaneous evolutionary process developed rules for trade (a form of boundary) and Rule of Three equity arrangements that allowed enterprise to prosper, even without a government bureaucracy capable of making fair rulings in complex commercial matters. Along with evolving boundaries and Rule of Three principles in what the British would call common law came the passions for making things and trading them—a supporting founding mythology for what Adam Smith would later call the "propensity to truck, barter, and exchange."[3] That propensity itself developed from marketplace experience. Given some small probability that a single marketplace experience would generate a profitable outcome, clearly cumulative marketplace success depends upon the number of experiments carried out. As entrepreneurial China captured more and more of the previously bureaucratically run state-sector productive activities, privately generated GDP growth would tend toward the exponential. The fundamental principle behind all marketplace success relates to the number of experiments an entrepreneurial economy can generate.

The fatal flaw underlying all efforts at state sector–led economic growth now becomes readily apparent: State efforts yield minimal numbers of experiments into what new technologies might generate exponential returns, and so most probably will generate negative returns, having failed to recoup initial investments. The situation grows even worse when private entrepreneurial activities strip a bureaucracy of the operating money it needs to perform its most important task—which is to match revolutionary technological advances with the infrastructure evolutions

[3] See Dr. Smith on the Division of Labor in *The Wealth of Nations*, 1776.

those advances require in order to thrive. This appears to have been the case in Ming/Qing period China. The fundamental principle: Nations thrive when government activities support private technological discoveries—and not the other way around. But this still leaves a critical *why* question.

We do know that productive enterprises formerly run by state bureaucrats became captured and operated more profitably by private entrepreneurs, and that this accounted for declining state tax revenues, but that is only the *what* of the matter. The *why* becomes apparent when we add in the knowledge that Chinese dynastic rulers left a long history of frequent falls from power due to rent-seeking behaviors on their parts: in a word *corruption*: Powerful bureaucrats padded their personal nests with payouts from entrepreneurs acquiring state-run enterprises.[4] Government corruption consists, after all, of personal bribe-taking that benefits the individual government official at the expense of the nation's general welfare. Through this process, which likely also involved acts of nepotism, the Chinese state became hollowed out—as though eaten from the inside out by cankerworms. So, even as the overall population of a China made larger through the Manchu-enabled additions of northern lands and people to imperial control, public resources diminished; population grew from perhaps 100 million at the turn of the common era to some 450 million under the later Manchu Dynasty, but government resources actually shrank at the same time.[5]

The remaining factor accounting for the Chinese decline that set in by the 19th century and beyond came from a residual feudalism that Chinese emperors, beginning with the Qin, had never fully snuffed out. In periods of weakness in the administrative state, individual feudal lords challenged the state for control of areas traditionally ruled by them. Without the peaceful working out of conflicts through the Rule of Three, conflicts will get worked out using military force.

At roughly the beginning of the 18th century in Western chronology, then, the situation stood somewhat like this for the Chinese: Two hundred some years of a growing propensity to truck, barter, and exchange had created a Chinese working class and middle class whose members held

[4] See Appendix C for a disturbing look at government corruption in recent times.

[5] We have used a goodly number of online sources for our estimates of likely GDP and population numbers both here and earlier in our document. Ultimately, such figures represent a best guestimate upon our part, made from other guestimates.

within themselves internalized models about how the world works based in such propensities. The new model told the Chinese that hard work and striving carried out in the marketplace would yield a new kind of personal—and more importantly—family security. The Chinese people in this manner had created a new founding myth revolving around a China called into being by Ming-era entrepreneurship.[6] Then, everything began to unravel. As the ability of the administrative state to supply law and order public goods declined, the warlords assumed greater and greater power. By the dawn of the 20th century, the Chinese peasant had come to possess an internalized model that told him to work very hard and to truck, barter and exchange, but also to place himself under the protection of his local warlord—but not too much so, for his own warlord might steal from him as well as a rival warlord. And so, the *yin* and the *yang* of an increasingly precarious existence shaped the emotions and perceptions for each Chinese.

The downfall of the house of Manchu had appeared immanent for years, but it nevertheless came with a frightening suddenness in 1911–1912. There is a lot of ruin in a nation, but bankruptcy, when it comes, comes quickly. In the following chaos, what might be done to restore Chinese power and success? Understandably, the men vying for leadership in a new China directed their focus toward how to unify a nation split into many factions. One faction that formed around the rump of Manchu-Chinese rule attempted to reform the old structure—doing such things as eliminating age-old Confucian training for the bureaucracy, developing modern educational programs for some of the people, and attempting to play catch-up technologically with the West and with Japan. Other factions sought a new beginning by in effect creating and communicating through propaganda a new founding myth for a new nation—a vision for a modern China. Not surprisingly, these factions regarded the founding principles that had arisen in the West, in Japan, and in the new Union of Soviet Socialist Republics.

The first significant ideological leader, Sun Yat-Sen, set out a basic philosophy of governance consisting of three points: nationalism, democracy, and socialism (or "the livelihood of the people"). This all appeared terribly derivative and cross to thousands of years of Chinese governance

---

[6]Basic entrepreneurship still accounts today for the Chinese peoples' propensity to truck, barter, and exchange—and for their success as immigrants in other countries. It seems that they do best outside China, just as the Scots have done better outside Great Britain.

which had always been very authoritarian. Only the third element—livelihood of the people—had a root in Chinese tradition: Emperors had always feared what would happen if the people lacked enough food to eat. Sun's simple formula simply could not carry the splintered nation along with him. One should observe where failure stemmed from: Sun the man himself lacked the practical knowledge of how political economy actually works; unlike the American founding fathers, his was a worldview shaped by the ideological socialism emerging from 19th-century France and by academic trends in Great Britain and the United States—and then by recent Soviet thinking. No one in the new socialist academic *avant garde* thought in terms of the Scottish enlightenment philosophy it was supplanting—that school that saw the importance of common sense perception and observation, and the recognition of spontaneous evolutionary processes that had over thousands of years finally yielded up such principles as liberty, boundary limitations, and the Rule of Three.

No one of an ideological bent at the time fully recognized the contradictions in any party platform presenting democracy and socialism as comfortable bedfellows. Instead, following German philosophical tendencies, Western and Soviet socialist thinking increasingly operated on the basis of converting abstract ideas into reified general variables that could then yield to authoritarian impulses: "Workers of the world unite!" In scope, the entire human world could be reduced to just the proletariat and the bourgeoisie. Lost in the reification of real flesh and blood people was the reality that "the proletariat" was merely a theoretical construct, that many men over their working lifetimes began as simple wage earners and moved into the ranks of small craftsmen and *kulaks*—the group of often quite successful capitalist farmers that the Soviet intelligentsia spoke of with dripping scorn.

In the early part of the 20th century, the Republic of China, after some truly nasty infighting, eventually failed and disintegrated into something almost feudal in overall structure as the warlords competed for power whilst under the nominal leadership of Sun's successor, Chiang Kai-Shek. Under the urging and tutelage of the Soviets, a competing ideology and party organization then began forming to the north of Chiang's Kuomintang: Mao's People's Republic. Far more efficiently organized for authoritarian brutality, Chairman Mao eventually would capture control of China. The failure of one and the control achieved by the other reflect Chiang's Christian missionary upbringing leading him, like Sun before him, to emphasize the democracy Western missionary tutelage brought him. Sun and, later on, Chiang would favor the American tradition for a democratic republic as a new form of government for China, even to the point of suggesting a Rule of Three overarching principle meant to mimic the then-current American experiment in soft socialism: nationalism, democracy and socialism. Mao, of course, from out of Soviet influences, instead favored hard, authoritarian socialism. Indeed, at the most fundamental level, all socialism is at its heart authoritarian: You will be made to…. And in the end, "democratic socialism" constitutes an oxymoron. Both republics attempted, through propaganda, to reshape basic Chinese beliefs away from traditional founding myth and into the realm of the new emerging Western philosophy based in general, broad ideological categories. Mao's form of socialism, of course, won out—but at a high cost to the Chinese people.

During the first half of the 20th century, the country was wracked with the ugliest manifestations of civil war. Food shortages and even famine did occur. During the opening war with Japan and then during World War II, an uneasy peace was struck between the two Chinese republics. Then, the war ended, and the Peoples' Republic rather quickly defeated the Kuomintang. Chairman Mao then set about radically changing the political economy of the nation, helped and encouraged by the Soviets. The first action took the form of the Agrarian Reform Law of 1950, the purpose of which was twofold: to redistribute agricultural land, working animals, and machinery from private owners to the landless peasants in a communistic form, and to break the power of the private owners. The Party encouraged the peasants to try "evil landowners" in what amounted to kangaroo courts. Guilty verdicts had serious consequences. As many as a million landowners were summarily executed; those not executed got trundled off to special "re-education" camps purposed to eliminate any residual propensities to truck, bargain and exchange. In a few short years, 400 to 500 years' painfully acquired knowledge in entrepreneurial agriculture disappeared from the land. Private banks got the axe as well, replaced by a massive state banking operation. With the private banks went centuries of knowledge related to financial support for a primarily agricultural economy.

Unsurprisingly, the Maoist land-use reforms did not end well. The culling of agricultural knowledge possessed by landowning farmers got followed by a complete reorganization of work on Chinese farms—a collectivization scheme that yielded extraordinary resource wastage, especially in the form of idle farm labor. To make matters worse, party apparatchiks dictated radically disastrous farming practices received from a Russian crank and pseudoscientist named Trofim Lysenko that included close planting and deep plowing. By 1958, the combination of killing deep knowledge about agriculture, collectivizing labor in the most inefficient manner imaginable, and employing destructive crank ideas in farming practices had set the stage for the world's greatest 20th-century famine, one in which some 35 million Chinese starved and death.

It gets worse. Right around the time of the great famine, the Chinese leadership decided to decouple itself from the Soviet heavy industry model with its emphasis upon large-scale production utilizing accumulated capital from out of agriculture. After all, Chinese agriculture could throw off little accumulated capital in the first place. As a low capital-intensity fix, China would forgo painfully and slowly building up industrial capacity, and instead use surplus rural labor to run backyard steel furnaces, rather like distilling whisky in the American back country. The experiment, of course, failed splendidly, not only due to the primitive technology, but also related to the state setting up offshoots of agricultural communes to make steel. So, the peasants got themselves frustrated fooling about with hopelessly inefficient technology, the Soviets pulled their support for Chinese industrialization that had abandoned the Russian model, and the farming commune workers took to eating the working animals in order to stay alive. "Yes, there is a lot of ruin in a nation."

After rectifying rural China, Chairman Mao turned his attention to the Chinese city populations who, he believed, had become too bourgeois to fulfill his purposes and assure his legacy. August 1966 then saw the beginnings of the Cultural Revolution. Schools shut down. "Elitist" individuals became targeted for harassment and eventually for "re-education" camps. Not even Politburo members could live in safety; one such member, Deng Xiaoping, found himself under arrest and assigned to such a camp. The Cultural Revolution also set the cities' communistic youth organizations—called the Red Guard—against the adults. Utter chaos followed, and for roughly 10 years, the children ruled over the adults. From an outsider's view, China had seemed to go from one ill-conceived experiment to another for 30 years from 1949 to 1979.

Numbers, imprecise as they may be, illustrate the fall of China from the golden era of the Ming to 1979. In the late Ming/early Qing period of 1660, The Chinese population had reached the then-stunning number of somewhere between 160 million to 220 million. Population expansion from 150 million in 1600 increased significantly as the Qing rulers added more northern, Manchurian area to China. In 1660, GDP per capita for China reached $600. In 1900, per capita GDP stood at $652 with population at 400 million; GDP stood at $260 billion. By 1952 when the Peoples' Republic cemented its grip on power, per capita GDP stood at $54. By 1962, it had risen only to $71, and by 1972 to $132. In 1978, GDP reached only $150 billion. China appeared to have entered an inescapable death spiral. In actuality, the decline for China had set in well before the Maoist experiments, and in fact had begun by 1700. In that year, China generated a per capita GDP of 52% of 1990 Great Britain. By 1800, that number had fallen to 29%, by 1850 to 20%, by 1900 to 12%, and by 1950 to 7%.[7]

While Chinese sources readily blame the tanking GDP upon the 19th-century encroachments made by the West, particularly Great Britain, that yielded the Opium Wars, the Boxer Rebellion and such events, one should regard these admittedly real factors with caution—remembering the causality principle: Correlation never speaks truth about causality. That China slew its entrepreneurs and placed massive barriers to economic advancement in the way of enterprise truly contributed to the great decline, as successive Chinese dynasties forced the nation to look inward and reject the previous foreign trade routes that had made the nation great. Ultimately, the British no more caused China's massive failures than China caused the failures of the feudal nations it had earlier conquered. The fault, dear Brutus, is not in our stars but in ourselves that we are underlings.

Gold, Frankincense, and Myrrh—The Persian Middleman Story

Ancient Persia, now Iran, became powerful largely through an accident of geography: The three great world centers of economic power—Mediterranean Europe and Africa, China, and India—unfortunately lacked good means of intercourse between them. Separated by thousands of miles of frequently inhospitable arid plateaus capped by high mountains, their desires to "truck, barter, and exchange" amongst themselves got systematically stymied, until the desert tribes of Persia supplied them

[7]See Broadberry, Stephen and Hanhui Guan, "China, Europe and the Great Divergence," *Social Science Research Network*, July 2014. Other data appear in *Wikipedia* and other contemporary sources.

an invaluable service. As best we can ascertain, the Persians hit upon a strategy of encouraging international trade by building and maintaining an intricate network of pack animal trails that came to be known as the Silk Road. The Persians apparently provided security services as well to the merchants traveling betwixt the great continents. The Persians also found themselves in a handy position to acquire the know-how for making splendid luxury goods themselves.

The making of this, the second, Persian empire began around 200 BC, coinciding with Han Chinese interests in trading with the West and with India. One should note here that international trade from the period roughly 200 BC into the 17th century had a rich variety of desirable goods going every direction, with Persia acting as a switching yard where shipments got redirected along complex routes that eventually reached beyond Egypt, up European rivers, broadly into west Africa, and deep into India. The notion that the West produced nothing the Chinese cared for arose from a much later period, after the Manchu interlopers took control and began a long-term program of import restrictions. In a sense, it all became a self-fulfilling edict: The barring of Mediterranean fine products eventually caused wealthy Chinese to become forgetful of them. And of course, at some period, Chinese pride in Chinese luxury items only kicked in. At that point, the Europeans could only acquire Chinese luxury products, particularly silk and porcelain, by paying cash on the barrelhead so to speak, and tribute—in silver. That in turn threatened the balance of trade for the Europeans—and eventually sparked the Opium Wars.[8]

If the Persians acquired their position through a fluke of geography, they then lost it through the very conscious efforts at conquest launched by desert nomad Arabs after the rise of Muslim beliefs in the 7th century. The Persians exhausted their strength resisting Muslim incursions; the eventual creation of the Ottoman Empire broke up the old Silk Road

[8] The huge nature of international commerce in the period 200 BC to 1700 AD becomes readily apparent when one considers the trade in silver. After the Spanish had captured the monopoly on South American silver production during the 16th century, some 40% of all silver produced annually ended up in China. International trade was a big deal. The silver concentration in China, in turn, came about because the great inward-looking government actions that started in the late-Ming era in turn collapsed support for the paper money regime that had begun with the Han. The Ming Chinese rulers learned to their chagrin that paper money floats upon trust. Trust, once gone, takes hundreds of years to restore—if ever.

trading routes, and with them, the strategic advantage the Persians had enjoyed, and their major source of wealth. The Western nations could, and did, replace those routes to the Far East with merchant vessels capable of weathering the Cape of Good Hope. The Persians had no such option.

Ancient Persia/modern-day Iran has had the immense good fortune for geography to favor it—not once, but twice. Who says lightning does not strike twice? The first strike, of course, was the good fortune to be located at the great ancient world trading nexus between China, India, Egypt, Mediterranean Europe, and the northern Slavs. Wealth followed—until this geographic advantage got wiped out by the new and overwhelming power in the Middle East, the Muslim Arabs.

The Persians had to wait some 1,300 years for lightning to strike again—this time in the form of a vast underground lake of black liquid gold—oil. The American government saw the potential for using Iran to achieve something close to Middle Eastern hegemony by helping rescue a collapsing Iran, allowing it an entry into the ranks of modern nations. So, in 1953, the CIA engineered a coup that replaced a power vacuum caused by the earlier collapse of the last ruler (who had played footsie with the Europeans) with a new monarch—Reza Shah Pahlavi. With American aid, the plan called for creating a modern, secularized state—one that with American aid did bring about significant economic growth and improvement in the lives of its people. However, beginning in roughly 1950, the Iranian parliament commenced its ultimately successful efforts to nationalize an oil industry hitherto controlled by Western companies. By the 1960s, regional efforts had begun to form a regional monopoly on all Middle Eastern oil—an effort succeeding in 1969 with the creation of OPEC. The economy grew at some 14% annually, and the population doubled—giving Iran the youngest average age population in the region. A thriving middle class developed. By the early 1970s, all looked well in Iran, and the Americans plans for a secular, liberal state looked golden. Then came 1978.

Treated Like Slaves: The Russia Story

> Work is the curse of the drinking class.
>
> Oscar Wilde

Russian Slavic roots trace back to the damp, gloomy, heavily-timbered forests of the southern Baltic region, where arable land and agriculture scarcely existed at all. The life of the sea with its sometimes-rich fisheries assumed outsized importance. Human life hung on a knife's edge much of the time. Threats from warring tribes, both Slavic and Scandinavian, always hung over every common man, the Vikings being a particular terror. No wonder that slavery formed the life story for most of the people who would eventually push southward to populate the future Russian Empire. Only by attaching themselves, body and soul, to a powerful chieftain could common men gain some measure of protection against dismemberment, or being traded as a slave to a foreigner, probably Muslim, and probably traded several times to end their wretched days and years worked to death in North Africa.

Again, geography played a role. Major Russian rivers run south; east-west travel was challenging. The Russian chieftains, at home as much on water as on land, pursued trade, and conquest, downstream after the orderliness of Silk Road Persia gave way to warfare between Mongol hoards and Persians. Eventually, the Slavic fighters of a region called Muscovy, from which Moscow received its name, came to control a vast area, in the north from Mongolia to Eastern Europe, in the south to the Balkans where southern Slav populations blocked them, and southeast until running up against Ottoman warriors. Eventually, too, the Muscovy Slavic rulers began to settle in this whole vast region and to make progress toward civility. The old practices regarding slavery as the fit and proper place for most men, and women, still remained—as did the strongman founding mythology for this mighty empire.

When time reached the later 19th century, European civility began to affect the Russian Empire, but slavery still existed as the reality for most Russians. Enter the 20th century, and that *status quo* came under strong challenge from various factions of ideologues busy adopting the new German thinking about assigning people *en masse* to the most general of categories, such as "workers of the world." Many of the small-time capitalist farmers, toolmakers and such that comprised the leadership and practical knowledge base of traditional society found themselves eliminated in the conflict that was to come when they were executed or exiled on a wholesale basis. Death to the kulaks!

The Russian aristocratic leadership destroyed the continuity of the nation by running poorly armed or unarmed, and poorly trained, soldiers against the German war machine. Once World War I ended, the country readily then fell to the radical factions who defeated other factions standing for democratic, Western governing principles. After some brutal sorting out amongst the radical factions, a new thing on earth formed itself, a totalitarian socialist regime that would with vicious efficiency create the new Soviet Man, regimented beyond anything previously imagined and permitting little, if any, space for a private life. Life became directed by those two out of every ten men who had Party affiliation and who could snitch to the dreaded secret police upon anyone found on their wrong side. Soviet justice, of course, aimed at convicting anyone caught up in the snitchers' nets: "Show me the man and I will find you the crime" as Lavrentiy Beria, the head of the Russian secret police, would proudly put it. The Russian behemoth expanded through conquest of weak neighboring states to form the vast Union of Soviet Socialist Republics.

Through the brute force of carrying out five-year heavy industry production plans, the Soviets achieved high levels of basic materials production rapidly, but by the 1960s it began to appear that brute force would not gain them entry to the league of advanced consumer societies, nor the ability to make complex, miniaturized electronics and such. The Soviet economy differed significantly from those of the Western democracies: A major goal always involved the syphoning off of surpluses to devote to military dominance and adventurism. Soviet socialist doctrine called for agriculture based upon communes, which proved about as inefficient as in their Chinese counterparts. Crackpot pseudo-science helped tank agricultural production as well. The lack of market-based price mechanisms for capital assets particularly caused massive asset misallocations. The gargantuan, and impossible, task of simultaneously setting many thousands of consumer and producer goods prices also caused horrendous misallocations: At one point, farmers bought bread to feed their cattle, because it was cheaper than raw cereal grains.

By the 1970s, Soviet citizens had become deeply depressed, turning increasingly to vodka to dull the pain. Vodka production for the government exemplified the old adage: "Damned if you do and damned if you don't." Cut back on vodka and risk outright rebellion; boost vodka production and watch citizens become ever more dependent and dysfunctional. "We pretend to work, and they pretend to pay us." Indicative of the rapid decline in the Soviet economy, gross national product growth fell from the 5.2%recorded officially in the late 1960s to 2.2% in the late 1970s. Agricultural output actually fell 0.8% annually in the late 1970s.[9]

---

[9]See *Encyclopedia Britannia* article on the Soviet economy under Leonid Brezhnev.

The Child of Hope and the Home of the Brave— The Israeli Story

> The land of Israel needs a people, and the people of Israel need a land.
>
> Israel Zangwill

> The original settlers sought to create an economy in which market forces were controlled for the benefit of the whole society.
>
> Israeli professor Avi Kay

Immediately after the United Nations gave nationhood to the geographically minimal new state of Israel, the surrounding Muslim nations attacked. This, the first war fought by the new nation, had an existential nature: Defeat surrounding enemies or die. This existential challenge forged a founding myth and a nation out of Jewish people drawn from many areas and very different cultures. Unfortunately, the conflict also forced some 600,000 Jews from their dwelling places throughout the Muslim Middle East, and encouraged Muslims living in Jewish Palestine to flee to what became permanent refugee camps. The bifurcation divided Jews and Muslims and made them enemies of each other—reflected by three more wars. The new nation remained dedicated to a socialistic form of government and society—until it no longer yielded positive results, beginning around 1965. Today Israel stands out as one of the two most remarkable entrepreneurial "start-up" nations in the world—the other being Singapore. As recently as 50-some years ago, Israel stood out as the premier small socialist country on earth. Then something remarkable occurred: Israel transformed itself from a failing socialist statelet into an entrepreneurial powerhouse. Why a socialist state, and why the transformation?

Every modern-era socialist movement of any significance has had prominent Jews amongst its intellectual forerunners and its leadership—especially in Germany and Russia. These two countries, and their satellite captive nations, eventually turned on their fellow socialist Jews. During World War II, they executed millions of Jewish people, including many prominent Jewish socialist intellectuals. Some of these Jewish leaders remained loyal to the Nazis and the communists—even aiding the execution of their fellow Jews. It was as though these men and women wanted only to be the last ones eaten by the totalitarian crocodile. Why did such a pathway to unspeakable cruelty come about?

Two explanations seem likely; both probably contain elements of truth. The first argues that the Jews have always possessed strong utopian ideals; their brand of intellectual idealism always contained a core element of "brotherhood of man" wishful thinking following Saint-Simon and the first modern socialist utopian movement in early 19th-century France. According to this theory, Jewish society has always had a strong utopian component to it, and this led Jews to sympathize with early Nazi national socialism.

The other explanation sees the source of the Jewish adoption of socialistic ideology as originating in the 1,000-some years of rejection that many Jews experienced coming from the ruling elites of many European countries. Beginning in the late 19th century, some intellectuals within the Jewish elites sought a way both to security for them and their families and for local prominence and power through a process of ingratiation toward European native elites. Jews who had lived in European communities for centuries had still found themselves regarded as foreigners and interlopers. Ingratiation drove Jewish intellectuals toward at first a rather mild form of middle-class socialism. Eventually, in a forlorn hope for acceptance, some few Jewish intellectuals went much farther and became leading actors in totalitarian socialism, sometimes sacrificing their own people.

When the surviving European Jews who managed to get themselves to Israel after World War II joined the existing Zionists on the ground, they reinforced the already existing socialistic tendencies of the pioneers who had formed agricultural communes, or *kibbutzim*, to achieve basic subsistence living, and also joined workers at government–owned and operated enterprises. Clearly the Jewish settlers—having been subjected to poverty, blatant discrimination, forced exile, and even extermination for some 1,500 years—desired deeply to take advantage of their new nationhood to forge a totally new thing: a country built from the ground up on a foundation of complete equality. The institutions used to create such a planned utopia consisted of the Histadrut or General Federation of Labor and the political Labor Party. Their foundational belief saw capitalism as exploitative of labor, and the only means of preventing the robbery of the worker consisted of placing all the means of production under state control.[10] The Histadrut soon unionized pretty much every job in Israel.

[10] See Lee Edwards, "Three Nations That Tried Socialism and Rejected It", *The National Review,* 14 October 2019.

In 1961, the first murmurings of resistance appeared—in the form of the new Liberal Party that espoused market economics.

The Israeli socialist model worked astoundingly well—until it didn't. From roughly 1955–1975, the Israeli economy grew at 12% annually—at the expense of a loss of income equality. Midway through this period, in 1965, the first rumblings of approaching danger appeared—in the form of Israel's first recession—perhaps brought on by the inflexibility of Israeli socialist economics. Then, the 1967 War hit the country, limiting any effective government responses to the downturn. Unemployment quickly tripled. By 1973, the inflation rate had reached 17%. The debate over socialist versus free market economics began in earnest that year, with Nobel Prize winner Milton Friedman crying out to the socialist government, "set your people free!" Also in that year, the Likud Party, strongly nationalistic and market oriented, took form through the efforts of Menachem Begin. By 1977, Likud had created a coalition with enough smaller parties to capture control of the government—until an election returned power to Labor, and then Likud again after that. One needs to recognize the sheer audacity of the historic Israeli achievement, but also pay attention to the peculiar parliamentary form of government that the new nation put in place, driven by shared desire to create a totally egalitarian state and society.

The new Jewish state created something never before known on earth: a people destroyed as a nation some 2,000 years ago now reunited. This year in Jerusalem! Because of the manner in which Jewish people got drawn from all over the world back to an old-new homeland, their nation-state government had some pretty unique concerns about representation in its new democratically elected Knesset, concerns magnified in importance by the new country's socialist roots—and the desire to create a democratic socialist state. To ensure that even the smallest groups be given some power in parliament, the Israelis adopted proportional representation rules—which have led to continual political churning over the issue of size of support for a group to gain a seat in parliament. To what degree should the rules of electoral politics guarantee representation for the many small ethnic and religious minority groups resident in the country? How small should things go? Too large a cut-off would mean disgruntled citizens; to small would make parliamentarian government practically impossible regarding such basic purposes as the election of a ruling government. It appears that the Israeli leadership has consistently confused the rules for election with the desired outcomes. Perhaps eliminating mandated proportional outcomes in favor of "first past the post" elections would merely force small groups to reach consensus and join together before parliamentary elections, rather than after. Of course, then, the splinter factions could no longer enjoy parliamentary argument and the prospect of forcing frequent elections. How much is such liberty worth?

Election rules caused much churning that probably kept government from focusing upon the failures inherent in socialistic enterprises. Agricultural communes proved inefficient and generally incapable of generating needed results. State-controlled industrial enterprises also proved inefficient. Necessary innovation got stymied, particularly related to water desalination for an arid land where water scarcity abounded and conflicts with Arabs over water rights seemed pretty much continual. By the 1970s, the future economically did not appear very bright, and then came the fourth, Yom Kippur Arab-Israeli war of 1973. By 1978, nearly everyone perceived the need for some radical changes.

The Birth of the New Republic—Great Britain and America

> All that progressives ask or desire is permission to interpret the Constitution according to the Darwinian principle; all they ask is recognition of the fact that a nation is a living thing and not a machine.
>
> Woodrow Wilson

Herbert David Croly seems like one of those rare individuals bred to a purpose and fed as by mother's milk on a revolutionary new formula. Both parents pioneered in writing what would become progressive journalism. Herbert Croly himself had an outsized influence upon America's first progressive president, Theodore Roosevelt. His influential book, *The Promise of American Life,* published in 1909, defined the progressive project for the 20th century: to assure that all members of a community received a fair share of the benefits brought from economic association where previously and presently those benefits accrued to only the few. He espoused positive rights for all people replacing the negative rights of Jeffersonian democracy and the evolution of institutions to succeed the outdated, fixed institutions of the old constitution: in a phrase, a "living constitution." Strong labor unions and powerful government would become the tools for accomplishing progressive goals.

When Mr. Croly launched a new progressive magazine in 1914, he named it far better than perhaps he realized: *The New Republic*. For a new republic to come into being, of necessity an old republic must pass away. The life, liberty and pursuit of happiness that yielded up the earlier American experiment must in turn give way to the new rule of experts replacing American individualism. While life, liberty and the pursuit of happiness had produced a continual evolutionary dynamic within American political economy and society, it would have to yield to the rational processes of a power elite's adopting institutional changes favoring particularly the losers in the great game of life. Yes, that title—*The New Republic*—captured brilliantly the totality of purpose behind the large and radical progressive agenda. The progressives sought for nothing less than the total transformation of America into a new socialist utopia.

Whilst the thinking of Croly and his associates seemed to burst fully grown onto the American landscape early in the new century, it actually had its roots in three separate movements founded in the previous one: the women's movement, the good government movement, and the new economics movement based in communitarian and socialistic beliefs founded by a younger generation of American economists who received training in Germany—perhaps best represented by Richard Ely. They sought to replace natural rights and natural law principles with Hegelian historicism and with Darwinian imagery. Their chosen battleground concerned property rights, and how redefining such rights would make the country more democratic and eliminate poverty.

The good government movement appeared the least threatening to more traditional Americans—and produced the most effective results: a trained cadre of professional managers replacing corrupt political machines in cities great and small alike. Direct democracy's recall petitions and propositions enabled inept managers to be replaced and institutional changes to come about quickly. Progressives pointed proudly to how professional management expertise had eliminated costly duplications of public services in such areas as utilities provision to the public. To this day, benefits of the good government movement do still accrue to some areas of municipal and state regimens.

The other two legs to the progressive agenda yielded a less acclaimed result. Seeking to overthrow all traditional moral principles and judgments, women such as Cady Stanton unwittingly gave birth to a progeny that not only included a women's right to vote, but also the eugenics movement, adopted by the Third Reich, and eugenics' sterile provider, abortion. Within economics, private versus public property rights became an ongoing battle, with the progressives arguing for more public ownership, or at least control, over industry. Progressive economics shaped the New Deal and its progeny, all seeking to make America over into a socialist utopia.

We have linked America and Great Britain together in this story of the pursuit of the New Republic, because similar efforts and similar philosophies reshaped Britain at roughly the same time. The British progressive movement had a somewhat more formal beginning that its American cousin—in 1884 with the birth of the Fabian Society. The Society's name, however, had a more fuzzy meaning than did *The New Republic*: It referred to the Roman general Quintus Fabius Maximus Verrucosus who had fought a delaying action against Hannibal during the second Punic War, circa 220 BC. The Fabians apparently expected British toffs to perceive the Fabian Punic War strategy as analogous to their own efforts to stave off the Marxist threat to make Britain communist. Leading first generation Fabians included the playwright George Bernard Shaw, Graham Wallis, and Sidney and Beatrice Webb. Second generation, 20th-century Fabian thinkers included Harold Laski and C.D.H. Cole—who became a good deal more radical than the run-of-the-mill sort. Labor Party politicians—such as Roy Jenkins, R.H.S. Crossman, and Dennis Healey—shaped much of the left-of-center agenda for modern British politics. The Society still hangs on as a think tank for the moderate sort of British socialist.

The philosophical roots for Fabian socialist principles came from collectivism—the belief that the rights of the individual must be suborned to a social collectivity such as state, nation, or social class. It seemed apparent to them that substantial government interventions would be required in order for the average individual to flourish. This meant, in turn, that the government would have to control industry—an eventuality that became real after World War II when the labor government under Clement Atlee nationalized railroads, airlines, utilities, steel, waterworks and many others, as well as education, nutrition, housing, and care of the sick and aged. The Fabians saw this sort of activity as only a logical extension of the provision of municipal public services by local government and believed that through a process of "permeation", more and more of the British economy and society would fall under the public domain—and it did.

The Great Depression had given socialists in both countries the necessary boost to threaten the free market *status quo*. At that time, America probably had the more toxic labor relations, dating back to the post–Civil War conflict between the skilled workers possessing technical knowledge and mill owners possessing the capital. When the new Wagner Act of 1935 took real effect in 1937 after a Supreme Court challenge to its constitutionality, wages jumped in some industries by as much as 30%, and in 1938, the country experienced the pain of a recession within a depression. The American labor situation rapidly became so toxic that the government likely could not have supported Great Britain in the war to come without the alliance formed with the USSR after Germany's invasion of Russia. The reason: Unionized America regarded the USSR as America's future and would not push its members to work hard at the war effort until the alliance formed.

After the war, of course, the Labor Party won a majority in parliament and promptly nationalized most major industries. The American trend toward socialism remained comparatively weak, largely because the country emerged from the war poised for a remarkable growth. What did develop in America was a powerful trend toward institutionalized strife between Big Labor and large-corporation management. By 1951, the American economist John Kenneth Galbraith was prophetically writing about the need for a "countervailing power" coming from government to balance out the competing labor and management forces within the economy—something we might identify as a new Rule of Three dictum. Galbraith proclaimed that labor needed to grow powerful enough to form a "countervailing power" to that of the major corporations—with government help if need be, which labor got. Labor conflicts yielded onerous work rules and a near-constant threat of strikes—all tending to reduce America's productivity and hinder technological advance. The Americans remained busy substituting free market continual labor-pricing movements with prices driven by labor-management negotiations and the Federal Reserve's attempts at managing inflation.

By the 1970s, Great Britain had fallen into a downward economic spiral related to a still worse labor situation, one where even in the many nationalized industries, unions bosses could, and did, call their workers out on strike with growing frequency and over the most trivial work rules quibbles. The union bosses had become the new lords of British industry—being seemingly more powerful than a string of ineffective Prime Ministers. Eventually the British people would tire, and then become quite angry, at the inconvenient slowdowns and strikes imposed upon them by the labor lords.

The first Arab oil embargo of 1973 put both countries deeply into recession driven by runaway inflation—in turn driven by their respective governments' attempts to cope with the dire emergency through petrol rationing and general price controls. With their economies no longer functioning within a free-enterprise relationship, by 1978, conditions in both had sunk precipitously—and then 1979 arrived. That year, the second great Arab oil embargo resulted from the Iranian Revolution overthrowing the westernizing Shah. Even though oil prices rose only moderately, some 4% or so, the American and British economies proved themselves too constrained by regulations to allow prices to adjust demand to supply. The command economies had for a second time in the decade failed—and were failing gloriously.

Section Three: 1979–2019
The Great Inflection Point and What Followed

What happened in the run-up to 1979 occupied us in the first sections of this chapter. Then, events around the time of this auspicious year revealed the beginnings of significant changes politically and socially for all six countries we have examined, changes reflected in each nation's GDP results. What happened, then, around 1979, and in the 40 years following?

China

In 1978, China still operated as a tightly controlled, backward country following discredited Marxist principles and policies that kept the people poor and the economy stagnant and horrendously inefficient. A private sector, as such, did not even exist. Meanwhile, its impoverished population comprised almost totally of peasant farmers continued growing at an exponential rate, approaching close to one billion—up from 400 million 75 years earlier.

In 1979, China took its first hesitant steps toward allowing a market economy to come into being—something completely attributable to the second-time resurrected Party leadership by one Deng Xiaoping. Shortly after the death of Chairman Mao in 1976, the "Gang of Four" had briefly exercised power and had once more purged him from the high Chinese leadership. The disintegrating nature of the Chinese economy and social order led to his restoration, and shortly thereafter to his assuming overall Party leadership. Mr. Deng was nothing if not a brilliant politician and survivor.

We may regard his two biggest lifetime achievements as being: creating a market-based shadow economy to the official, State Owned Enterprises (SOEs) one, and adopting and enforcing the one-child population control strategy. Western sources tend to attribute the resulting economic growth to the West's sort of prying open China, begun by the American President Richard Nixon in 1973, for Western business interests to form an invasion, and indeed in the first years of the 1980s this perspective had some truth to it.[11] One must never, however, fail to attribute the Chinese economic powerhouse status to the hard work and initiative of Chinese entrepreneurs and their workers—people who had always thriven in business after immigrating to other countries lacking the homeland's controls upon enterprise. Something approaching the 20/80 rule can get applied here: Some 20% of China's working population created 80% of its new wealth. The workers who made this actually happen responded to pay incentives, incentives lacking in the official, government-run economy. Incentives to industry, not a door forced open, ultimately made the Chinese "miracle" happen. Indeed, the government economy resembled a Potemkin village, a Chinese showcase, behind which the frequently run-down-looking private businesses actually made the things for domestic needs and international export.

The largest abuses of what Deng himself would call *market socialism* came from the lack of a capitalist economy's ability to properly value assets; in communist China, state mandates determine where capital investment will go, and the result would become the many "ghost cities" now dotting its landscape.

Deng's second significant achievement went right to the heart of the declining domestic output per capita problem in the country: too many often nonproductive mouths to feed. Population control had to get forced upon Chinese peasants; farmers as a body behave very conservatively—knowing how close to starvation things can get, and did get in the early 1960s. Lacking a trustworthy retirement trust fund to draw upon, children, many in fact, remained a farmer's best work force and retirement fund.

---

[11] See *Cowboys and Dragons: Shattering Cultural Myths to Advance Chinese/American Business* for a first-hand recounting of these early years in Chinese-American business interests.

And, the greatest threat to any Chinese emperor has always been a shortage of food for the people. By the second decade of the 21st century, Deng's great error came clearly into focus: China's population was shrinking and ageing, perhaps too quickly and too much. As some wag writing for the *Economist* magazine once put it: China will be the first country to grow old before it grows rich.[12]

The final act in the 40-year Chinese play began in 2012 with the appointment of a new Paramount Leader in 2012, Xi Jinping. With Xi's succession to the top job, China began moving away from Chairman Deng's attempt to implement a form of democratic socialism all the while continuing to "hide our capabilities and bide our time; never try to take the lead." Legal changes would narrow the liberties of the Chinese people—something of an echo from the past of Qin Dynasty legalism.

Mr. Xi began a very public policy of financing intercourse with other nations, much of it along the old Silk Road routes. This time, China would not passively accept Silk Road activities carried on by the Persians; instead Chinese infrastructure projects all over the world would be carried out as loans to receiving countries—who then would have a dependency relation making them captive buyers of Chinese products. It constituted a very bold move toward regional, and even world, dominance. Reflecting his newly established power, Mr. Xi had himself made Core Leader in 2016—once more echoing a Chinese tradition originating within the deep past: Mr. Xi has, in effect, become the next Emperor of a new Chinese dynasty.

Persia/Iran

Just before 1979, the Americans were still busy creating a new free-market Iran, but they, and perhaps the Shah as well, had underestimated the growing power of Shiite Muslim fundamentalism. For the Iranians, fundamental Muslim beliefs had long before become a founding myth for the nation, displacing its earlier myth of the ancient trading dynamo producing vast wealth from foreigners. Resistance to the modernizing Shah's rule from Shiite clerics grew steadily throughout the 1970s—threatening all the Westernizing projects, and also the continuation of

[12] See the 15 May 2017 article in *The Economist* entitled "What is China's Belt and Road Initiative?"

Western aide—which had become superfluous anyhow thanks be to the 1973 oil embargo and permanently elevated oil prices. By 1978 the whole American effort began to look like a house of cards as Western capital flight reached something like $40 billion. Then came 1979, when the Iranian mullahs engineered a coup of their own—the capture of the American Embassy in Tehran. Nineteen seventy-nine brought the Iranian revolution and the replacement of its progressive government with a theocratic state led by Ayatollah Ruhollah Khomeini. The Americans lacked the moral courage to do more than rescue the Shah they had once placed into power.

Nineteen seventy-nine in fact brought a year of revolutions to the country. The new government nationalized all domestic industry including NIOC (National Iranian Oil Company)—and also the banking system. A new constitution passed in the parliament, a document seeking to allow a smaller private sector to operate within an economy dominated by state-owned enterprises. A cooperative sector permitting state and private enterprises to join together for some purposes got included as well. The overall economy world thenceforth fall under the central control of the government, driven by successive five-year plans, very much on the Soviet model. Lastly, any vestiges of marketplace capitalism would disappear as a central authority would thenceforth set all prices and distribute subsidies to favored government enterprises.

Despite efforts to unify the Muslim Middle East, originating from Egypt's ruler Gamal Abdel Nasser, and despite massive new oil revenues, the region exploded into war as the 1,200-year quarrel between the two branches of Mohammedanism flared up—made even more horrific than before by modern weaponry. The Sunni Muslims of Iraq led by Saddam Hussein attacked Shiite Iran in 1980. The war endured for eight long years until peacemaking efforts through the UN finally brought it a halt. By 2019, Iran had become the chief world exporter of terrorism and actively sought to create a Shi'ite crescent empire extending from Turkey and Syria through Iraq—all directed by Iran in the southeast. The Iranian crescent peoples would challenge Sunni Saudi Arabia, its allies, and even Egypt in an effort to triumph in the 1,300-some year inter-Muslim bloody conflict. Lastly, any possibility of free-market capitalism and liberal democracy coming to dominate the country got buried by a succession of cruel totalitarian clerics—strongmen in black robes.

The Soviet Union and Glasnost

In late December 1979, Soviet troops invaded Afghanistan. The Afghan war had begun a year earlier, in 1978. The conflict raged between a new communist central government comprised of formerly warring people's party factions supported by Moscow and indigenous Muslim guerillas. During 1979, what had become a Soviet client state ruthlessly purged the country of opposition and began a series of land and social reforms aimed at making the country more like a Soviet socialist republic and less like a traditional Muslim peasant land where agriculture, including major opium operations, comprised nearly the entire economy.

The insurgents, collectively identified as the *mujahideen* ("those who engage in jihad"), appeared likely to overthrow the ill-disciplined and poorly motivated Afghan army that enabled the puppet government to hang onto control of Kabul and other major cities. The Soviets apparently worried that should they lose their newest client state, others amongst their Muslim-majority socialist republics might attempt to escape as well. So, in a decision that was to have major ramifications for the next 40 years and more, the Kremlin leaders sent in some 30,000 Russian troops to quell the rebellion—figuring, no doubt, that they could be recalled by summer. Perhaps that might have been so, if the United States under its new President Ronald Reagan had not commenced supplying the mujahideen with weaponry that included shoulder-launched guided missiles capable of taking out Soviet aircraft and tanks. The Afghan war would stretch out for nearly 10 long years, readily becoming a killer drain upon an already crumbling Soviet economy. As the Soviets poured more money into the military, Soviet education and medical care reached a point of being a national disgrace.

In 1982, the long-serving head of the USSR, Leonid Brezhnev, finally died. He had largely overseen the Russian attempt to make communism really work, before finally giving up and proclaiming the new goal of attaining *developed socialism*. In his last few years, he had lost control of the country. The KGB no longer directed the expression of Soviet arts and culture; new flames of nationalism threatened the many republics' one-state policies of the Brezhnev era. An interregnum of sorts followed Mr. Brezhnev's departure, with Yuri Andropov, that supreme politician, slipping into the top job as party leader and president. Mr. Andropov believed that there was nothing inherently wrong with the Soviet system; what needed fixing involved the exploding rates of corruption, absenteeism, and alcoholism. Before he could prove himself right, Mr. Andropov, however, joined Mr. Brezhnev in the great beyond—replaced by the 72-year-old Konstantin Chernenko who would shortly die himself, of terminal cancer. How much the Soviet medical establishment contributed to these deaths we may never know. The figure of Chernenko perfectly symbolized everything wrong with the entire empire.

Mikhail Gorbachev slipped into the role of next party leader, and for once the Soviets had someone not already brain dead and likely to live out a long life. Now the Russian people had someone who recognized the need for a total remake of the existing "command-administrative system" as the radical reformer Zaslavskaya put it. Mr. Gorbachev set about creating a revolution that would be controlled from above and driven by two basic concepts: *perestroika* and *glasnost*—the first meaning a "restructuring" of all Soviet economic and social arrangements. What Gorbachev had in mind came down to such things as worker participation groups, decision-making local authority for managers and participation by local soviets, and a general increase in what could be called social justice reforms. *Glasnost* meant "openness and transparency." Glasnost, of course, suggested that the critical decisions within the empire would no longer be made by Party diktat out of sight of the people.

Mr. Gorbachev failed his first major *glasnost* test—waiting some 18 days before releasing official confirmation of the Chernobyl disaster. Presumably the experience forced upon him the importance of reducing the totalitarian role of the Communist Party that he headed up. He held, early in his leadership, that the Soviet system only required some minor tinkering—in this sense resembling Yuri Andropov. His plan for goosing the Soviet economy, however, differed greatly; rather than attempting to motivate workers, he focused upon increasing capital investment so as the boost productivity as the West had done. Soon realizing the error of his early thinking, he began approving some market-based alternatives to the Soviet rigid planned economy. By then, perhaps it was already too late, as rationing of consumer goods had become necessary in order to compete with America's defense spending initiative. This all involved *perestroika* at work. Afghanistan plus Mr. Reagan's strategy of spending the USSR into bankruptcy would in the end triumph—and that end fast approached. The ruin of a nation comes slowly; then, bankruptcy happens in a heart-beat. In 1987, Mr. Reagan gave his famous speech in Berlin in which he called out, "Mr. Gorbachev, tear down this wall!" In 1989, the Berlin wall did come down, and the centrifugal forces around the periphery of Mother Russia blew the Soviet Empire apart.

The *glasnost* element to his thinking took the form of actions aimed at some degree of democratizing Party rule. Sadly for Mr. Gorbachev, his less-than-halfway measures in both economic liberalization and governance created the conditions for precisely what he and his predecessors had hoped to cure—a form of chaos that this time would drive the breakup of the whole Soviet empire. As the American Mr. Jefferson noted of southern slavery, when one holds a wolf by the ears, it is very tricky indeed to let go.

When Mr. Gorbachev let go by replacing the Party's central committee for running the economy with a parliament structured on Western models, and moved the empire toward a Western-style executive presidency, he opened the country up to his own overthrow by Boris Yeltsin—a hard-drinking proponent of Republic of Russia primacy amongst the collection of Soviets comprising the Union. In 1990, Mr. Gorbachev had initiated a Soviet-wide referendum on a new Soviet federation; the vote came in as a resounding yes, but Mr. Yeltsin defeated Mr. Gorbachev for the new role of President. In 1991, the Yeltsin regime moved to make the Russian Republic the more equal amongst equals. To save the Russians from a federation limiting Russian power, the agencies traditionally keeping control over the people, such as the KGB, initiated what became a coup of sorts. At year end, the USSR ceased to exist. The resulting crash of the hermaphrodite command-free market economy cut GDP by one-sixth and created a massive hole in the Russian Republic's operating budget. By 1998, Mr. Yeltsin himself—something of a loose cannon—began losing favor with the people. A man named Vladimir Putin, at first favored by Yeltsin, began a rise to power. By the early years of the new century, the Russian republic—with its cosmetic democratic institutions—appeared well on its way back to rule by a strongman. The strongman had, after all, ruled Russia since time immemorial, and that part of the founding mythology of the country would not yield to Western imports in governance.

The New Nation Israel

> The state is wise, and the market is stupid [or is it?].
>
> John Maynard Keynes

> I got the whole Sinai, but all poor Menachem got was a piece of paper.
>
> Anwar Sadat

In March of that auspicious year 1979, Anwar Sadat and Menachem Began signed the Egyptian-Israeli peace accord, for which both men received the 1978 Nobel Prize for Peace award. A single fact illustrates why this peace accord amazed everyone at the time: Both principals signing the agreement had been what we today would call terrorists earlier in their lives, being involved in murdering members of opposing religions, Jews and Muslims. Later on, Mr. Sadat had led the 1973 Egyptian/Syrian Yom Kippur sneak attack upon Israel. For Israel's Menachem Begin to treat with a man regarded as wicked and treacherous truly did amaze the entire world. The other thing they held in common related to political economy: Both men believed in the superiority of market economics over central planning and pricing by diktat.

Remember, the *what*, *where*, and *how* questions in life are easy; *why* is difficult. Why did these two men, who surely hated one another, reach a peace agreement? Certainly, both men took high-risk gambles in so doing; Mr. Sadat himself fell victim to radical Muslim terrorists who murdered him in Cairo in 1981, and even before that, Egypt got run out of the organization of Arab states. Certainly, too, that much-maligned American President Jimmy Carter had much to do with it; Mr. Carter, after all, brought the two together on neutral, American turf and skillfully led them toward an agreement, and Mr. Carter's wife Rosalynn perhaps exceeded her husband's own diplomatic skills. But the Carters were part of the *how*.

It takes two to make a peace. The Israelis have lived under a constant existential threat to their very existence from the surrounding Muslim nations. It would always be in Israel's own self-interest to swallow its anger at Arab treachery in order to remove one or more of the many threats to it. For Egypt, the *why* appears a little more obtuse. Of course, Mr. Sadat recognized that despite coming close to defeating Israel in the Yom Kippur war, the Muslim world would likely never succeed in wiping out the Jews. One might suspect that the Egyptian attack commencing the 1973 war had been designed to gain a platform for future peace negotiations, as the Egyptian initial attack came close to success and forced the somewhat arrogant Israelis to recognize that the Egyptians possessed some prowess and courage also.

In human relational terms, Mr. Sadat had warmed to Mr. Begin after being warned of a likely assassination attempt against him discovered by Israeli secret agents. Mr. Sadat, possessing by training something of a British officer's sense of honor, perceived that here was a Jew he might deal with. Also, Mr. Sadat had come to despise heartily his Soviet advisors who really did regard their Egyptian charges as a lot of country bumpkins. He happily expelled the Russians and accepted aid and military training from the Americans, who curiously had bailed out the Israelis in the war—supplying them promptly with war material and aerial reconnaissance flights. The lesson we can easily see: Reasons for both war and peace may be complex and many generations old; sparks initiating war or peace often, however, come from the subjective perceptions of the immediate actors involved who often possess very imperfect information.

The aftermath of 1979 we should regard as instructive. The Israeli political war between socialists and free marketeers continued well into the 1980s. The economy stagnated, and inflation roared ahead—reaching 450% by 1984. Government spending and the national debt soared. The tricky thing involved how to unwind the tentacles of socialism that ran through the entire social order. The Likud government asked the help of that famous American Jew Milton Friedman who advised and detailed out a set of policies for going slow. Then in 1983, the inflation bubble burst, and the economy pitched headlong into a steep decline. There is a lot of ruin in a nation, but then bankruptcy comes with shocking speed in the blink of an eye. The Histadrut industrial empire collapsed. Many private companies and individuals went bankrupt. Perhaps the entire nation would have collapsed and its people been exterminated by its neighbors, when the American President Ronald Reagan and his Secretary of State George Schultz made the Israeli government an offer it could not refuse: Receive a \$1.5 billion grant, with the *quid pro quo* that it abandon socialistic rules of the game for some good old-fashioned American entrepreneurial capitalism. Within a year, inflation shrank to 20% and the budget deficit disappeared. Finally unleashed and at liberty to innovate, the Israeli private sector took off like a rocket. Remember, the European Jewish settlers ran out of Europe taking with them some of the finest higher education and training on earth. Perhaps, too, their IQs had been honed by those 2,000 years of existential threats? Foreign capital investment shortly increased by some 600% over the bad old days. Parliamentary democracy also blossomed, even though the Israelis retained their love for splinter parties and frequent elections.

For Egypt, sadly, the outcome has been profoundly disappointing. The only thing growing has seemed to be its population. The government has remained a socialistic dictatorship. In the 2011 Revolution, one dictator, Hosni Mubarak, got overthrown by a radical mob action carried out by radicals who blamed him for Egypt's grinding poverty. Mr. Mubarak shortly got replaced by another dictator. In reality, the country's problems cannot be solved by swapping one strongman for another. Sadly, too, the Egyptians, while keeping an at-times tenuous peace with Israel, never embraced their wildly successful neighbors and failed to learn any valuable lessons from them. Technology transfers have not come about. The Egyptians perhaps have looked down their noses at the uppity Jews. Pride cometh before a fall.

The Anglo and American Resurgences

> Now is the winter of our discontent
> Made glorious summer by this sun of York;
> And all the clouds that lour'd upon our house
> In the deep bosom of the ocean buried.
>
> From William Shakespeare, *Richard III*

> In the end, more than freedom, they wanted security. They wanted a comfortable life, and they lost it all—security, comfort, and freedom. When the Athenians finally wanted not to give to society but for society to give to them, when the freedom they wished for most was freedom from responsibility, then Athens ceased to be free and was never free again.
>
> Attrib. Edward Gibbon

Nineteen seventy-nine, that year of audacity, introduced stunning changes to both Great Britain and the United States. In each case, change began from within a nation rather than being triggered from without. And each case involved the voters' overthrow of long-entrenched social-democratic policies, and the ideologies driving those policies—replacing them with free-market principles. In this year, to-be-Lady Margaret Thatcher carried the new "dry" Conservatives to victory over a floundering Labor administration. The Conservative "wets" got relegated to the political wilderness for nearly a generation. In America, former Hollywood actor Ronald Reagan swept to victory over the Democrat Jimmy Carter, whose perceived domestic policy failures overrode his peacemaking diplomacy regarding the Israeli-Egyptian accord. Mr. Reagan's policies would power the United States political economy for nearly a generation as well. In each case also, a conservative era began with the new leader commencing a war of independence. One leader, Lady Thatcher, did lead Britain to fight a hot war—the 1982 Falkland Islands confrontation—fought upon a principle, the principle of free determination of who shall rule a people. In this case, she fought for the right of Englishmen not to live under a foreign nation's rule. [The same principle would direct her war protecting the rights of Northern Irish loyalists against the radical IRA.] The new American leader fought the Cold War against the Soviet Union in the same 1980s decade: "Mr. Gorbachev, tear down this wall!" Mr. Reagan also pursued a major build-up of the moribund American military, forcing Mr. Gorbachev's government to spend itself into bankruptcy trying to keep up. Soviet Russia did not go quietly into the night; the Americans pushed it.

In Great Britain, the Conservative Party in 1975 had been taken over by a woman calling for radical economic changes—a junior minister within the Edward Heath Conservative government. None of the male senior party leaders had had the moral courage to challenge the Party and the nation to make a change in course, the whole lot of them being too intimidated by the Labor lords. The thing that brought everything to a head occurred in the winter of 1978—the "winter of our discontent" brought on by a series of major labor strikes. Lady Margaret Thatcher swept into office promising an end to British labor unrest and declaring a new dawn of individual liberty, of freeing the people from the near-total constraint government had placed upon their lives. Some of the new Tory government actions undermining Labor's ability to organize and call strikes: banning the closed shop, requiring union leaders to poll their memberships before calling strikes, forbidding sympathy strikes, and holding members' unions responsible for strike-related damages. The clash between labor and government boiled just beneath the surface, until 1984 when the government announced the closing of some 20 coal mines—called *pits* by the Brits—it declared redundant and uneconomic to operate. The National Union of Mineworkers declared a nationwide strike shutting down coal production in a sometimes-hot war raging for nearly a year. Considerable collateral damage in terms of people living in the cold and businesses closing occurred. If the Labor lords thought she would buckle they were sadly mistaken; unlike her weak-kneed predecessors, the Iron Lady refused to make a single concession. The unions buckled, and the shape of the British political economy changed forever.

Lady Thatcher's other agenda targeted the industries earlier nationalized under the first post-World War II Labor government. All except the nationalized healthcare industry returned to private ownership, creating millions of new ownership shares, and huge new opportunities for average Britons to become shareholders. Much of the housing stock in the country had been rebuilt by the post-war government, which rented units to private citizens. Few Britons had the opportunity to own their own dwellings. Privatizing 1.5 million housing units in government estates changed all that as well. By the end of the 1980s, shares ownership in Britain had tripled, and home ownership came within reach of many citizens.

Under Mr. Reagan, the Americans fought a domestic war as well, but unlike in Great Britain, this war did not involve a human institution such as labor unions; the American government battled inflation. A few weeks before Mr. Reagan won election in 1979, Paul Volcker assumed leadership of America's central bank, the Federal Reserve. American inflation had been a mere 1% in 1965; by 1980, it would hit 14%; unemployment would go from 3.5% in 1969 to 9.7% by 1982 as a recession appeared to set in. The stock market tanked, and corporations largely ceased investing in the future as the prime lending rate shot up to 21%. Yet by 1983, these depressing statistics had begun to reverse course, with inflation falling remarkably to 3.2%, and by the following year the great 1980s boom era had begun. What was the *why* that happened to reverse this frightening downward spiral?

First, we should focus on the expectations inflation had already generated. Once more, perceptions matter greatly. Both individuals and corporations quite rationally had come to expect high inflation as the upward trend in prices over 10 years had become apparent to all. Borrowing to pursue investments likely to beat inflation had been increasing dramatically. The Federal Reserve, to put things very simply, had been pursuing the goal of keeping the price of bank reserves at a predetermined level—thereby assuring that the banks could keep lending to speculative investors. The growing money supply then simply fed increases in the general price level, goosing inflation and stimulating more speculative borrowing by people and institutions that were speculators, not investors. In a radical move under Mr. Volcker, the Fed in 1979 began to control the growth of the money supply itself. The result: Interest rates on borrowing soared, and warning signals regarding a recession began to flash on the dashboard of the Fed. But, in fairly short order, something a little over two years, the Fed successfully squeezed speculative behavior out of the economy—and with it, runaway inflation. But, what about that nasty specter of a serious coming recession—our second issue here?

The answer, of course, came in the form of *supply-side economics* and the successful nostrums recommended by America's greatest economist Milton Friedman and economist Arthur Laffer of Laffer curve fame. These two men laid the philosophical foundation for supply-side economics: monetarist economic growth theory and tax theory. Their whole argument could nicely get captured by a single formula: MV = PQ, where M is money supply, V is the velocity at which M turns over, P is the price level, and Q is economic output measured as quantity. Because V remains stable in the short run, changes in the money supply could affect either prices or output, or both.

Until the 1970s, Keynesian demand-side theory had shaped American monetary and tax policy beliefs. Keynesian economists told a succession of American administrations that the manipulation of interest and tax rates could guide the economy on a stable growth path and balance the federal budget over time—by affecting the demand for goods and services. Excessive growth and inflation could be throttled by increasing interest and tax rates, thereby reducing consumers' ability to purchase products. Economic downturns could be corrected by cutting those same rates. The scheme had worked reasonably well—until confronted by the 1973 oil embargo. Then, interest rate hikes had failed to reduce fuel demand enough to stabilize petroleum prices: Welcome to *stagflation*—a dreadful state in which inflation increased but economic growth did not. Rather than allow prices to rise to balance supplies to demands, the Nixon, Ford, and Carter administrations had adopted various forms of overall price controls—very predictably triggering rationing and black-market activity. By the mid-1970s, the economic situation appeared desperate enough for some rethinking to occur.

Dr. Friedman appeared as America's short-term savior—by reversing the Keynesians' thinking. For Dr. Friedman, supply and not demand determined P and Q, where P times Q equals GDP. In the short run, the growth in the money supply permits economic growth by funding investment at profitable interest rates—but only absent tax and regulation restraints upon growth. Otherwise, growth in M merely creates price inflation. The supply-siders argued for a money supply growth commensurate with the economy's ability to generate inflation-free output. In a sense, Dr. Friedman's thinking validated the old 19th-century truism called Say's law: "Supply creates its own demand." Say's Law in turn reveals the mechanism by which growth occurs in a free market economy. Increasing the supply of entrepreneurial risk takers increases the experiments running within the economy; those risks that pay off generate in turn demand for labor, goods, and services—and so on and so on.

What then, under supply-side thinking, prevents money supplies going into boosting P rather than Q? Here for the supply-side thinkers, the Laffer curve comes into play. Reducing tax burdens upon business, and also reducing regulatory restrictions, puts more working capital into the hands of entrepreneurs. The resulting effects through Say's law makes the costs for generating more Q fall, and prices remain stable whilst Q and GDP increase. The increased economic activity largely offsets the "cost" to the government of cutting business taxes in the first place. While such thinking quickly got challenged by orthodox economists, supply-side effects did in reality boost the economy—a clear case of theory working out in practice. One might note that the British experience driven by Lady Thatcher's resolve displayed some similarities to the Reagan revolution in America—but without the theoretical underpinnings. By 1990, it seemed that free market economic policies had triumphed in both countries. The great philosophical treatise presenting the *why* of all appeared in 1988 with the publication of Friedrich Hayek's *Fatal Conceit.* And yet, by the turn of the last century, the resistance movement in favor of socialism had already begun, and in 2019 the very survival of market economics and individual liberty have become threatened with extinction.

Conclusions

Beware of what men do in the name of good.

An old Dartmouth College credo

All six countries we have selected made some efforts toward socialism in the preceding century. Three countries have had authoritarian governments during this period; three have had democratic rule. At some time in this past century, three countries have experimented with democratic socialism—Israel, Great Britain, and the USSR. America has had a political movement toward democratic socialism actively going on twice, during the Great Depression in this the new century. Two countries engaged in empire building—China and the USSR. [Britain, of course, lost an empire during the same period.] That has not worked out well for the

Russians, and probably will yet fail for the Chinese. Iranian efforts at empire construction appear likely to be stillborn, yielding a deconstruction of Iran as a clerical tyranny.

Our overall summary: None of our six countries has made a socialistic command economy work. Likewise, democratic socialism has failed, being as much an oxymoron as "liberty and equality" within 18th-century French experience. The reason, as we see it, is quite simple: The prosperity of a nation depends upon its citizens individually, and its businesses corporately, possessing the liberty to experiment with potentially revolutionary technologies. It matters not that some nine-tenths of these fail: One cannot know ahead of time whether two geeks in a garage will create the next Apple. At the philosophical level, then, the Scottish Common Sense philosophers got it right with regards to the workings of spontaneously evolutionary processes being superior to central planning. Functionalism says that wherever a *system* exists, someone must have planned it; but this is wrong. Orderly processes come into being with no master planner at all; in fact, a master planner could never even imagine the results achieved through markets. America, Great Britain, and Israel all have created growing material abundance for ever-broader numbers of their citizens through free market political economic policies. China not so much. Russia and Iran have simply failed to do so at all.

But how can we say that about China, you may ask? Certainly, Chinese GDP over the past 40 years has grown faster than any other country on earth—in nominal GDP. But what sort of wealth has resulted? Drawing upon that quintessential political economist, Adam Smith, we may define *wealth* as the annual output of goods and services that an economy provides for its people's happiness—not as the previous-to-Smith, mercantilist definition of wealth as a hoard of gold, held by the wealthy. By this definition, China has generated rather little real wealth for all its people—and certainly none for the disfavored classes within its overall population, such as the Uighur Muslims. By neutering free market economics, China has built dozens of huge "ghost cities" filled up by—no one. Sitting upon a hoard of American bonds extracted by creating conditions yielding massive trade deficits really constitutes the 21st-century version of 17th-century mercantilism's pursuit of gold bullion balances extracted through tariffs and trading regulations favoring one party over the other.

<>

Discoveries:

Boundaries are essential for any nation pursuing the happiness of its people. Looking at our six examples, we might first of all observe that the building of empires does not conduce to human happiness within those empires, or even to stability and harmonious relations amongst its peoples. Empires always must get constructed through the violation of physical boundaries—as was the case for both the Russian and Chinese empires and for Iran's striving to build a fertile crescent empire recently. These violations, made in order to build a growing empire, always yield dismemberment and chaos because the costs to maintaining an empire grow geometrically as the empire grows arithmetically. Much of the total costs relate to the need for a constantly growing network of spies and snitches; in the old Soviet Russia some 10%, or even 20%, of the people did nothing but spy and snitch upon the rest.

Boundary matters go far beyond border walls. Laws, rules, and regulations all also function as boundaries—between legal and illegal conduct. The protection of property rights extends beyond the material into the intellectual. Boundaries provide the patent protection that motivates entrepreneurial risk-taking. Perhaps even more importantly, boundaries serve to protect the people from government overreach. Boundaries also serve as protections for individual life and liberty. The real issue between democracy and socialism? Individualism versus collectivism. Socialism becomes indifferent to the well-being of the individual. The goals of socialism require that the government enforce a collective will against that of resisting individuals, as we see in China and Hong Kong today. You will be made to….

The device employed to accomplish collective ends involves the reification of the many localized cultural variables existing in any nation—bunching them all together into just a few that then can be communicated to an entire nation through mass media propaganda. Propaganda, remember, is the employment of mass media in order to change the founding mythology of a nation. The people must be made to accept these reifications—the most basic being the workers versus the bourgeois capitalists. We should note here in passing again

(*Continued*)

that the reification tendency shaped the fields of economics and sociology in ways taught by the new research universities of Germany. Consumers versus producers. One social class against another. In Darwinian terms, the weak versus the strong. Divide and conquer.

The other kind of totalitarian rule, ancient in origin, still exists in the shape of the traditional strongman dictatorship, backed up by a military junta. Strongman rule traditionally had no overriding ideological structure or purpose. The strongman simply wants to have power over others and to extract any economic surpluses his people may produce—which usually adds up to little because the expropriation of the wealth of others hardly acts as an incentive to productive labor. When combined with an overriding ideology, however—such as international communism, strongman rule may initially yield high outputs of basic commodities. Recall what the horse in George Orwell's classic book *Animal Farm* had to say about the shortcomings of other workers: "I will work harder." Yes, but for how long?

Dyads are inherently unstable. Within our framework of analysis, three countries have evidenced wild and destructive undisciplined government behaviors, unbalanced by any restraint or compromise. Both the now-defunct USSR and militant Chinese governments have, during the 119 years since the 20th century dawned, directly caused the state-sponsored extinctions of nearly 100 million innocent people; add in the killing fields of other socialistic regimes such as that of Cambodia, and the total reaches perhaps 110 million.[13] These deaths may get attributed both to experiments with bogus science and forced collectivization—and to punishment meted out to outgroups perceived by government to constitute threats, such as the kulaks and the Ukrainians in the 1930s and Uighurs today. "One death is a tragedy, a million is a statistic"—a chilling formula

(*Continued*)

[13] See Wikipedia article entitled "Mass killings under communist regimes" for an excellent review of literature on this subject.

(*Continued*)

attributed to Joseph Stalin. Countries lacking a balancing factor between government and people also have the just-mentioned tendency to engage in territorial aggrandizement at the expense of other nations—usually driven in part by the need to draw attention from domestic failures.

Only one means of preventing the emergence of totalitarian collectivism has thus far ever been conceived of in the mind of man or carried out by the efforts of people. Remember: Every battle is first won or lost in the human mind, before it is ever played out on the field of conflict. The Rule of Three constitutes that thought; achieving and keeping it working in the world require great moral courage and the physical and emotional effort of the whole man. While primitive versions of the Rule of Three at work appeared in ancient Chinese, Israeli, Greek, and Roman states, the Rule really came into its full force and power from out of the English Civil War and the American Revolution. Nothing like it emerged in the East, other than for the hierarchy of Confucian pairs in China—an early Rule of Three. The Rule of Three functions only under the rule of law, not of men, and works to have one member of the three adjudicate a conflict between the other two. The great example, of course, comes from the American Founding Fathers who established government comprised of executive, legislative, and judicial branches. Perhaps in the future we may all evolve to a point where the fundamental Rule of Three becomes: the passions, the interests, and the Golden Rule (which in its weak form signifies a basic concern for others than oneself; in the strong form, it equals love).

People respond to passions far more readily and powerfully than they do to interests. The most powerful movers for a nation take the form of founding myths—stories deeply ingrained within the psyche of every citizen of a nation. In order for a government to change something so deeply imbedded in every soul, propaganda must be employed. The challenge for the progressive and socialistic movements

(*Continued*)

in the 20th century has been the changing of founding myths which frequently contain elements from primitive, tribal periods into mythologies supportive of their new ideologies. A particularly nasty example: Nazi propaganda sought to modify ancient tribal myths regarding Teutonic warrior kings to accept the Nazi superman lies. The Chinese and Soviet governments attempted to replace what they termed *bourgeois* market capitalism beliefs with a "new man" of communism or socialism. Very significantly, despite 20th-century revolutions, warlord chaos, and Maoist attempts at crushing "truck, barter, and exchange" practices, the Chinese people—outside of China—always became successful entrepreneurs—just like their Ming-era forerunners. The same hard work–success mythology still remained in the Chinese mainland where significant Chinese people responded to the incentives offered under Chairman Deng; such people drove the Chinese economic revolution of 1979–2019.

As the general rule, *all attempts at creating new founding myths supplanting the old failed*—in every one of our six countries under consideration. Such efforts have failed everywhere in fact.

Case closed.

Part Two Conclusions

THE PROGENY OF INFORMATION INTERCOURSE

No guts, no glory.

American Air Force Major General
Frederick C. Blesse, 1955

Europe was created by history. America was created by philosophy.

Lady Margaret Thatcher

The Trade in Ideas

Whilst the Agricultural Revolution stimulated fundamental changes in how human beings in groups govern one another and stimulate trade for agriculture-related livestock, food stocks, tools and for some luxury items, it did nothing to advance intercourse in *ideas*—either about innovation or about human organization. And without such intercourse, advances in both areas took literally millennia to work themselves out.

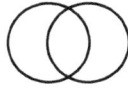

We have made the case here that the Printing Revolution created the technology for mass communication in such ideas, where learned thought and expression had formerly required laborious hand-copying of precious manuscripts that then needed to be also laboriously circulated. In this regard, the Printing Revolution not only facilitated intercourse regarding governance; it also made possible information and idea mass exchanges that facilitated all subsequent technological revolutions and innovations within those revolutions. Printing explains why radical changes in human governance required only decades to take root, rather than millennia—and also how new thoughts and ideas themselves provided stimulus for their next generations.

The Evolution of Thought

> A poor player that struts and frets his hour upon the stage and then is heard no more.
>
> William Shakespeare, *Macbeth* 5.5.2

> And some seed fell among thorns, and the thorns grew up, and choked it, and it yielded no fruit. But other seed fell on good ground and yielded a crop that sprang up and increased; and brought forth, some thirty, and some sixty, and some an hundred.
>
> *Mark* 5:7–8

The Printing Revolution stimulated the number of experiments conducted in thought directed at a wide range of human needs and wants; thoughts made by many players in the great game of discovery multiplied exponentially. Thoughts piled upon thoughts, ideas expanding like vegetables. Most thinkers themselves resemble Mr. Shakespeare's "poor player who struts and frets his hour upon the stage and then is heard no more." Yesterday's thinkers become like dust motes in the air, but the Great Printer keeps strewing forth new ideas and new thinkers daily. Thinkers' intercourse with the Great Printer keeps on generating more and more progeny. Most thinkers' thoughts die off immediately like a male insect that performs his lifetime's reproductive deed and then departs. In this regard, the sexual analogy to the classical meaning of *intercourse* takes hold.[14]

---

[14] See Appendix B for a short, playful recounting of how the combined notions of a number of overstimulated writers can create a veritable chaos of false information growing wildly until it finds itself deflated by objective facts on the ground.

Some ideas, however, take firm root in the ground fertilized by all the thoughts and ideas within the Great Printer's memory banks, now held online in the world wide web, and those thoughts and ideas yield the next generation of revolutions, small and large—revolutions both technological and within the governance controlling their applications to humanity, or perhaps to inhumanity. Just how this evolutionary sorting out works, in a version of natural selection, itself appears confusing. Very likely, some combination of ongoing marginal improvements in outcomes and the intuitive insights of genius thinkers capable of seeing all related ideas over all time in a view from 30,000 feet, and then expressing them all to one another, comprise the great intercourse between humankind and the whole created universe: MV = PQ.

We have established that the rich soil of Western thought with its voluminous experiments has yielded the best outcomes in terms of governance and technology yielding peace and plenty. Western liberty simply generates more experiments, and more freedom to the many thinkers who attempt to thinks things through. Welcome to the year 2019.

Part Three

Anno 2019 & Onwards

From Our Present Age to the Age to Come

Some say the world will end in fire/Some say in ice.
From what I've tasted of desire/I hold with those who favor fire.
But if I had to perish twice, I think I know enough of hate
To know that for destruction ice is also great
And would suffice.

Robert Frost, *Fire and Ice*

Future Light and Darkness/Yin and Yang

What does the future hold for humankind? Will it reach the bright shiny uplands of peace and plenty, or will it descend into a new Dark Age, lit only by the deceiving light of perverted science? Or, perhaps more likely, a world condition somewhere in between and very mixed in outcomes. In this last Part, we have a look at the tendencies in world affairs toward both authoritarian darkness and the light generated by the Rule of Three. Unlike the people of the East who foresee a never-ending interplay between the forces of light and darkness, Western thinkers hope for light to triumph permanently, rather than for two opposing forces forever to experience a cosmic interplay. Yin and yang versus utopianism.

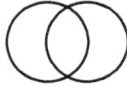

How Shall the Growth of Nations Happen?

In the last couple of decades leading up to 2019, we witnessed the collapse, and the rebuilding, of Soviet and Chinese empires—and the beginning recreation of a former ancient empire in Iran. In the immediate future, questions as to the viability of a Middle Eastern empire and of Russia's rambling pseudo-empire shall surely become resolved—probably in failure. The problems facing empire governance will become more and more apparent: growth by way of conquest inevitably leads to the revolt of conquered peoples—and then likely to extinction. The democratic West has traditionally grown, either or both in population and territory, through assimilation. While messy, assimilation possesses the virtue of creating new voluntary bonds to a people's new nation, without destroying earlier and more primitive bonds formed around small group affinities.

Two forces shall battle for supremacy, then, in the world to come: the ideological impulse for some form of world government versus the continuing trend toward the birthing of new nations out of the shells of the old. The United Nations presently contains 193 nations—most of them formed since the dawning of the 20th century. Do these new nations offer hope for progress, or a retrograde force for chaos and poverty? We see the growth of nations in number as, on the balance, more than benign—in fact a good, when not stimulated by revolutions caused by strongman rule.

Barring, then, the triumph of the strongman within totalitarian states both small and large, Rule of Three assimilation will triumph, but for the democratic world, vigilance regarding both autocracy and mob rule needs must be continual. Threats emanating from authoritarian ideologies will make the survival of some democracies a close-run thing indeed. Be very scared, for new technologies meant for good may easily get perverted into ill.

Of National Psychologies and Psychoses

The Scotch brigade went over the top.
They thought they heard a penny drop.
Inky dinky *parlez vous.*
from a popular World War I Western soldiers' song.

It is very difficult to comprehend the behaviors of states tending toward the totalitarian. It helps to see nations as possessing distinct personalities—psychological makeups if you will. Thinking in raw psychological terms, both individuals and nations may choose to employ *projection, displacement,* and *sublimation* in order to gain security and some measure of relief from guilt. At some point—for both individuals and groups even as large as nations, such defense mechanisms cross over a warning line from the normal to the psychotic. We make the argument that authoritarian impulses all rely upon projection and displacement in order to win converts and protect their power bases—in the process heading full tilt toward the psychotic. Individual liberty, on the other hand, along with the laws of life and the pursuit of happiness, make up a grand Rule of Three that tends toward a psychological normality of a nation.

The nature of darkness is the oppression of the many; the nature of light is individual liberty. The great gain for mankind under liberty is the sheer number of experiments in every area of human life that liberty generates, thereby creating a powerful force for a healthy evolutionary progress in technology and governance. Authoritarian monopolies upon ideas and thinking merely yield misery—partly for want of experiments.

Of Natural Communities and Bridges

It is a fundamental principle that people at liberty tend to congregate together around common, shared *affinities*. In so doing, people form what may be termed natural communities. Within primitive tribal cultures, people possessed single affinities, tribal in nature, and so belonged to only one natural community. In modern civil societies, the same individual may claim membership in a number of natural communities—extended families, churches, ethnic clubs, sports teams, local towns and neighborhoods, and of course states, regions, and nations. Each comprises a natural community, and those communities often have a hierarchical nature sorted by each individual in order of his or her own ultimate concerns. Many of these communities possess a voluntary nature; one joins because one wishes to join. Of course, communities involving governance do have some measure of compulsion placed upon membership, and here assimilation works to minimize frictions amongst individuals and communities.

Such nestings of natural communities develop natural bridges connecting each to each, bridges that form largely out of inter-community intercourse—trade in goods and services, beliefs and ideas, and labor. We make the case that the last best hope for all mankind takes the shape by analogy of an archipelago of islands, great and small, connected by robust bridges of human intercourse. It is far easier to build a bridge than to rebuild a nation. In this great scheme of things, those natural communities higher up the totem pole receive by natural contract only limited functions from the far greater number of people in natural communities below them—functions such as defense of the realm, coinage, and the protection of universal, existential liberties to be possessed by all—such as life, liberty itself, and the pursuit of individual happiness.

This suggested third way has recently become supercharged by the third and last technological revolution that we see as radically changing how we may be governed in the future, a way offering far greater hope than either straightforward warfare or playing games with balance-of-power strategies. This last technological revolution we term the Intercourse Revolution, for its technological basis lies within its internet-focused radical efficiency gains for every area of business, governance, and diplomacy.

You may well inquire as to what then would ensure that another natural community would not hold ideological beliefs inimical to its own—beliefs favoring slavery or racism for instance. One protection would always take the form of the existential beliefs stated within a natural community's founding documents—such as life, liberty and happiness. The other recourse would be that of shunning and shaming—tools that the English and American Quakers for example used to good effect. Bridges of intercourse can be blocked—as America currently has been doing with regard to several authoritarian regimes in the Far and Middle East. Like assimilation, these tools take some time to achieve their ends, but they offer the great benefit of maintaining high levels of peace and plenty whilst they work their results out.

Public Servants and Private Corruption

Without a doubt, the gravest threat worldwide to peace and plenty takes the form of the private vices of public servants—in a word, of corruption. Private vice amongst public servants interacting with their bedfellows and with corrupt private sector miscreants exists the world over and has no easy answers solving this existential and perennial problem. It exists within authoritarian states and democratic states under the Rule of Three alike, often forming international nests such as the one that took shape around the wealthy private citizens and public servants of the Ukraine and high government officials within the United States and other Western nations. While corruption springs eternal within the human breast, we will end this tome by considering the worst solutions to ending it other than all the rest.

Chapter Seven

What Happens Next?

To put the world in order, we must first put the nation in order; to put the nation in order, we must first put the family in order; to put the family in order; we must first cultivate our personal life; we must first set our hearts right.

Attrib. to Confucius

The disintegration of a regime often starts from the ideological area.... If the ideological defenses are breached, other defenses become very difficult to hold.

Xi Jinping, 2013

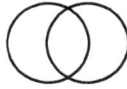

Overview: *What, why, how*? The themes for a study of what has happened and may happen in the future frame our study for Part Three of this book. By 1989, apparent triumphs for post–Cold War Western liberalism, and also Eastern dynasty making, created sensibilities projecting a new world prosperity—and even the end of history. What happened? What caused victory to hang fire? We trace the thinking of the dominant Western foreign policy elites as disappointment replaced utopian thinking. Their focus upon culture as an explanation merely confuses description with cause. What went wrong needs a look under the rug—as in the case of Middle Eastern violence being driven by the cult of the Strong Horse. Assimilating people from deeply strongman-oriented founding myths means that any assimilation by these groups will take far longer than the usual three generations. Assimilation versus extermination may be the future for much of the world's transient populations.

Introduction: Whatever Happened to Victory?

> The whole world is festering with unhappy souls/The French hate the Germans, the Germans hate the Poles….
>
> American Kingston Trio, *The Merry Minuet*

In the West following 1979, a great fear overtook the liberal foreign ministers' establishment: The crazy cowboy-actor in the American White House will get us all killed in a Russian nuclear Armageddon! Then came 1989 and the fall of the Berlin wall, and the liberal West began debating the nature of the new world order. In the East, the dragons nodded sagely; they kept their heads about them and worked steadily to become richer.

By 2009, China had become very wealthy indeed: It appeared to the mandarins that after five rebellions/revolutions in the land, occurring over a 100-year period, a new Chinese dynasty had indeed received the mandate of heaven. China would resume its rightful dominant place in the world. In the West well before 2009, many people wondered, "Whatever happened to our victory over the Evil Empire? Why have we not found peace and plenty?" By 2009, Middle East turmoil followed by the beginning of the Great Recession had shattered America's confidence.

Perhaps this has to do with world leaders putting the nation at the top of their concerns, rather than following the ancient Chinese maxim of building a healthy nation from the bottom up: right relationships, family, and work unit done well in millions of cases yields national harmony.

The dominant Thesis: What Could Possibly Go Wrong?

> Not just... the passing of a particular period of post-war history, but the end of history as such: that is, the end-point of mankind's ideological evolution and the universalization of Western liberal democracy as the final form of human government.
>
> Francis Fukuyama, *The End of History*

When we began our exploration for the sources of harmony, or peace and plenty upon earth, our first shock came from considering Dr. Stephen Pinker's 2011 book *The Better Angels of Our Nature: Why Violence Has Declined.* As has most of the Western world thinkers, we had imagined that the just-passed century generated more violent death than any previous one. Wrong—in a relative sense. Violence had steadily declined per millions of population—a *what* happened matter. We then wondered *why* this pattern pertained. Here, we found ourselves parting company with Dr. Pinker, and we also discovered a whole recent trail of Western thought that apparently led him to his explanation. That explanation, to put things simply: the triumph of Western liberalism. But does this explanation hold up against the facts? After all, as the 18th-century American lawyer-statesman John Adams put it: "Facts are stubborn things."

The trail begins with a landmark 1992 book by Francis Fukuyama entitled *The End of History and the Last Man.* As quoted from above, this entertaining work saw the culmination of all human history arriving after the Cold War—in the form of Western liberal democracy—bringing with it the final evolution to the *New Man*. That's it; it's all over: maybe not quite Nietzsche's Superman, but close enough. Right before Fukuyama's book appeared, the First Gulf War of 1990–1991 had already blown up his thesis. The American 9/11 event closely followed after, blowing up with it the dream towers of liberal academia. In military language, the two events made for a "straddle." The reply to the failed liberal New Man thesis came in the 1996 book entitled *The Clash of Civilizations and the Remaking of World Order* by Samuel Huntington. The new Western liberal thesis advanced by him held that *cultural* and religious identities would become the future source of the world's conflicts: Future wars would be fought between the world's eight basic cultures, rather than between countries—a comforting thought. And so we had it: the final word regarding the sources of conflict. Wars would still continue to be fought, destroying hopes for harmony, but a different lot would be fighting them—thanks to Western democratic liberalism. And then along came Dr. Pinker to tell us not to worry, violence has been going steadily down, relatively. What could possibly go wrong with the basic democratic liberalism causality thesis?

Well, we saw continuing conflict betwixt co-religionists in Muslim regions, whilst the various Christian denominations worldwide pretty much made peace amongst themselves. ISIS rose up in an infantile effort to recreate something like the Ottoman Empire. The post-religion

European Union began a trip to dis-union. Nominally Catholic South Americans began putting liberation theology into practice against one another. China began fearing, and frightening, its Hong Kong cousins. Pressures rose and fell within the North-South Korean boiler of contention, raising ominous red flags regarding nuclear war. All in all, it has seemed as though the peoples of the same fundamental cultures warred more against one another than against other cultures—partly, to be sure, because of proximity. It appears easier to operationalize hating one's neighbor than hating the Russian bear or the United States bogey man. Meanwhile, the American democratic liberal establishment has declared war upon its fellow Americans who resent their globalist outlook—a war that will continue to play out for another generation.

The above-mentioned democratic liberalism trio of post–Cold War thinkers did not have the field to themselves, however. In fact, the earliest entry into the rethinking-world-order game came, not out of left field, but out of right. This line of thinking saw the apparent triumph of the West coming from market capitalism, rather than from democratic socialism. The book we have in mind appeared in 1988 under the title *The Fatal Conceit*, by Friedrich Hayek—a scholar who saw the defeat of leftist empires arising from out of the marketplace's ability to bury the socialists' dreams for world conquest in an explosion of productive might yielding prosperity. The *fatal conceit* (a phrase from Adam Smith) was the left's belief in the superiority of non-market socialism. Dr. Hayek, too, forecast peace and plenty in the coming world order, but coming through marketplace capitalism's wealth-generating power. This alternative view got buried under a storm of anti-capitalist propaganda, a reaction creating the great American political conflict to come.

These bitter American political conflicts will continue into the future because that country's democratic liberal establishment cannot bear the overthrow of its fundamental racism thesis, a belief set that has driven its favorable stance on globalism for some 60 years now.

The Sirens' Song: Oh, Culture!

> When people see a strong horse and a weak horse, by nature they will like the strong horse.
>
> Osama Bin Laden

What went wrong? The West listened to the sirens' song of culture. In a sordid history of the attempted undoing of its previous blatant scientific racism, Western thinkers, in a fit of sublime sublimation, seized upon a handy, guilt-assuaging tool, borrowed from cultural anthropology. Culture, they reasoned, could explain all of the nastiness emanating from people: People do nasty things? Their racist culture explains it. Culture has become the single factor explaining everything—as Dr. Huntington would have us believe. And, because culture has become the grand bulwark against previous claims of scientific racism, culture can never get challenged: Challenge culture, and you become *de facto* a racist yourself. The fundamental flaw in the culture paradigm, of course, is this: Anything claiming to explain everything explains nothing, but simply stands out as a tautology—a truism, but a meaningless one.

In reality, culture as an analytical term has two fatal flaws: It floats on the surface of any significant issue; it is descriptive, not analytical at all. It also represents a summary result of complex underlying issues, not a cause of them. Culture fails as an explanation for behavior. It tells us nothing about why people choose to behave in the ways that they do (more about this in the next chapter). This does not signify that culture as a descriptive set of categories has no intellectual value. Quite the opposite; the tools of cultural anthropology may display to us issues that require deeper exploration and understanding. Our prime example here appears as a book that reveals previously unrecognized distinctions present within the out-migration from Britain to its American colonies: *Albion's Seed* by David Hackett Fischer. Fischer's overview of that period in Anglo social history largely gets driven by the results obtained from cultural anthropology. We show in our Chapter Five the roots of these four great out-migrations and why and how they shaped the whole American experience, roots that make trivial such cultural facts as how each migrating group prepared their food. Cultural anthropology puts paid to the idea that the American colonists constituted a culturally homogeneous group that really loved one another; in reality, each group of colonists thoroughly hated the others—just as left and right in America today. Why the four groups behaved so differently, however, forces us to look into their deep pasts, to their founding mythologies.

As a case study in exploring the behavioral roots of a culturally defined group, consider the matter of Middle Eastern Muslims—one of Dr. Huntington's eight fundamental world cultures. Muslim culture, of course, does not present a homogeneously peaceful face to the world:

Whilst some Muslim groups exhibit pacifist behaviors—such as the Sufi—most do not, and most make war, first and foremost, amongst one another. The first clue to an understanding of *why* so much violence occurs: Its people desire what we have previously termed strongman leadership. Dig a bit deeper into the history of the Muslim movement, and you discover a theme that comprises a major part of the founding mythology of its broader culture: strong horse/weak horse. Always follow the strong horse. As Lee Smith writes in *The Strong Horse,* violence rules this culture's politics and social order—and also its relations with all outsiders. Osama Bin Laden got it partly right: Some people will always choose the strong horse.

The strong horse image itself dates back some 1,500 years, and likely arose even before Islam's founding era. It comes, of course, from out of the desert nomad Arab tribal experience, the strong horse raiders, and got shaped by tribal thefts and violence directed toward the then-new agricultural societies of the fertile crescent. The strong horse ethic, then, probably arose some 3,000 to 4,000 years ago—in all, a long time to keep fighting. Even the Scots-Irish immigrants to America declared peace in only a few hundred years. We do see the dim-past shadows of the Arab strong horse leaders in the overthrow story of the ancient Persian Empire that once controlled East-West trade along the Silk Road routes of western Asia. Persian rule then yielded to the overwhelming fighting ethic of the strong horse Arabs who created an Islamic Persian Empire in its place. That empire, of course, fell to Alexander the Great—but enough of this story. Suffice it to say, modern Islam has deep roots in the past.

This brings us to an important variant upon the Rule of Three: It takes at least 3 generations for an in-migrating group to assimilate into its own members the founding myths and values of its new land. The assimilation process involves the first-generation immigrants, their native-born neighbors, and their second-generation youthful progeny—who may begin to do such things as learn a new language and adopt the social relations of their birth nation. Normally, by the third generation, most immigrants have lost the desire to cling to their grandparents' language or social arrangements—all summed up in a culture that they will largely abandon. So went the assimilation pattern in the new American nation, and for that matter in the developing Chinese nation—both old empire and new nation-state. The Chinese case, of course, got marked at one point by its own overthrow by its assimilating northern neighbors, the Mongols.

The pattern appears deeply embedded in the American experience, as well as the experiences of many other nations. For example, a first generation of Chinese (or Italians or whatever) followed by a generation of Chinese-Americans (*hyphenated-Americans* as the saying goes) followed by succeeding generations of just-Americans who eventually become curious about their country-of-origin roots.

Sometimes, however, the Rule of Three for assimilation becomes a case of arrested development. Assimilation may take more than three generations. It may take 100—or even more. The Arab strong horse founding myth still rules much of the Middle, and Far, East even today. Its adhering generations could well exceed 100. Some of us come from tribes of very slow learners indeed. It seems that we only learn through experience, and she is a harsh teacher who begins with us gently, but when we do not learn only increases the pain.

Assimilation or Extermination

> The man of system, on the contrary, is apt to be very wise in his own conceit, and is often so enamoured with the supposed beauty of his own ideal plan of government, that he cannot suffer the smallest deviation from any part of it. He goes on to establish it completely and in all its parts, without any regard either to the great interests, or to the strong prejudices which may oppose it. He seems to imagine that he can arrange the different members of a *great society* with as much ease as the hand arranges the different pieces upon a chess-board. He does not consider that the pieces upon the chess-board have no other principle of motion besides that which the hand impresses upon them, but that, in the great chess-board of human society, every single piece has a principle of motion of its own, altogether different from that which the legislator might chuse to impress upon it.
>
> Adam Smith, *The Theory of Moral Sentiments*

Only two means exist for pacifying the population of a nation, or of absorbing another group, of culturally distinct peoples: *assimilation* or *extermination*. Assimilation has the unfortunate quality of taking a long time, at least a generation for foreigners to grow into citizens. The grease that moves things along is called liberty—which allows future citizens broad freedoms within which to learn a nation's founding myths and principles for ethical conduct. One might note in this regard that the United States successfully assimilated every current one of its states into a new nation, not without some initial violations of liberty with regard especially to African Americans, Catholics, Irish and Mormons. In the end, the constitutional mandates of liberty won out. A strong horse leader may only keep moving the people like chess pieces in the game of life by applying brute force. Within triadic governance, each chess piece possesses a power of movement all his or her own.

On the surface of things, one might regard the totalitarian nations as having inherent advantages with regard to stability and staying power. The Rule of Three, after all, does appear to be inherently, well—messy. However, one should regard Mr. Churchill's admonition that "democracy is the worst form of government—except for all the rest." Underlying all the messiness, triadic nations may add either people or territories without recourse to force merely by allowing its people who want to join it maximal free rein—degrees of freedom—to pursue their own predilections. In so doing, triadic nations allow new people to discover for themselves the beauty that has already been wrought by a nation-state's founders contained within their founding mythologies. The seemingly weaker way of nation building turns out to be the stronger.

Without the benefit of assimilation, a nation has no choice but to use force of some form to conform peoples and territories to its will. Any nation that does so becomes an empire. By definition, empires use force to subjugate citizens and new non-citizens alike. Over the centuries, a number of extermination strategies have been employed by growing empires: physical exterminations, yes; but also by employing massive relocations of group populations, setting minority groups against one another, and through various forms of slavery—all the while using propaganda and "the lights of perverted science" to enforce ideological mandates. In the last century, the Soviets and the Germans employed such techniques. The Soviets followed mad agricultural science, and the Nazis practiced inhuman medical "experiments" upon concentration camp inmates.[1]

The empires of old, such as Persia, Rome, and China, with their limited means of mind control through propaganda, could successfully

[1]The Nazi regime also debunked the emerging science around nuclear fission as being "Jewish science"; following their own Arian science, they bombed out on developing a nuclear bomb.

enforce obedience to a far-away and foreign-to-the-people power to a limited degree—and therefore survive for centuries. The Chinese people, for instance, traditionally claimed to have great freedom: "we can do anything we want—so long as we don't get caught"—all made possible by very ingenious people and inefficient bureaucracies. Not so in the modern world of immediate communication and tightly controlled intercourse generally: In spite of great gains made in snitching on people, modern growth-empires such as the USSR, Nazi Germany, and Japan lasted mere decades: The people, not only the bureaucrats, may take advantage of greater information. The new Iranian empire may turn out to be a stillborn monster-child. It turns out that forcing ideological conformity upon a people's traditions of many centuries, which all empires attempt to do, has become an ugly and vicious exercise in failure. It will, sadly continue as one pattern in our future history.

We may conclude that a corollary to our earlier technology principle—that technological revolutions yield changes in governance—must get introduced. That corollary simply states that the changes resulting from technological revolutions may be either for the good, or for downright evil purposes. The movable type revolution in England yielded the mass communication of public opinion and the modern democratic nation-state driven by it.[2] In dyadic countries, mass-communicated propaganda has yielded immense power for harm to a country's ordinary citizens. In some populist movements, especially in Latin and South America, the excesses of the mob have destroyed the prosperity of whole nations—Venezuela being the primary present example of the results of strongman rule.

All of this said, we cannot help but conclude that the present Chinese effort to impose ideological conformity will yield some severe negative consequences. The conundrum: Will the CCP ideology of Chairman Xi, who is the latest emperor, overcome the thousands-of-years-old requirement that the Emperor act under the Mandate of Heaven (*Tian*)? Emperors who fail the test of virtuous leadership lose the approval of heaven's gods. Disasters, including those of the natural variety, could and may still be interpreted as indicators of such loss. Will massive crop and livestock failures provoke a loss of the mandate? How about international trade failures? Rebellions? Will the Hong Kong uprising trigger the withdrawal

[2] See Appendix B for a somewhat humorous example of how the technology allowing mass communication also can create virtual flash mobs when rumor goes viral.

of mandate? Or, will all work out well in the end, and will Chairman Xi's China Dream triumph? We cannot know. On the other side of the world, it appears at least as likely that the ongoing destruction of America's stabilizing founding mythology carried out by its progressive movement will tear it apart. How this ideological warfare will end, nobody knows.

Chairman Xi is quite correct regarding dyadic regimes: "The disintegration of a regime often starts from the ideological area." This is precisely the hazard that the present Chinese regime faces. Can the brutal enforcement of an ideology imposed upon the Chinese people during the current 70-year period overcome the traditions of over a thousand years? Will another Chairman like Deng appear to balance out *yin* and *yang*? Stay tuned.

The present situation in China has three possible longer-term outcomes: Successful strict dyadic control over its people, and neighbors; internal rebellion leading to severe dislocations in governance; a new movement toward authoritarian triadic government. One reasonable viewpoint sees the Xi dynasty as merely an interruption to China's healthy progress toward the triadic form of authoritarian rule, one in which people's rights and the rule of law pertain everywhere.

In truth, East and West differ radically regarding ultimate possibilities and goals: The East, at a deep level, believes that the constant struggle between *yin* and *yang* will always bedevil us. The pulse of Chinese history has cycled through periods of benign authoritarian rulership under a Confucianism that resembles the Rule of Three and then to strict law and order and outrageous corruption.[3] The West tends to view future possibilities in a utopian light: perfection is indeed possible. The cynic holds that the East will be proven right.

Conclusions

The patterns of theft and violence against human harmony—peace and plenty—displayed by some groups will continue to shape the ongoing history of the world for the foreseeable future. History did not die out peacefully when the Soviet Empire fell. Underneath the polite veneer of Western liberal democratic thinking about culture, the harsh reality of a terrible deep past will continue to well up to horrify those of us who do not wish for the strong horse to win.

[3] See Appendix C for an examination of the pernicious effects of corruption.

But this will not be the whole story. It will remain only a part of what may happen next. Looking on the sunny side of life, the *why* of what has happened may lead us to the *how* of changing the age-old pattern of *what*.

***

Discoveries:

What will happen in the future? It appears that the Western liberalism has not triumphed post–Cold War.

Continued international conflict seems most likely, without some significant changes in the present world order.

The dominant consensus on what happened following 1989 cannot stand up to scrutiny, and appeals to culture ring hollow.

Culture has proven a failure as an explanation for what has happened—being merely descriptive, not analytical.

Strong horse/strongman mythologies appear likely to dominate the behavior of many nations.

Cases of arrested development have blocked the pattern of more primitive groups led by dictators assimilating peaceful approaches to governance.

Extermination rather than assimilation has and will continue to threaten any efforts at peaceful solutions to conflicts.

Corollary to the revolution-evolution model: Sometimes technological revolutions yield dark-side governance evolutions.

The cult of the strong leader threatens all efforts for peace and plenty and assures continued efforts at exterminating rivals.

Ideological conformity must be enforced by strongman nations—or else.

Chapter Eight

The *Why* for What Will Happen

Overview: Why have so many leaders chosen a fork in the roadway of history that leads to impoverishment and even death for their countrymen? The unholy triad, the pursuit of wealth, power, and sex is a very good place to start. Why not choose peace, plenty, and joy? Our search for answers leads us to the matters of face, deception, and self-deception as explanatory principles. Psychotic personalities, of leaders and whole nations alike, manipulate the unwary—including themselves—by employing the psychological black arts of projection, displacement and sublimation. At the extreme, powerful members of government create crime families akin to the Mafia in order to build personal empires of vast wealth and power by, in effect, becoming whoremasters who infect entire governments through their corrupt actions. Sleep with a whore and get the pox.

Introduction: An Unholy Trinity

When you come to a fork in the road, take it.

Yogi Berra

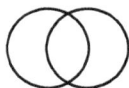

It seems from recorded history that men who seek to lead others often get motivated by what might be termed an unholy trinity: the pursuit of wealth, power, and sex, where power fills the role of a mediating leg enabling the other two. When this triad replaces that of peace, plenty, and right relationships, quite literally all hell breaks loose. What has happened, and will continue to happen, then, involves murder and rape, theft and destruction, and general mayhem.

One of the basic postulates of microeconomics states that more is better than less—which explains much of what drives us, the acquisitive species. The historical corollary states that it is far easier to steal than to build—in order to get more. It may take hundreds of years to build a temple or cathedral, and only a few hours to loot and burn it down. Why labor under the burning sun to raise food crops when they may simply get stolen from some poor sod at harvesttime? Grow it or steal it: a fork-in-the-road time for choosing for each individual or leader. When you come to a fork in the road, take it.

When you boil everything right down, each individual fork-in-the-road choice helps determine the direction that entire nations and civilizations will take—like the proverbial butterfly flapping its wings in China: Will it be that fork leading to peace and plenty, or the other leading to conflict and poverty? *Why*, we wonder, do people so inerrantly fail to take the right road at the fork?

It will do no good to attribute bad behaviors to bad emotions or characteristics. We so often encounter the pejorative term *greedy*—as though greed explains some nasty behaviors. In reality, greed only describes some conduct, not that conduct's source. The same holds true for two others of the bad emotions' triad: envy and lust. They also lack explanatory power. It simply will not do to screech out the bad triad and expect that bad behavior will change. We must dig deep below the surface of bad behaviors to comprehend why the bad and the evil exist, and often thrive. Very deeply down in each person's soul, anger and fear live—kissing cousins in the darkness of the human heart. Resolving these two primal emotions can lead a civil social order, but only if they can be brought out into the light of understanding.

At the human race's development/evolution level, the resolution lies within the passions/interests paradigm—of how passions evolved into principled interests. What most of us desire to replace gut-level reactions from the passions takes the form of civilized conduct shaped by concern for the other as well as for the self—ultimately defined by one of the three forms of the Golden Rule: "Do unto others as you would have them do unto you." By at least 2,500 years ago, the Golden Rule had been recognized and spread through written intercourse within the world's great civilizations: Chinese, Hebrew, and Greco-Roman. By some 400 years ago, the Printing Revolution spawned mass intercourse debating and refining the civil interests of social orders. Still, behind public images, conflict and extreme violence have prevailed—in absolute terms greater than ever. *Why?*

Face Masks

> ...and people loved the darkness rather than the light because their works were evil. For everyone who does wicked things hates the light and does not come into the light, lest his works should be exposed.
>
> *John* 3:19–20

> One may smile, and smile, and be a villain.
>
> William Shakespeare, *Hamlet* 1.5

> If you can practice these five things with all the people, you can be called *jen:* courtesy, generosity, honesty, persistence, and kindness.
>
> Confucius

We learn from the same big three ancient civilizations that the matter of *face* matters greatly. For the ancient Chinese, two words with differing meanings evolved, as we have noted in our Chapter Two. *Mainzi* connoted social position; one's manner should communicate that position, framed within the five Confucian pairs. *Lian*, on the other hand, communicated familial obligation: the one more public, the other more private. A person came to possess *jen* or *ren*—fundamental humaneness, something akin to Western *honor*—when one's deeds over time matched what one's face projected. Ancient Chinese opera utilized face painting to create masks symbolizing various virtues and vices. Of course, even Westerners have some familiarity with Chinese masks—if only from videos of Chinese New Year celebrations. One of the most popular of such masks depicts the dragon, an image the we have used extensively to represent the public face of Chinese government and business leaders, and in fact for China generally.

Ancient Greek drama, both for tragedy and comedy, employed actual masks held up by the actors, masks that employed exaggerated expressions to project the physical appearances of extremes in character.

Big smiley and frowny faces, masks that the actors changed as they played various roles. The actors remained hidden behind the face masks. Tragedy and comedy. Face for the Greeks conveyed a sense of merely distinguishing the physical appearances of each individual, somewhat akin to Aristotle's care to distinguish analytical categories by physical characteristics. For the Greeks, what you see is what you get. For the ancient Hebrews, barred by Mosaic Law from making images, an overriding concern involved hypocrisy—the quality of appearing to be one thing whilst doing another.

Face, then, in all three traditions had something to do with the matter of making good impressions; the complexity came within the possibilities opened up by deception. One may smile and smile and be a villain: masks of virtue versus an underlying nature of vice. A basic *deception story* ran through the many spheres of ancient life, particularly the military. Indeed, Chinese military strategy as presented by Sun Tzu made deception into an art form, as did the Renaissance Machiavelli for politics. And Clausewitz taught us that warfare consists of policy carried out by other means. A good deal, then, of the impetus behind theft and violence came from the possibilities of employing deception to fool one's target of opportunity—thereby making theft far cheaper than growing something. The same deception story plays out again and again to this day, often in the form of public virtue/private corruption—and will continue to do so for the foreseeable future.

Face masks, then, play a powerful role regarding theft and violence, but the ancient world appears to have neglected, or never perceived, the more malicious masks that humans may adopt. The ancients appear to have largely assumed that the individual behind the mask knows perfectly well his, or her, true nature as a deceiver. What if this turns out not to be so? What if the most harmful masks consist of the ones that an individual, or a group, uses to hide a true identity from his, or itself—masks achieving self-deception?

There are just a few stories, and the deception story inherently possesses the most wicked complexity of all. An archetypal example: Two tribal hunting parties detect each other in a large forest. The leader of one group presents a friendly face to the other group who let down their guards. The first group then suddenly attacks and subdues the members of the second. They then procure for themselves the other group's game and weapons. Simple deception. The infuriated leader of the second group threatens violence upon their release, his face taking on an appearance of murderous delight in the thought of it all. Members of the first group cannot be sure if the threat is real, but they see murder in his face. The first group's members then come to believe, from the ferocity of the threats, that the second group had intended to capture and kill them all along; the first group had fortunately acted first, they believe, to protect themselves. Those second tribe guys were really intending to kill us! In a frenzy, they slay all of the second group members.

Then, the first group begins to feel remorse. Maybe they did not mean us harm. Now, it becomes more than simple deception. The simple passion of the moment—greed one might say—has become mixed in motive. It has become a complex act of self-deception. To cover the guilt stemming from their actions, the first tribe's leader announces that he knows the second tribe intended to steal and rape their women. "We did it all in self-defense," he proclaims. It turns out that the first tribe had the previous night worked itself into a wild and drunken frenzy, a frenzy in which they had acted out precisely what they intended to do the that other tribe in the area and its women. Deception/self-deception. Fear + hatred = guilt.

Those of us from civilized tribes of course would never perform such primitive acts—or would we? If you believe yourself free from such crude behaviors, do have a look at William Golding's classic *Lord of the Flies*, a book written in our own modern era, for it will chill you to the bone: The imaginary beast that seems to appear to one of the boys stranded on a Pacific island, that beast who threatens to kill them all, has a reality behind its false image. The Lord of the Flies lives within us all—ancient and modern alike.

Psychological Masks: Personalities and Psychoses

> Psychological projection is a defense mechanism in which the human ego defends itself against unconscious impulses or qualities (both positive and negative) by denying their existence in themselves while attributing them to others.
>
> *Wikipedia*

> The fault, dear Brutus, lies not in our stars/But in ourselves that we are underlings.
>
> *Julius Caesar* I.iii.140–41

> *Sublimation* (*psychology*): The diversion of the energy in a sexual or other biological impulse from its immediate goal to a more acceptable social, moral, or aesthetic nature or use. …a purification or refinement; ennoblement.
>
> *Wikipedia*

The psychology (the science of the mind and of behavior) of the individual personality unsurprisingly developed after the physical and biological sciences, and even after the social sciences of economics and sociology. The reason for such a progression from the study of the inanimate to the study of human intimacy: It is very difficult to permit one's self to get examined under a microscope—stripped bare for all to see. Rather than undergo such humility, most of us choose to obfuscate, and our favorite means, our triad of little darlings, are what modern psychologists call *projection*, *displacement* and *sublimation*. We have noted a common definition for projection above; we have also used a line from Shakespeare's *Julius Caesar* to illustrate in a quite brilliant manner the rejection of displacement: We human beings individually appear all too readily willing to blame our failures upon others—be the other our boss, a political rival, a family member or a friend, or an enemy soldier. Gaius Cassius in Shakespeare's play renounces to Brutus the displacement of their own failures onto Caesar: The fault lies within ourselves that we are underlings.

Groups of people and whole nations also possess what we might call personalities—perhaps displaying strong behavioral tendencies still within the range of normal—such as "dour Scots" and "carefree Polynesians." Some social scientists will even refer to Western versus Eastern personality traits. Here, we have an interest in how projection, displacement, and sublimation may be examined to understand better the behaviors of entire nations—especially those nations of an authoritarian tendency, where national personalities may cross over into psychosis—a trip from reality to unreality. The fundamental principle: Such regimes require enemies—real or fabricated—from without to dispel rebellion from within. Classical displacement.

The Nazis came to power in the 1930s by using a combination of unlawful force and propaganda. Propaganda had two facets: a false claiming of a perverted version of a Prussian founding myth and a false creating of an outside, existential enemy—the Jews, the betrayers of the nation. The twin tools worked to create projection and displacement.

Then, in order to assuage guilt, and do a great deal of shame dumping, the country's leaders projected their own wrongdoing upon minority groups perceived as evil or unworthy: Jews of course, but also the mentally ill, gypsies, communists, homosexuals, and greedy capitalists. These twin pathologies resulted in acts of indescribable evil. And then, postwar, many German people attempted blame shifting, claiming that they had been kept in the dark as to their leaders' evil conduct. The sins of the fathers are visited upon the sons, even to seven generations—although this time it took but two. Again, displacement. They all knew—tacitly, they all knew.

Conquest, famine, pestilence, and death—the four horsemen of the Apocalypse. These four, armed horsemen in ages past brought their terrible consequences to innumerable tribes and nations. Their long reign may soon be ending—to be replaced by their new age equivalents: lawfare, hidden sexual abuses, extortion, and character assassination. The original four bestial wrongs modern men have sublimated into these the new four: After all, we are far more humane today than in ancient times; we don't actually kill anyone. And the modern four horsemen ride together in a troop called *corruption.*[1]

Forming the abnormal personalities of corrupt nations, then, these three psycho-social sicknesses distort and dirty entire nations. Projection, displacement, and sublimation together constitute an unholy triad, a Three-Legged Stool from the dark side—one in which the third leg, sublimation, allows the internal guilt generated by wrong conduct to receive relief—a safety-valve of sorts. Sublimation says to the soul: After all, I am doing this for the good of the nation—or my clan, or family, or my son. That's how members on the dark side sleep at night, though perhaps fitfully.

Within traditional governance, sublimation took the form of kingship or divine right. In our own age, in the West particularly, it has taken the form of the public servant heroes "working for the little man." If some kings of old operated, in effect, "crime families," large governments today frequently comprise numerous crime families—and this holds for both West and East, Cowboys and Dragons alike. The task for the present age is to bequeath to the future age a human world stripped bare of such totally corrupt creatures.

---

[1]See Appendix C for a detailed look at corruption in high places.

At the highest levels of play, the corruption game pits two Rules of Three against one another: the dark side trio wealth, sex, and power obtained through the psychological tools of projection, displacement and sublimation versus the Rule of Three giving light—life, liberty, and the pursuit of happiness attained through love, joy, and peace—or as the East would say, through harmony. In a sense the battle resembles the Taoists' idea of *yin* and *yang*, primeval forces continually battling one against the other in a never-ending dualistic conflict. The powers of light needs must remain ever vigilant lest the darkness overwhelm us all.

Within the Middle East, the Persians of old-turned modern-day Iranian Islamists seek to build a new empire. So, too, has ISIS, and even modern Turkey. All engage in the same national predilections for displacement of their own hatred upon the other—the Jews primarily, and America. The danger in this scheme is that one might run out of manufactured enemies, and then what? Invent some more.

Without an outside, manufactured enemy, a ruling tyrant taking advantage of his power becomes vulnerable to challengers claiming that he has ripped off the people of his own country. When internal conditions do in fact bring misery to many—usually caused by the corrupt leader and his party siphoning off economic surpluses through extortion, outright theft, and bribery—the impoverished masses, eventually backed up by the military, will agitate for a replacement leader, one strong enough to force a palace coup or populist uprising. He will appear as a man "of the people"—very likely wrapping himself in Lady Democracy's robe, for one election. When the chaotic mob democracy becomes bad enough, this new "man of the people" will seize power—backed up by the military and the disenchanted poor. The old strongman will have the peasants' anger displaced upon him by the rising new strongman. Dictator and peasantry alike project their own passions for death and destruction upon the other: Each imagine that its enemy wants to do to them what they wish to do to their enemy. Knowing only the impoverishing stability of a dictator, the impoverished majority will always throw their support to another strongman, believing that only a strongman can successfully protect them. Several such situations playing out over time inevitably lead to the creation of a culture of the strong man, or strong horse. The charade will continue—perhaps for hundreds of years more. Latin and South America have lived in the strongman trap now at least since the 18th century—and under primitive totalitarian empires such as the Mayan, for far longer.

Strongman beliefs held in the deep heart of a people represent the fundamental reason why migrants from amongst them seeking refuge from tyranny will always threaten any well-ordered civil society into which they move. Even within that new nation, they will unerringly support strongman public figures. The Rule of Three applies here: It will normally take three generations for strongman beliefs to die out in such an immigrant group, before the foundational myths of their new nation begin to take hold.

The best to be hoped for under traditional dictators, then, consists of a strongman who allows his people some measure of local independence and who can, like a prize bull, breed sons who will follow in his semi-benevolent footsteps. It is better to bear those ills we have than to fly to others we know not of, as the great British bard put it.[2] Sadly, the supposedly enlightened democratic nation-states have traditionally tolerated dictators for other nations—in return for economic favors; as the American President Franklin Roosevelt famously said of Samosa, the dictator of Nicaragua: "He may be a son-of-a-bitch, but he's our son-of-a-bitch." "Vanity of vanities, saith the Preacher, vanity of vanities; all is vanity."[3]

What may break the traditional strongman pattern cannot be the emergence of a democratic nation-state; the passions of the impoverished can never get converted into the interests of an informed citizenry. Instead, the rule of traditional dictators has only been threatened, and frequently overthrown, by a charismatic new leader propounding an equally new ideology—such as liberation theology. In our own time, in South America, that ideology has been born the bastard child of authoritarianism got upon Christian belief by the theology of socialism. Unfortunately, the new creation will always turn out to be a disease far worse than the old—an authoritarian ruler whose regimented minions enforce their dehumanizing ideology against every area of liberty formerly possessed by the people. Then, darkness descends—even at high noon.

Beware the tyranny of the strongman and the things powerful men do by utilizing the masks of deception.

---

[2] *Hamlet* 3.1.4.

[3] *Ecclesiastes* 11:11.

Tales of the Whorehouse and the Pox

A pox on both your houses.

William Shakespeare, *Romeo and Juliet*, 3.1.90-92

Pox: a transitive verb meaning to infect with a virus causing a pustule or with a venereal disease such as syphilis.

[Chinese] *Xingbing*, meaning venereal disease.

Beware of the inevitable infection that deception, and self-deception, cause in the entire body politic. That infection has a name: and its name is *corruption*. Corruption has a way of infecting an entire populace, beginning with its power brokers and eventually reaching all receivers, many of whom also become smaller-time brokers. There is a ready marketplace for power, wealth and sex, and all who play in it eventually become infected, and infect others. To put an image to this marketplace: It is like the story of the Whorehouse and the Pox. Sleep with a whore and likely get the pox. Then become a whoremaster and pass the pox on to a new group of unwilling victims—first to the young women seduced by money into sexual bondage, who then pass the pox on to other men. Like the infection rate from a viral pandemic, the pox readily infects much of a whole population.

Consider how the corruption paradigm plays out in the founding of an American public crime family. A politician who gains a strong foothold within government—by employing the techniques of deception to win elections—then uses that position of power to gain wealth by signaling his openness to accepting bribes for private favors. He becomes the whore who sleeps with a number of "clients"—who all get the "clap" from him. At some point, the power of self-deception kicks in, and the politician begins to project his inner guilt upon his political "enemies" and to displace his own corrupt actions onto some vulnerable group whom he creates—often out of whole cloth. Consider the example of how powerful politicians ginned up the big lie of impoverished Chinese people constituting the Yellow Peril to the American nation back around 1900.[4]

[4]Diana Preston in her book *The Boxer Rebellion* provides a good look into the so-called Yellow Peril virus running through American journalism at this time. Her work is but one out of many on the subject.

He then turns whoremaster and leverages his position through favors-marketplace intercourse to gain more power for himself—and to empower various family members. *Voila*, a crime family in the making. He sleeps his way to some of that power by seducing vulnerable women and making deals with powerful women—in bed. Each of his "victims" then proceeds to practice seduction and bribery upon others. All in all, he gives full meaning to the old term *intercourse*. Eventually, one person's initial actions may reach the point where an entire government bureaucracy becomes infected, and he and his crime family seduce and bribe entire foreign governments. The initial fork-in-the-road decision has now led to the wholesale theft of a country's integrity, and a substantial portion of its economic gains, to the disadvantage of a basically honest populace. Of course, the sex-power game can, and has, gotten played out as a same-sex power game as well.

In order to cover its traces, such an administration at some point must create a villain to blame, all in order to retain power and the support of a disgruntled populace. Then, the virus becomes a pandemic, and if not somehow controlled, it will lead to international conflict and even major war—all brought on through displacement and sublimation. Consider in this regard the various fascist and socialist-communist regimes in modern history.

CONCLUSIONS

Face masks, deception and self-deception—and a large dose of corruption—constitute that unholy triad creating the world's regimes of unremitting, impoverishing violence. One may indeed smile and smile and be a villain. This triad constitutes the *why* for what people of goodwill worldwide desire but lack: harmony—or peace, plenty, and joy. All in all, not a pretty picture. Without some radical rethinking, what has happened since 1979 will continue to happen.

The question now remaining regarding this merry minuet, this dance of doom: *How* might people of goodwill the world over change the nature of the dance?

***

Discoveries:

The unholy triad: Wealth, power, and sex—where power empowers the pursuit of the other two.

Face masks: The deceptive devices that leaders hide their identities behind.

The world's two most powerful stories: The deception story and the self-deception story.

Psychotic personalities: Engage in enough deception and self-deception, and you lose all sense of reality.

The personality of the strongman emerges from out of psychotic personalities.

Corruption constitutes the end-result of self-dealing in the unholy triad. It always creates the environment of the whoremaster and the pox. The moral lesson to be learned: Sleep with a whore and likely get the clap.

Chapter Nine

THE *HOW* FOR PEACE AND PLENTY

OVERVIEW: How might the continual conflicts plaguing the world get resolved peacefully? Thanks to the latest technological revolution, human governance now has the possibility of evolving toward a third way—beyond offensive warfare and purchased balance-of-power strategies—for reaching peace and plenty. The third way may be modeled from out of the metaphor of an Archipelago World. We lay out the fundamental components for such a world's emergence and growth toward the sunny uplands of peace and plenty.

INTRODUCTION: THE CHOICE SET TRIAD

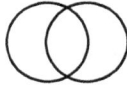

Three possibilities regarding international relations now exist—a triad of choices. One, major world powers, whether defined geographically or culturally, will continue striving for either the defeat or the complete dominance of their rivals large and small. Their weapons: aggressive diplomacy, economic bribery, and diplomacy by other means—which means open, invasive warfare. Most nations would then become parts of a one-world or world-area empire, or vassal states to a superpower. The recent developments in the Middle East suggest an Iran aiming for option one. Two, dominant nations play off one another, continually seeking advantageous balance-of-power arrangements so as to minimize any chances of option one coming to pass—against them. Germany and Japan attempted option one; Great Britain for centuries has played at option two. In the East, China has traditionally played option one, although one might characterize China's Vietnam-era strategy as a power-balancing move: a form of option two. Smaller Southeast Asian nations have attempted to execute balance-of-power strategies betwixt themselves but have been overshadowed by the elephant in the room—China. Eastern European nations have been trying their hands at the balance-of-power strategy. Neither of these two choices offers hope for peace and plenty amongst all the peoples of this world. Wars and rumors of war continue.

Three, a new way does now exist—expanding the choice set. The third way arises from out of three factors. First, the recent Internet Intercourse Revolution can now facilitate fundamental changes in peoples' governance. Second, these evolving governance changes can now reflect peoples' basic desires and needs for natural affiliations, rather than ideological conformities forced by dominant powers. Third, the technology-driven Internet Intercourse Revolution facilitates as never before the effectiveness of a peace and prosperity-creating triad: *toleration, shaming*, and *shunning*. These factors will drive our development of a new international relations model—one that we call the Archipelago World.

Radical Individualism and Common Ties

> No man is an island/Entire of itself,
> Every man is a piece of the continent/A part of the main....
> Any man's death diminishes me/because I am involved in mankind.
> And therefore never send to know for whom the bell tolls/
> It tolls for thee.
>
> John Donne

> *Xiao: Xiao* is love for the immediate family and then society. It is the principle of love of parents for their children and of children for their parents. If every family is united and happy, the society will prosper.
>
> Attrib. to Confucius

Radical Individualism and Cultural Uniqueness

A strange pattern has developed over the past 100 years or so in the liberal West. On the one hand, opinion leaders from out of academia and mass communications have seized upon ideas that see each individual and each human culture as being unique: radical individualism. Individuals seek self-actualization through their uniqueness; cultures likewise possess uniqueness, and so each one of the many cultures must receive respect and protection.[1] On the other hand, these same opinion leaders demand that all people march lockstep into relatively few ideologically-defined *communities*—mainly consisting of the ideological categories of race, ethnicity, and sexuality. Membership in one or more of these communities cannot be optional: You will be made to acquiesce.

Not only that, the communities that the opinion leaders promote receive treatment within a hierarchy of value—to be enforced by the liberal democratic state. Members of the Black Community receive positive points for their historical received oppression, whereas members of the White Community receive negative points for their historical oppressing. Where each stands on the grievance scale determines the nature of its treatment by both the grievance industry and the grievance adjudication divisions of governance. However, disagreements run rampant over which subgroupings should dominate other subgroupings. How do Black Women scale against Gay Men? This invented set of complex subgroups has evolved into the pseudoscience of *intersectionality*. Presumably without conscious intention, Western opinion leaders have created a different sort of deeply divisive conflict, one betwixt complex grievance categories and subcategories, a conflict that appears ready to rip whole nations apart. The demands that intersectionality become the rule of the land barely disguise an otherwise naked totalitarian instinct at the heart of the whole enterprise. The exquisite double-dealing here confounds all rational thought. The totalitarian ideological beliefs of the East—workers versus the bourgeoisie for instance—appear to have gone down whole, without any corrupt influences from their Western intersectional partners.

---

[1]The term self-actualization derives from the researches and writings of the American psychologist Abraham Maslow who postulated that each unique individual possesses within him or her a stepladder-like hierarchy of material and psychological needs that scream out for fulfilling—one at a time from bottom to the top wherein self-actualization lies. Within this structure, liberal government should assist and even subsidize each individual's reaching the top rung.

The New Puritans

Puritanism: The haunting fear that someone, somewhere, may be happy.

H.L. Mencken, *A Mencken Chrestomathy*

The result of the Western movement from radical individualism and cultural identities to intersectionality has been the creation of a new Puritanism. Intersectionality has castrated the earlier idea of respecting the individual above all else—not an ideal situation but one that the Progressive tribe may hold to without great harm—amongst themselves. This tribe has, however, moved on to threaten all the other natural communities comprising a Great Society with some form of annihilation upon refusal to conform. Snitch on your neighbors. Free speech for us but not for you. Above all else, it appears that these folks simply cannot tolerate the idea that anybody else might have fun disagreeing with them, or indeed have any fun at all. You will be made to.

There are Just People

I am a Jew. Hath not a Jew eyes? … if you prick us, do we not bleed?

Shylock in *The Merchant of Venice* 3.1.58 ff

Against this pseudoscientific juggernaut, researches into human similarity and commonality of beliefs have gotten drowned out and pretty well buried. That does not mean that commonalities do not exist, and they do. Take for instance, the large matter of property rights. Despite communistic outrage, nearly all people everywhere perceive that some possessions, material and of conscience, rightfully belong to each person, rather than to the state or other community. A man in a gulag may cling to his hair comb, now missing many teeth, as his only remaining humanity dignity. Regarding right and wrong, all people believe that these two categories do exist, and that some institution should adjudicate disputed behaviors. A moral order to the human universe does exist, beyond and above the flow of *yin* and *yang*.

There are just people: "We hold these truths to be self-evident, that all men are created equal." Underlying any and all cultural differences lie the bedrock triad sought out by all people of goodwill: "Life, liberty, and the pursuit of happiness." Harmony in the Eastern world. Property rights and moral conduct represent two of the three legs upon which civil society rests, everywhere. The third leg takes the form of *affinity*. Nearly all people throughout the world—regardless of such categories as race and sex—need close affinity with like-minded souls in order to prosper: Life, liberty, and happiness do not become realized within an individual's solitary domain. "No man is an island, entire unto himself." Affinity breeds group cultures, and not the other way around.

The liberal West's ideological tendencies to reify the many variables within human experience into the few now reveal themselves as being quite poisonous, and one of the worst reifications goes to the heart of economics as a social science, and that is the consumer-producer category set. Western economists insist upon putting all people into one these two boxes. In reality, every person is both—consumer and producer. Consumers and producers have no real existence, outside economic thought. This false dichotomy drives a stake in the heart of that balancing third leg in the natural community triad: affinity. Whilst the dichotomy has very important uses within the economics craft, it leads people away from trading first and foremost with those they share affinity with.

The dichotomy creates a false sense of cost, excluding from marketplace calculations the longer-term costs of *dis-affinity*, costs that eventually hollow out every natural community that buys into the false narrative of being consumers only whenever they buy. Your purchase of the cheapest present cost products impoverishes every natural community member in the longer run, as like unto a grim reaper; rewarding work falls to the ground and dies, killed by whatever big industry you favor with your trade.

Starting with this triad of principles, an entire structure for peace and plenty, for harmony, may be constructed—within any civil government and amongst all governments. Of course, there will always be outliers, both individuals and groups, refusing to accept property rights, moral conduct, and affinity for others. Fortunately, an immunization against their threatening conduct does exist.

The Internet Intercourse Revolution

Of Technology Revolutions and Governance Evolutions

The world's third great technological revolution (following agriculture and printing) with regard to effects upon governance evolution consists of the ongoing radical technological advances made for furthering human intercourse. This revolution began in the West in the 1840s with the advent of telegraphy, and it continued on to telephony and then wireless telegraphy and telephony. Rapid intercourse in government instructions would henceforth prevent such catastrophes as the American 1814 Battle of New Orleans, fought with great slaughter after the end of formal hostilities with Great Britain had officially been declared. Of course, it early on became apparent that such swift intercourse could also wreak harm upon others—as when the German nation employed telegraphy and telephony to set in motion a war plan before actually declaring war. Naughty conduct. The Intercourse Revolution continued apace throughout the entire next century—wireless, wireless voice and video, and then the *piece de resistance*—the World Wide Web.

Synergy results whenever the whole exceeds the sum of its parts, and the Internet Intercourse Revolution surely meets the definition of synergy. The revolution's power resides not so much in its individual technological discoveries as in their linkages—not just between voice and data, but between knowledge and its ready availability, between the virtual and the material, and between the nearby and the far away, quite instantaneously. Every significant technological revolution has radically changed the feasibility set for governance over, and perhaps for, the people—opening up new avenues for both attaining peace and plenty, or for accelerating conflicts and resulting poverty.

Regarding the Internet Intercourse Revolution, think back for a moment to the intercourse situation from the Old Silk Road until the revolution in transportation technology wrought by deep-water steam power and wireless. East-West intercourse in, let us say, 1100 could take as much as three years for a one-way journey—or even more. Enterprising travelers might get robbed and murdered along the way, with the nature of their demise unknown to family and friends. Eighteenth-century innovations in both ships and navigation, bringing faster East-West intercourse, still meant a round trip sailing journey of a year or more—still with significant risks of total loss. New England ship captains' houses had prominent "widow's walks" on their roofs for good reason: Some wives watched for years for never-to-return husbands consumed by sea or pirates. Deep water ventures brought about the creation by Lloyd's of London of insurance markets for such ventures, and the limited liability stock company permitted the sharing out of losses as well as gains, but on the whole these ventures remained wildly costly—as did the goods they conveyed.

Limitations in affordability and timeliness still meant that for all nations, and right down to local community levels, most consumer and producer goods would still largely require local sourcing—or no sourcing at all. This in turn meant that shortages, starvation, and resulting grinding poverty would remain the lot of most people. Powerful kings and princes, in this environment, rightly saw invasion and conquest of their lesser neighbors as a best approach to assuring better supply, particularly of foodstuffs, avoiding unrest at home. As attested to by the chroniclers of the tiny, ancient nation-state of Israel, invasion was for many millennia a sounding death knell for the small and weak. Something of a Darwinian situation, all in all. Then the conditions for smaller nation-states began to change—gradually at first, but recently, all in a rush.

Picking up upon our narrative, the steamship revolution steadily reduced passage times—one could by World War I reliably reach America from England in five days compared to two to three months under sail. The linkages between sea transport and cargo timing, however, would remain weak until very recently. Thanks be to the current Intercourse Revolution and its tight linkages, a supply chain can now deliver parts from dozens of countries spread over the world to one factory in the quantities precisely needed for the very next day, and today's production can be shipped out around the world before tomorrow dawns. Literally everything can be obtained readily by anyone nearly anywhere at any time—and everything will become much more affordable for many more people.

The Internet Intercourse Revolution will also reduce the vulnerabilities of smaller and weaker nations to exploitation by the larger and more powerful ones. The whole capture versus trade calculus will continue to favor peaceful trade, the world over. As many nations will in the future be able to restructure their productive enterprises, taking advantage of rapid and secure intercourse in inputs, and when needed, for outputs from their productive processes, they will discover that in the longer run it costs less to buy locally than to import, thus securing local well-being. Produce what you can effectively make, and then buy the rest.

The significance of rapid goods movements and tight linkages confirms earlier economic theorizing. The theoretical gains from trade and comparative advantages economists imagined 100 years ago have now become mundane realities. Even small nations can now produce what they can and trade for the rest of what they want—and the costs of trade have plummeted. The continued poverty endemic to some nations can now be traced to government corruption, rather than basic economics. Prosperity has become radically more affordable. With the gains from acquiring goods from other countries by force dropping, the situation for smaller nations and communities has correspondingly improved. Herein lies the opportunity to reshape the nature of governing units themselves. It turns out that "smaller is beautiful" can change from a slogan of the hippie '60s to a promising reality.

Archipelago World

> O brave new world /that hath such people in't.
>
> William Shakespeare, *The Tempest* 5.1

O Brave New World

Consider what a brave new world may burst upon our scene. In the 16th-century world of *The Tempest*, Duke Prospero and his 15-year-old daughter Miranda have been stranded, presumably shipwrecked, upon a remote Mediterranean island for some 12 years. Miranda knows nothing of the wickedness of the world of mankind. She stands amazed at the appearance of some also shipwrecked courtesans landing upon the island—brought thither by her father employing white magic. The new unwilling immigrants turn out to be neither brave nor noble in demeanor. The mask falls. Things are not what they seem. *The Tempest* stands even today as a powerful emblem for the human condition.

Fast-forward some 325 years, and Shakespeare's brave new world reappears to shock the Western civilized nations: Aldous Huxley sees his cynical, dystopian novel *Brave New World* published, in 1932. In it, Huxley sees a future in which all the might of perverted science and a single ruler and ruling class have been turned upon mankind in order to create the dark-side universe of communistic totalitarianism with its accompanying single workshop of the world: test-tube babies assigned social class prior to birth and manipulated to conform to their predetermined higher or lower classes. To a significant degree, Huxley stood as prophet for a new world order that dark-side forces and ruling classes today strive to birth. All this merely points to the corollary to the basic rule of technological revolutions—that such revolutions may bring about either good or bad governance evolutions. Add in the speech control—"newspeak"—of George Orwell's *Nineteen Eighty-Four*, and what you get will raise the hair on the back of your neck. So much for a quick look at the dark side.

The Tempest stands for a world of isolated communities having no means of outside intercourse—a world best described as an archipelago of distant, isolated islands of base humanity vulnerable to invasions. The Internet Intercourse Revolution awakens a possibility of yet another form of human governance—neither isolated nor warring. This brave new form we term the Archipelago World. Imagine, for a moment, a metaphorical world consisting of many islands and islets, literally thousands—perhaps something like the geography of the South Pacific region. Some islands contain large populations. Some consist of a number of islets formed in the shapes of atolls surrounding one or two somewhat larger islets. Some islands and islets exist very far apart indeed from any others. All the islands and islets possess very different manners of doing things—cultures—developed over many centuries of living apart. Voyages betwixt the various lands have always been time-consuming and very dangerous. Intercourse therefore has always been limited. In the place of actual knowledge about one another, the occupants of each island tell stories about how bad the other, distant islanders behave. Warning signs go up: Beware The Other. Then, seemingly in an instant, bridges appear connecting each island to each other island. What happens then? How will such an Archipelago World evolve?

Model for an Archipelago World

Where traditional forms of governance have always evolved from out of top-down conquest by the strongman, the Archipelago World will evolve up from out of *natural affinities*. The building blocks for a new world order facilitated by the Internet Intercourse Revolution consist of a triad: natural communities, cultural facades, and bridges. Bridges compose the necessary ameliorating third leg to the first two.

Natural communities consist of just people drawn together by shared affinities. Natural community members share cultural identities evolved over many, many years of living together and underlying, bedrock natural law beliefs in property, justice, and the goodness of affinities themselves. Cultural facades consist of the particular practices each natural community has adopted over time. Cultural facades hide the natural-law-shared values that every community possesses. The cultural practices of each natural community may indeed be very good, and they may play an important role in creating affinities, but nevertheless they stand out as facades blocking a view of people's commonalities. If you prick us, do we not bleed? Because of the frictions and conflicts amongst natural communities caused by cultural facades, the necessary third leg to the ground-up triad consists of bridges connecting natural communities.

Bridges go from one place to another—A to B. They do not broadcast a message in a multilateral manner but contain and direct intercourse, one-to-one. They will take a number of forms. Obviously, advanced engineering may actually enable some remarkable vehicle bridges to be built where none now exists—as has happened in such places as San Francisco, or the Mackinac Straits, or the Isle of Skye, or Hong Kong-Zhuhai-Macao. [Probably no such bridge will ever link Los Angeles to Hawaii in order to fulfill a Green Dream for the elimination of air travel.] Bridges go far beyond the literal, however. Bridges will include air and sea travel as well, and all forms of materials delivery. They will include digital communications regarding commerce, government affairs, and entertainment—the one area where single messaging to multiple locations works.

The power of virtual and physical bridges to create change, however, comes in one specific area: commercial intercourse. The power of linkages created by the Internet Intercourse Revolution supercharges business activity. Efficiency goes up; cost goes down. The new intercourse vastly increases the gains made through relative comparative advantage. One result: people from very different natural communities will now be able to afford to carry on intercourse between each other. This intercourse may be either virtual, people relating online, or better yet physical, people coming physically together and beginning to share such amenities as local food and entertainment—and even humor. [Humor, it turns out, is not universal; some cultures need to learn what is funny for others.] Eventually, people begin to examine why and how they do things, things seemingly very different. Then, they begin to discover that they possess underlying beliefs about what really matters in life; they enjoy differing cultures, and they value holding the same basic beliefs. Bridges of this sort in reality constitute discovery pathways. Who are you? Who am I? We share the same basic things! Why should we ever fight? Businesspeople constitute the great adventurers traveling across bridges; they fertilize the soil for others to grow relationships within. In this sense, out of many, entrepreneurs are the world's greatest benefactors.

What basic things do we members of the *homo sapiens* tribes share? Yes, our respect for others' property and personhood; these things should never get violated. Also, we share desires for affinity. Here, the wisdom of the East founded in Confucius may appear: We all need family, beginning with the mother-child bond. Then, we all thrive upon relationships with friends and neighbors. We come to love the customary practices that we share together, the basic good things such as infants and children, food and games, and even memories of our ancestors who have helped shape us into who we now are. We *homo sapiens* like to work, but we like to work together; so, we create other bonds, amongst fellow workers. We all desire the good life, and that life becomes richer when we expand our relationships into other natural communities other than the one(s) we presently know.

A Humorous Look at East and West

For the Chinese people, conditioned by many centuries of uncertainty and frequent crop failures and war, this simple triad resonates deeply: family, relationship, work unit. This can become the defensive Dragon-in-his-lair posture that many Chinese adopt toward American Cowboys. For the Americans this traditional triad has evolved over time, driven by good fortune and few disasters, into the ASS triad: *advertise, sell, and systematize*. Americans learn from early on in kindergarten show-and-tell to advertise themselves, to sell themselves to prospective buyers, and to systematize everything. For them, family and relationships still matter, but not so much as they used to. Work units have evolved into play units. Americans love team sports, and so they make their business work units perform like football teams. In order to do so, they systematize everything, in a manner resembling an American football team's playbook. They make work exhilarating and fun. And they love jokes. The Chinese have learned over many centuries that life is very hard, no fun at all. So, one of the disconnects between East and West takes the form of failures to understand humor.

Modeling a Hierarchical World

Of course, few of us live *upon* actual physical small islands. Instead, we live *within* more than one natural community. I may have my American business friends and also my Chinese friends; I may thus belong to at least two natural communities. You may live amongst American friends and also perhaps among Scottish friends. We may also belong to such institutions as sporting teams or churches or synagogues or temples. We may belong to hyphenated-American clubs and enjoy hyphenated-food together. Some of us may belong to political clubs—parties as they are called. However many natural communities you live within or enjoy relating to, all of the same principles behind "getting to know you" apply: We meet, we share, we question—we dig through our cultural facades, and we discover what we really like in one another despite our outer differences.

This makes good sense, as far as it goes. A knotty complexity, however, must get introduced: within our model for a new world order, not all natural communities are equal. No natural community is an island—and perhaps in reality never has been. This complexity goes beyond surface differences defined by cultures. Nearly everywhere, multiple communities, both natural and artificial, exist that take the form of hierarchies. The hierarchies may consist of market-based ones such as production workers and managers; they may consist of levels of political or military governance. Even within the spiritual realm religious hierarchies exist. So, it is one thing to consider how just people may break down cultural barriers to reach mutual understandings. It is quite another to wonder how basic natural communities should relate to higher-level communities—especially those created by the very acts of governance that also may seek to create peace and plenty.

Having said this, it turns out that the answer to the question that our overall model poses actually is quite simple: The same building blocks apply to hierarchical communities as for basic natural communities. The application of our basic natural law principles—property and justice particularly—work to create affinities, the third principle. A valuable part of each nation's created affinity comes through the evolution of founding mythologies that bind us together. Also, the fundamental Rule of Three works itself out in the manner in which property, justice and affinity receive protection under law. Justice and right dealing between the various levels of hierarchical communities evolve out of basic needs for peace and plenty. So, in America a civil disagreement between people in a small town will get adjudicated in a county court—and so on and so forth until the adjudication may rise up three levels to the Untied States Supreme Court. So long as founding myths continue to hold fundamental affinities together, the whole structure will possess inherent stability—like the Empire State Building versus the Leaning Tower of Pisa.

Modeling Conflict and Conflict Resolution

But you may say, quite rightly, that all of this has something of a Pollyanna nature to it. What about world poverty, about racism, about sexism and the sex trade—and all those testy intersectionality issues concerning so many people in the West particularly. If we take a broader, historical view of this huge problem in human and governance relations, we find that these matters tend to pulse between two different states or conditions of dealing. Like *yin* and *yang*. The first, primordial state involves the passions. Tribes respond to their own felt needs by taking what they need, likely from others. Tribal rivalries may then create real human devastations. At some point, usually dominated by overall exhaustion, some form of peace gets cobbled together. *Yin-yang*. In a more civilized time period, battles got fought over the very nature of what the goals of governance should be; after the horrors brought on by English Civil War, the fighting factions finally declared a peace, returning to the status antebellum. They had learned the hard way to accept a large measure of *toleration* for the differences that had brought about the conflict in the first place. *Yin-yang*.

Recently in the West, people and central governments alike appear to have lost the capacity for toleration between each country's own natural communities as well as for other nations, and along with toleration its kissing cousin called *compromise*—the art of which the Americans had invented in the first place. The whole American foreign policy exercise toward the Middle East has been driven by either overt warfare for one side over the other—to protect access to a single resource, oil, now in abundant supply—or by the power politics of balancing off competing sheikdoms. How might such situations get handled differently under our model for future peace and plenty? The answer lies in a triad composed of toleration, shaming, and shunning—at the overall governance level, not at the personal level. Call a government to account for aggressive policies but never blame the country's people—a fundamental principle of harmony. For that matter, never blame a nation's ruler or chief executive; point out the harms done by a nation's policy decisions. Mobilize the forces of world opinion against the policies but allow a leader some wiggle room, a way out of the policy. Always remember, a trapped lion can be very dangerous.

The toleration principle to our Archipelago World model works as follows: First, all nations need to learn to tolerate all practices of other nations—and of their own people for that matter—except those that pose existential threats. An existential threat is one that causes the loss of life, basic liberty, or means to live above impoverishment by government actions denying Rule of Three judicial practices for all. The ongoing existence of the international sex slave trade constitutes such a threat from any nations permitting it. Existential threats may get dealt with by using the traditional two means of disarming threatening behaviors that all tribes and nations, and even small natural communities, have used since time immemorial: *shaming* and *shunning.*

Shaming communicates disapprobation, and may over time change attitudes held by postures that natural communities come to disagree with. A classical example: the anti-slavery movement in 19th-century Great Britain conducted by William Wilberforce and his little band of committed evangelical Christians. Slavery in Britain itself and in much of the British Empire got disbanded—peacefully. Shunning, of course, has always taken the basic form of refusing to have anything to do with a disapproved other community. The brave new world of the modern Internet Intercourse Revolution makes possible high-tech, high-speed shunning, and shaming as well, by effectively withdrawing trade, and perhaps imposing economic sanctions—which is the negative form of trade intercourse—upon bad actors. When a number of nations agree to shun a nation or natural community for its misbehavior, change will follow—without warfare but perhaps taking quite a period of time. Take for example Venezuela.

Controlling Corruption

The remaining issue threatening harmony relates to the ever-present existence of government corruption.[2] How shall this work within our model? *Corruption* works by theft from the many by the few. Corruption will never be entirely eliminated; one might speculate that the costs of trying to do so would be too high. That said, two classic approaches to cutting corruption exist, and both can get made to work far more effectively thanks to the Intercourse Revolution: corrupt practices become more difficult to hide—although perhaps more easy to carry out as well.

The first approach: Starve the beast. Eliminate favors that government bureaucrats may sell to buyers of such favors—which implies fundamental changes to, and elimination of, government programs

---

[2] See both the last part of our Chapter Eight and our Appendix C for extended discoveries regarding corruption.

susceptible to favor trading. And eliminate corrupt bureaucrats themselves: Victorian Great Britain did much in these lines by choosing very wealthy people as ministers, reckoning that they had less incentive to steal than the more common men did. Ancient China under a healthy Confucian bureaucracy appears to have frequently gained control over corruption by strict schooling for bureaucrats-to-be. When character still mattered in the West, strict training in doing the right thing helped with the cure. Character qualifications appear quaint in most of the West now.

The second approach: Drive government program decision-making down to the level closest to where real benefits from such programs should appear. Hard programs—roads and bridges, for instance—may get monitored by watchdog agencies fairly easily, and they need to be. Soft programs—poverty-related for instance—will always be much trickier. The general rule: Always quantify expected and actual results from such programs. If you cannot measure it, do not do it. Always drive program management down to the governance level directly affected by each program. Make program managers responsible for results, reckoned at one level of governance higher up the totem pole. As a general rule, pay for outputs, not for inputs. Nothing so corrupts a person as a free ride, and paying for inputs does precisely that. A permanent salary is a sleigh ride to ill-gotten plenty.

One last word here regarding reducing corruption: favors granted to one political party by another will probably always remain—and may even sometimes benefit the common weal. Allow some of the practice to continue—stretching out over time. After all, handsome local government buildings do please the eye and imply that government is doing its bit. In the classic American system, this form of permitted minimal corruption got termed "log rolling." It did, and still has, the benefit of preventing intergenerational feuding amongst political parties. Dealings over time instill a certain honor amongst thieves by requiring them to keep their future obligations to the other party. If men were angels, we would need no government.

Conclusions

A third way does exist for the world's nations to carry on relations so as to achieve peace and plenty, or harmony as the Dragons of the East would say. Set against traditional policies of warfare and the balancing of power between enemies through paying one or another party to war against another, the third way seeks to generate peaceful attitudes toward other peoples through learning about the other. From this humble building block, peace amongst nations and plenty for their peoples may be achieved through just a few basic triadic relations: property, justice, and affinity—and the Rule of Three itself. Disagreements amongst nations may get dealt with through the toleration-shaming-shunning triad. The basic principles encapsulated in the Rule of Three make all of this feasible. The question is: How will people and nations alike regard the opportunities awakened by the new Internet Intercourse Revolution? Will our application of this revolution cause the nature of human governance to move toward the high and airy uplands of peace, plenty, and joy—or toward darkness at high noon? The future for this method for disarming mayhem presently looks promising—but never overestimate either the power of the forces of evil—or the intelligence of the leaders of governments.

***

A Fable That is Actually True

> And it is upon that rickety bridge that we've built up our relationship from a longtime friendship into the marriage we have today.
>
> Lynnette Li-Rappaport

> Black and yellow, red and white/They are precious in His sight....
>
> From a children's Bible song

There are just a few stories. One of the fairly recent ones, and also old ones, holds that Chinese women and Jewish men have been marrying at amazing rates—in America and largely amongst college-educated individuals. It also appears true that such marriages, within China itself, may well date back some 700 years—give or take a few centuries. Jewish people have had a presence in coastal China for that long. The Chinese-American woman quoted above has such a marriage, one fraught with interfamily frictions symbolized by what she calls the "rickety bridge(s)" she and her Jewish husband have built for themselves between each of their respective families. The challenge has apparently been great, for unlike most such Chinese brides, she had as a child become an evangelical

Christian. Nevertheless, despite the severe frictions between their parents' beliefs, their underlying beliefs in love, joy, and peace have held the bridges in place, still intact. Beneath even great cultural differences lie common beliefs about what is good between two people. Now, for a fable about a Chinese-Jewish wedding—one that is, though fictional, also true.

Li An had recently graduated from an American university in one of the Plain States. If her parents named her in the hopes that she would grow into the meaning of that name, their hopes surely had come true: *An* means "peace." She is indeed a lovely, shining, soft-spoken young woman always walking in an atmosphere of her own making, filled with calm. While at university, she had fallen in love with a young Jewish man named *Aaron*—Aaron Weisman. Now, as it turns out, *Weisman* descends from the German and means literally "white man", and so he is. Li An prefers to think of it as meaning "wise man"—as he surely is regarding knowledge of Jewish tradition; after all, the name *Aaron* carries the sensibility of one who teaches or enlightens. And so, Aaron has taught Li An the significances of a traditional Jewish wedding, so much of which she has found both charming and deeply meaningful at levels she knew not before. Of course, the Jewish emphasis upon family and tradition, and upon the preeminence of the mother-child relation she could readily relate to—as Chinese tradition contains the same truth. Also, she could understand and value the whole matter of mutual obligation captured within the Jewish sensibility for marriage—for this also has very deep roots in a traditional Confucian Chinese sensibility.

At the dawn of a couple's wedding day, Aaron told her, it is as though they shall both be cleansed of all past mistakes that each had made, forgiven and set free to merge into one new and complete soul. In all, this blessed day becomes a personal Yom Kippur for *chatan* and *kallah* (husband and wife) alike. Both will fast this day until after the afternoon ceremony: Fasting stands for purification.[3] The *chatan* will wear a *kittel*, a traditional white robe worn on Yom Kippur. The bridegroom and the bride do not see one another for the week running up to their wedding day—to build anticipation and excitement. They greet arriving wedding guests separately—a tradition called *kabbalat panim*. Then comes the *badeken*—the veiling of the bride by the groom. The veil symbolizes

[3] We are indebted to the *Aish.com* website for details about Jewish weddings. A number of other sites also provide such details.

modesty and means that whatever a bride's physical beauty may be, the underlying beauty of her soul matters far more.

The wedding ceremony itself takes place under the *chuppah,* or canopy, that symbolizes the shelter of the home they will create—without walls—open on all sides to invite in guests and to offer hospitality. The families of the bridegroom and the bride each escort in the *chatan* and the *kallah*. The rabbi then recites the *kiddushin* or betrothal blessings. Cups filled with wine get drunk by the couple—wine symbolizing the mutual joy that they will share. The prayer of sanctification follows. Then, the *chatan* provides the *kallah* with something of value—a gold ring to signify his giving her something of value. Only now has the marriage under Jewish law been actually completed. Then, the *ketubah* or marriage contract must get signed by the *chatan* who pledges his responsibility to support her—not only materially but emotionally as well. She will have a copy of the contract always available to her as an assurance that the *chatan* will keep his word.

Now, the second and final cup of wine gets drunk by the pair, as a part of the ceremony of the Seven Blessings pronounced upon them. We could go into much more detail, but it is easy to see *why* Li An has found these details so warmly rich and confirming of her desires to marry Aaron. Of course, the last thing that happens takes the form of the festive meal. This meal—because it so frequently seems to become an over-the-top outpouring of music, food, and drink—has come to represent the only thing people generally associate with Jewish weddings—sadly, because so much that is rich gets missed. One also might add that sometimes the contract becomes something akin to a secular property contract—more than hinting at the possibility of the marriage not lasting forever, and perhaps not for very long at all. Secular versus spiritual/theistic—what shall be the tone for each Jewish wedding?

It may well be that Li An will come to desire the theistic reality of Aaron's world, rather than the secular reality of her own—and perhaps not. Surely their shared sensibility for honoring their ancestors will make them feel even closer to their kin within the chain of being that brought them into this world. There is the story of two families with children boarding an airliner. The secular American family's children treat their parents with great contempt; after all, their parents are one generation closer to the apes. The children of the other family treat their parents with great respect; after all, their parents are one generation closer to the Patriarchs. This second family, of course, is Jewish. It might be Chinese.

Hopefully, the marriage of Li An and Aaron will last "as long as they both shall live." If the bridge that they are building between themselves and their respective parents has been well-enough constructed, it will. In the broader scheme of things, of course, their marriage stands as a trope or symbol for the millions of relationships that will get in the future formed betwixt people of different archipelago communities. Each of these future relationships will create values greater than the sum of their parts, for each will bridge the divides that have since human time began created misunderstandings and conflicts. Instead, these uncountable new relationships, as many as the stars visible in the heavens, will help create peace and plenty—life on the high uplands of joy. The harmony captured in the heavenly spheres.

One last matter, going back to the beginning of our book. Did we meet in this book by *chance*—or by *design?*

Fini.

***

DISCOVERIES:

There are just people: Behind the facades of culture, all people everywhere share the same basic beliefs.

The beliefs shared in common: Property rights, justice, and the desire for affinity.

Desires for affinity underly all human desires for peace and plenty, and joy—or, we may say, for harmony.

Basic building blocks for a peaceful world: natural communities, commonalities behind cultural facades, and bridges.

An Archipelago World: We may create a model for future peace and plenty within this metaphor for how a new world order might look.

(*Continued*)

(*Continued*)

A hierarchy of natural communities: Natural communities of like-minded people exist at every level of a great society and within all nations. Natural communities minimize intra-group conflict and should always receive encouragement from higher-level natural communities.

Of conflict resolution: Men are not angels, and so conflicts will always arise. Three institutions work to ameliorate conflict: toleration, shaming, and shunning. These replace open warfare and warfare by proxy.

Corruption: A threat within any institution of government, it consists of thefts from the people in general by self-dealing bureaucrats. It may get minimized, but never completely eliminated by starving the beast of corruptible government programs, driving accountability down to the lowest levels, verification of results one level higher, creating an ethos of honesty amongst government officials, and through log-rolling devices.

Eternal vigilance: Darkness at noon always threatens. Men are no angels.

Part Three Conclusions

Men are no Angels: The Existential Rule of Three

If men were angels, no government would be necessary. If angels were to govern men, neither external nor internal controls on government would be necessary. In framing a government which is to be administered by men over men, the great difficulty lies in this: you must first enable the government to control the governed; and in the next place oblige it to control itself.

James Madison, *The Federalist, No. 51*, 1788

We hold these truths to be self-evident, that all men are created equal, that they are endowed by their Creator with certain unalienable Rights, that among these are Life, Liberty and the pursuit of Happiness. That to secure these rights, Governments are instituted among Men, deriving their just powers from the consent of the governed, That whenever any Form of Government becomes destructive of these ends, it is the Right of the People to alter or to abolish it, and to institute new Government, laying its foundation on such principles and organizing its powers in such form, as to them shall seem most likely to effect their Safety and Happiness.

Thomas Jefferson, *Declaration of Independence*, 1776

We have met the enemy, and he is us.

Walt Kelly comic strip *Pogo,*
(perhaps borrowed from a 1970 Earth Day poster)

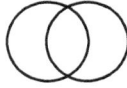

We Have Met the Enemy, and He is Us

> And this is the condemnation, that light is come into the world, and men loved darkness rather than light, because their deeds were evil.
>
> *John* 3:19, KJV

Men are no angels. Even men of good will frequently engage in very bad behaviors. Men who live on the dark side achieve frightfully evil deeds indeed. Part Three of our book has taken up the issue of darkness and light: In the future, how might more of all humankind live in the light, the bright sunny uplands of peace and plenty? What might be the prospects for such upliftedness and harmony?

The totalitarian state is the rightful place for men of darkness to thrive, as we have seen in Chapter Seven. Evil men own the dark. Be not misled: All deviant authoritarian dominance within human governance leads into darkness.[4] A woman cannot get just a little pregnant with good new life, and the impulse toward dyadic authoritarianism cannot yield just a little nasty growth.

We have emphasized within Chapter Nine the idea of natural communities achieving peace and plenty within themselves, through the right application of the Rules of Three, and bridging any intercommunity differences deriving from disparate cultures and institutions through mutual understandings developed through trade and ideas intercourse—in a word, through tolerance. Lest we should find ourselves misunderstood, we believe that some few things do rise above tolerance for such differences. Most differences between disparate natural communities must be tolerated in the interests of both national and international harmony and should be sorted out and ameliorated through intercourse in both trade and ideas over time. Existential threats to fundamental principles of individual wellbeing and living in the light do not fall into the amenable category.

The Rule of Three at the Pinnacle of Light

At the pinnacle of any nation comprised of disparate natural communities—such as America—a governance by a nation-state may appear.

[4] We do not wish to imply that normal law and order policing yields authoritarian rule; that is a fatal glass of beer argument. One glass of strong drink does not a drunkard make.

That government should perform only the few general and tasks of existential import to the whole nation, letting all others devolve to the natural communities—such as states, counties, towns and cities, and volunteer organizations and associations—that underpin overall governance. What then should the nation-state do for its citizens? National defense for certain. Coinage and regulation of banks certainly also. Market facilitating, yes also. Law as it relates to such national concerns as patent protections and other major property rights issues, crimes against the state, and some interstate commerce matters, yes, as well. What else might we wish to include?

One way that governments have chosen to regard this matter involves the issue of the rights of citizens over and against government—either in the form of negative rights as in America's Bill of Rights or positive rights such as rights of workers to form unions. Positive rights have simply exploded in the modern era, and not just within the United States. The positive rights movement generally gets driven by ideological beliefs held by portions of a nation's citizenry. At the extreme, policy positions held by the nation's ruling elites frequently force the adoption of measures that the populace at large does not approve of. In a word, something of a grab-bag approach to governance has come into being through the handout of free stuff or the favoring of one group of citizens over the others.

In all of this grasping for new areas for governance to control, is anything missing? We make the case that something has gotten lost in all of the positive law traffic in national governance—once more, not only in America but taking America as the representative Western nation. The truly existential has gotten buried under the inessential. Somehow, The American system has lost its founding purpose—stated so brilliantly by Thomas Jefferson in his world-famous Declaration, wherein Mr. Jefferson lays out the most fundamental, existential rights of each citizen of the American nation, just three in number—life, liberty, and the pursuit of happiness.

We have argued in this book that, whilst the Declaration in some sense is a list of fundamental priorities for the nation, it constitutes far more than just a list. Each of these three rights identifies an existential concern for every citizen—and an area of potential threat from a government. Not only that, but the three together form and shape the most simple and elevated example of the Rule of Three for the entire nation and all of its subordinate natural communities. The intertwined workings of the great Rule of Three appear really quite remarkable—whether Mr. Jefferson intended them so or not. In order to see this, perform a little thought experiment: For each of the three, imagine a country without it. Without protections for human life, all life, there would be neither liberty nor happiness for citizens deprived of it by forces of darkness. Without liberty, there could be no quests for happiness—some succeeding, some failing. There could be no responsive learning yielding an educated and mature citizenry. Without liberty, there could also be no protections for life—for without liberty, who could speak for the voiceless?[5] And without the pursuit of happiness, the value of life itself—and the whole purpose of liberty—vanishes into a deep, depressive totalitarian darkness. This great existential Rule of Three should always be at liberty to secure the most existentially important matters for all the government's citizens—everywhere in every land.

And so, a great American patriot summed it all up: "Give me Liberty or give me death."[6]

The Three Strategies for Dealing with Other Communities

For thousands of years now, tribes and nations have pursued one of two strategies for dealing with other communities: direct conquest or balances of power playing off some against others. Such strategies have for at least 5,000 years, East and West, involved the employment of overt force, using nearly continual warfare to achieve power over others or to reduce the power of some over the others. For the West, the penultimate period for what we might call chessboard diplomacy appeared during the first half of the 18th century.[7] During this period, the great emperors, kings, and at least one queen treated the landscape of Europe like a giant chessboard over which they could command the movements of their pieces in the shape of armies. The common folks of all Europe mattered for little or nothing to these heartless rulers who ground up people like so

---

[5]"First they came for the Jews, but I did nothing because I was not a Jew. Then they came for the socialists, but I did nothing because I was not a socialist. Then they came for the Catholics, but I did nothing because I was not a Catholic. Finally, they came for me, but by then there was no one left to help…." Martin Niemoller on self-interest under Nazi rule.

[6]Spoken by Patrick Henry to the Second Virginia Convention on 23 March 1775 at St. John's Church in Richmond, Virginia.

[7]See Reed Browning, *The War of the Austrian Succession* for a truly depressing in-depth look at how badly 18th-century royals behaved.

much cordwood. It was all extremely dyadic: chess masters and the chess piece armies moved by them. Then a new period in international relations emerged, one that Adam Smith grasped somewhat prophetically in 1759 when he wrote that the "man of system" no longer could treat Europe like a chessboard and countries like chess pieces; the chess pieces had begun developing a motive power of their own.[8] That power took the form of public opinion as enabled by a free press to behave almost like a virus within the body politick.[9]

This new, third form of international relations possesses a triadic, rather than a dyadic, nature: Each nation, or smaller community, stands upon its own resources and trades for what its people do not produce themselves cheaply enough—many sets of trading dyads result. As Adam Smith prophetically foresaw, peoples and nations would begin to redefine their wealth in terms of what they gained in standard of living through trade, rather in precious metal hoards acquired through aggression or corrupt trade practices forced upon weaker neighboring countries. Fair trade determines in a large measure the happiness of a nation. The third leg of the triad takes the form of national opinion—what Adam Smith termed "moral sentiments." Both within and amongst nations, a shared opinion forms regarding what may be considered fair trade; countries breaching that opinion find themselves ostracized, barred from trade, and eventually forced to conform. Within a nation's smaller natural communities, common moral sentiments determine what actions shall receive general approbation, or disapprobation. A moral sentiment resembles a thumbs up or down to public actions, but not given in a colosseum. Moral sentiments develop so as to check all undertakings against them on the part of a governing executive.

The fundamental changes foreseen by Adam Smith, and understood clearly by few if any of his contemporaries, worked themselves out through the American experience—largely through the wisdom of the country's first president. George Washington famously disavowed foreign entanglements—the necessary condition for the new strategy for dealing with other nations: We will fairly trade with all comers but empower none. As a sign of disapprobation, the new nation's new constitution would and did outlaw international trade in slaves.

---

[8] *Theory of Moral Sentiments,* VI.II.42.

[9] See our Appendix B for a look at how public opinion can run amuck, like a virus.

Within our present age, even as we sit here writing, the old dyads of conquest and power balances yield to a revitalized American international relations strategy that favors blocking trade to bad foreign actors rather than attempting the use of direct force, and the use of tariff favors and disfavors rather than attempts at forming threatening coalitions of nations against other nations. It truly is easier to build, or block, trade bridges than to rebuild bad-actor nations.

The traditional by-products of age-old destructive intermittent warfare, then, may finally draw to a close. George Washington would be pleased.

The Four Horsemen of the Apocalypse

> And I saw, and behold a white horse: and he that sat on him had a bow; and a crown was given unto him: and he went forth conquering, and to conquer.
>
> *Revelation* 6:2

> Sublimation (psychology): The diversion of the energy in a sexual or other biological impulse from its immediate goal to a more acceptable social, moral, or aesthetic nature or use. …a purification or refinement; ennoblement.
>
> *Wikipedia*

> When I think of the rollicking pleasures that earlier filled my life
> Lolly lo, lolly lo
> Like the time I beheaded a man who was beating his naked wife
> Lolly lo, lolly lo
> I can still hear his widow say/Never moving from where she lay
> "Tell me what can I do, I beg, sir, of you/Your kindness to repay"
>
> "Fie on Goodness" from Lerner
> and Loewe's *Camelot*

Conquest, Famine, Pestilence, and Death—the four horsemen of the Apocalypse. These four, armed horsemen in ages past brought their terrible consequences to innumerable tribes and nations. Their long reign may soon be ending—to be replaced by their new age equivalents: lawfare, sexual abuses, extortion, and character assassination. The original four bestial wrongs modern men have sublimated into these the new four. And the modern four horsemen ride together in a troop called Corruption.

Forming the abnormal personalities of corrupt nations, then, these three psycho-social sicknesses distort and dirty entire nations: projection, displacement, and sublimation. Together, they constitute an unholy triad, a Three-Legged Stool from the dark side—one in which the third leg, sublimation, allows the internal guilt generated by wrong conduct to receive relief. Sublimation says to the soul: After all, I am doing this for the good of the nation—or my clan, or family, or son. That's how members on the dark side sleep at night, though perhaps fitfully.

Within traditional governance, sublimation took the form of kingship or divine right. In our own age, it has taken the form of public servant heroes "working for the little man." If some kings of old operated, in effect, "crime families," large governments today comprise numerous crime families—and this holds for both West and East, Cowboys and Dragons alike. The task for the present age is to bequeath to the future age a human world stripped bare of such totally corrupt creatures. How might this get done? First of all, the perfect is the enemy of the good.[10] Accepting a small measure of horse trading that balances out taxpayer-funded programs favored by each party should be regarded as a small price to pay for relatively corruption-free governance—in a word, some small measure of logrolling which is horse trading spread out over time.

At the highest levels of play, the corruption game pits two Rules of Three against one another: the dark side trio money, sex, and power obtained through the psychological tools of projection, displacement and sublimation, versus the Rule of Three giving light—life, liberty, and the pursuit of happiness attained through love, joy, and peace—or as the East would say, through harmony. In a sense the battle resembles the Taoists' idea of yin and yang, primeval forces continually battling one against the other in a never-ending dualistic conflict. The powers of light needs must remain ever vigilant lest the darkness overwhelm us all.

Fini.

---

[10] Eighteenth-century British governance eliminated most corruption by, in effect, buying out a corrupt aristocracy's corrupt monopoly holdings—all in all a good deal for the British taxpayers.

Epilogue

The Fable of the Beavers and the Otters

Once upon a time, so very long ago, there lived in a large dark forest two tribes: Beavers and Otters by name. The forest was so large that the Beavers and the Otters occupied a neighborhood without any other mammals at all. Now each of these two tribes did what they always do: The Beavers worked hard all the summer and fall long, gathering sweet young saplings for winter food, and preparing large trees for felling to secure their dam across their favorite stream in case of springtime flooding. And they used tree branches to enlarge and strengthen their den with its underwater entrance secure against all invaders. That's what Beavers do. They respected the elders of their tribe, lining up in a row each morning for breakfast, biggest down to smallest. The biggest Beaver signaled the rest to begin breakfast by taking up a juicy sprout. And, oh, they also had older members of their company always standing guard, noses lifted and sniffing for any danger that might present itself to the tribe. At the first sign of danger, the senior Beaver struck a loud thwack upon the water with his flat tail. Who knew but what some foreign invader from another part of the forest might stumble upon them and attack? And then there were the Otters to take into account. Could they be trusted?

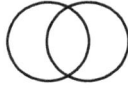

Now the Otters also did what they always do: They played. All summer long and well into the fall, they basked in the sun upon deliciously cool mud flats, and if they became too warm, they dove in the stream and frolicked together, their sleek, smooth bodies flashing in the sunlight. They also teased the younger beavers unmercifully whenever they got the chance. That's what they do—until the late fall panic set in: Oh, my gosh! Winter is nearly here, and we have not eaten enough to grow our winter coats of thick fat and fur! We'd better get going. They all found the work of fishing and hunting for meat, however, to be just *too* boring. So, the senior Otter of the tribe suggested that they make a game out of it! Let's see who can catch and devour the rich, delicious meat within the most crayfish in one day!

The whole tribe shouted with joy (Otters do shout, but in a funny, high-pitched squeal). While some of them fished alone, others formed teams and followed strategies for maximizing their collective catch. They had searchers for the best crayfish pools, and catchers, and butchers to sever meat from shell. The team with the biggest catch per member won the prize for the best team. That team's members shouted for pure joy! "Look at us, we're *numero uno!*" Occasionally, the hardworking Beavers would halt for a break and glare at the Otters disapprovingly. "They are so foolish! Do they not know that the cold winter will come soon," they asked one another. You see, Beavers take life very seriously. Otters love to laugh and play, and play jokes upon one another.

***

Unbeknownst to either tribe, a group of American college students had been walking through the deep forest and had observed these mammals at work and play. Some of them were Americans, and some were Chinese exchange students. The Chinese students found the mammals very interesting; they had not seen these creatures back home. They watched very carefully and kept quiet so as not to alarm them. The Americans quickly grew bored; they of course had seen both species in the zoos. One of the Americans burst out laughing. "The beavers," he proclaimed, "are just like the Chinese—so dedicated to hard work and so serious." The Chinese students nodded gravely in agreement: Yes, they are like us. Then an American laughed right out loud: "and the otters are just like us!"

Appendix A

1066: The Great Invasion

> The great events of the time were written down by the monks in their chronicles and so became history; but to the men and women who were living in the villages of England then, they were only oral tales of distant happenings, more or less twisted in the telling. Battles, the deaths of kings and rivalries of earls, were only important if they seemed to threaten the stable tenor of the village life, and the mutual kindness and custom that held it together; or worst of all, if they suddenly threatened to bring ferocious strangers tramping through the place, burning and slaughtering like the Danish and Norwegian Vikings in the bad old days.
>
> David Howarth, *1066*: *The Year of the Conquest*, 13

Introduction: Why 11th-Century Hastings Matters

In all human history, there are just a few stories. Of those few, one of the most significant has been the Conquest story. And because people are people, no matter the chronological time or material culture, one particular story well told and detailed can and may stand in for the innumerable similar tales throughout much of human history overlooked by chroniclers and forgotten by an aged, toothless and demented Father Time. And so, the story of the Great Conquest of 1066 may bring to life the realities faced by Hastings—and also by so many villages, towns and countries almost since historical time began, East as well as West. Hastings, England in 1066 possessed such depth and detail of story and untoward events that we may easily imagine and understand countless others like it;

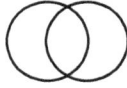

we may feel closer in studying it to a 9th-century BC village in ancient Israel or a similar village in Zhou Dynasty China at roughly that same time. For that matter, we may relate the Hastings story easily to warlord periods throughout Chinese history—or during the American cowboy Wild West.

Examine Hastings, and see a vast, visionary panorama of history unfold like an ancient precursor to 16-millimeter film—a Bayeux Tapestry analogue.[1]

Social Ordering in Anglo-Saxon England

> It was those [Viking] depredations in the past, more than anything else, that had given England the social structure it had in 1066. It was a farming country. Land was its absorbing interest; and originally, plots of land had been owned outright by the men who settled and cleared them, and inherited by their children. But such independent farmers had no defense against the Viking raids, or resources to tide them over other disasters like cattle sickness, a series of bad harvests, or fire or storm. In the course of time, almost every man in the country had attached himself by mutual promises to somebody more powerful, who could help to protect him and his family in times of stress. Small landowners had surrendered the nominal ownership of their land to their protectors—which in turn held the land in duty to somebody higher. This evolution has often been called a loss of freedom, and so it was; but absolute personal freedom had come to be, as perhaps it has always been, a dangerous illusion. Its loss was really a gain: the acceptance of the duties and mutual support of a social system, the end of anarchy.
>
> David Howarth, *1066: The Year of the Conquest*, 13–14

[1]The Bayeux Tapestry, embroidered by unknown hands in Bayeux, France shortly after the Norman Conquest of Anglo-Saxon England, tells the story of that conquest in some 70 visual images 19 inches tall, stretching over 231 feet like a pre-industrial film strip, telling a largely illiterate population the story of one of the world's most monumental human events. Perhaps its eight vivid colors of stitches got woven into great art by the nuns of a Bayeux monastery overseen by King William's brother Bishop Odo—prompted, legend has it, by William's wife, Matilda. Whilst telling the story from a Norman French perspective, it possesses an amazing correspondence to Norman and Anglo-Saxon written records.

On the surface, life appeared simple and very good in 11th-century Anglo-Saxon England. Almost all of it centered around each small village hewed from native forests that the average individual citizen lived within. Towns were few, and cities far fewer.[2] Trade intercourse offered a challenge, for the best roads in the kingdom dated back some 700 years to the Roman occupation—and those had had little maintenance for centuries. Food appears to have been sufficient, even bountiful, for the time period. Simple country life lived amidst clean air and fresh meadows and pristine forest land certainly seems attractive for a city dweller to contemplate today. But life also had a daily physically demanding, dull, and repetitious toll—a routine that wore out men and women alike before age 40. Indeed, life expectancy, even for those surviving beyond age five, scarcely exceeded 40. The harsh demographics very likely resembled the previous 4,000 years for the vast number of human beings born into the world, and the basic demographics would not improve much for another 800 years or so.

Life could be monotonous for years, and then leap into sheer terror driven by some outside, or inside, threat—such as Viking raiding parties, epidemics, crop failures and such. What could people do against such threats? Modernity claims that the people such as those populating Hastings possessed no insurance against the unforeseen—no fire, theft, or life insurance policies to pay, and that is true—only in a very literal sense. As for health care, well local wise women made available their herbs and potions—probably better care than in the following age of Heroic Medicine during which more people doubtlessly died of the cures than of the diseases. We encounter the idea today that people back then relied upon their children for support in old age—and this, too, is true, if only in a very narrow sense. And of course, there was not very much old age to support back then. But what emerges from the Hastings chronicles forms a very different picture for modernity to contemplate.

First of all, each Hastings family insured its own survival through networks of kin, neighbors, and people above them in a complex social hierarchy, one like unto a pyramid with a wide base comprised of serfs and servants, somewhat fewer commoners upon their individual plots of land standing above and controlling the serfs, and being themselves duty-bound to the local lords, each one overseeing several villages; then

[2] *Domesday* records show that fewer than a dozen cities in the country had populations exceeding 3,000; London, the largest, contained fewer than 10,000.

another layer of overlords, and then the great regional Earls—and lastly, a king, and the nation's *witan* or *witenagemot*, a counsel, literally, of "wise men" drawn from amongst lords and the bishops of the church, and perhaps some professional lawyers. Staffing the king's court, the lawyerly class ran the kingdom's courts, mint, and treasury—a fairly complex bureaucracy for the time.

The link binding all human relationships took the form of *duties*—usually stated in terms of days of labor owed to a superior, as opposed to days of liberty devoted to one's homestead—duties defined by tradition and largely self-enforcing, but with local courts to encourage obedience when required.

The concern of every man—serf, servant, commoner, and lord alike—lay with the land. Land had become itself parceled out into shires and hundreds, overseen by a class of lords called *shire reeves* and then by landlords over hundreds. The term eventually evolved into today's rather petty position of *sheriff*. Make no mistake about it, the shire reeves possessed great power within the hierarchy; we modern folk might remember Robin Hood and the Sheriff of Nottingham. No subject within the complex hierarchy of authority actually owned the land, however; residually, the ultimate control over all land fell to the ruling monarch, a condition that held in modern England until the 1970s. Clearly, over centuries, commoners traded away their original overall rights to land to their more powerful local landlords in return for protection from a wide variety of threats. [It turns out that modern-day "protection rackets" have a deep history from the past.]

The next thing to be observed: none of these complex hierarchies came about through *functionalism*, the planned structure of a system of relations. Functionalism says that wherever a systematic way of doing things exists, some smart people planned it. In reality, however, no ruling body legislated any human institution. Each evolved over time, perhaps for a thousand years or more, until it took on a sense of tradition, of simply how things were done from time immemorial—nobody stopped to consider *why*. Everywhere within Anglo-Saxon England, the whole intricate structure of social arrangements blossomed forth. For the present-day author David Howarth, these arrangements developed from a series of yieldings of control of individual plots of land in return for protection from threats, both human and natural. Freedom yielded to security. It appears from the historical record that the last remaining few pieces to the complete Anglo-Saxon governance clockwork fell into place just a generation or two before Hastings—just in time for its destruction at Norman hands.

The third matter to observe in this time capsule for human living arrangements: Everywhere, up to and including the monarch, institutional checks upon abuse of power existed. Should a local landlord attempt to squeeze his commoners for more days of service to him, a local court would almost certainly find against him. Even for the monarch, the institution of the *witan* could, and sometimes did, place a check upon any rapacious tendencies. As an ultimate check against the tyranny of the monarch, the witan could reject and work out the king's removal, and it could determine that the next king would not come from the current king's own progeny. All in all, the Anglo-Saxon social order did indeed run like a grandfather's clock—a bit cranky but nevertheless reliable for its essential duties.

What we must conclude from our study? The social order had its most fundamental and stable base within the Rule of Three: At every level from self to monarch, checks upon unwarranted abuses of power functioned remarkably well. The question this matter poses for us: *Why* and *how* did such an intricate clockwork evolve, without any human planning? Answering these questions for 11th-century Hastings—because people in all times and places possess similar behaviors—answers it for the totality of human evolutionary governance structures. In other words, we should be able to identify how the evolution of human governance, at a very granular level, actually worked out in ancient times and also why—and the same principles should apply even today.

Social Contract Theory and Governance Evolution

> **Social contract**, in political philosophy: an actual or hypothetical compact, or agreement, between the ruled and their rulers, defining the rights and duties of each. In primeval times, according to the theory, individuals were born into an anarchic state of nature, which was happy or unhappy according to the particular version. They then, by exercising natural reason, formed a society (and a government) by means of a contract among themselves.
>
> *Encyclopedia Britannica*

Notables amongst the 17th- and 18th-century intelligentsia occupied themselves with developing Social Contract Theory—a thought experiment for why and how governance by some of the people limited the actions of most of the people at least part of the time and for the hoped-for common good. The big names: Thomas Hobbes, John Locke, and Jean-Jacques Rousseau.[3] The model for this thinking begins with a condition (which is in and of itself a social construct) termed *state of nature*—an original state in which no governance by people over people existed. The model then postulated that people possessed two basic tendencies—self-interest and rational consent—leading them to join together into a social compact to benefit one another.

One should note that the whole notion of explaining any phenomenon through a thought experiment has about as much validity as explaining the created world as emanating from a god standing on the back of a great turtle. We are asked by the thought experiment folks to believe that a complex set of social entities sprang full-blown from self-interest; this merely begs the questions: How? Why? The problem for doing philosophy in the Age of Reason is simply that most of its thinkers lacked even a rudimentary understanding of the fundamental principle behind the development of governance: evolutionary processes.[4] Eighteenth-century understandings of human evolution, for instance, grasped the notion of "irreducible complexity," but could not formulate how complexity arose in the first place.[5] Likening the human being to a clockwork mechanism fails to explain anything about *how* timekeepers came to be—or *why* (other than, perhaps, by "design").

One might well argue that natural philosophers of this period really could not deal with either the evolution of governance, or with how prices change in an economy. [The two problems together, of course, comprise the basic dimensions of political economy as a discipline.] Taking a quick look at the price adjustment problem prepares us for considering the governance evolution problem. The Age of Reason thinkers became so flummoxed by the price adjustment problem that they corporately invented the concept of the invisible auctioneer: that this ethereal being called out prices in a virtual auction until somebody bought the entire lot

---

[3]And Thomas Jefferson whose *Declaration of Independence* stands out as a most remarkable statement of abnegation regarding the Colonies' relation with the British king. Its justification for independence works upon the notion that the King broke an existing social contract, thereby permitting the Americans' separation from a commonwealth.

[4]The history of the development of thought leaves this mystery for the Scottish philosophers of the 19th century.

[5]For an understanding of irreducible complexity, see Michael Behe, *Darwin's Black Box*.

of a product at some a market-clearing price. There never was an invisible auctioneer, of course. We now know, thanks to the late 19th-century Marginal Revolution in Economics, that prices adjust on the margin as a reflection of the many small price movements caused by the sometimes myriads of individual buyers and sellers willingly trading for small units of a product. Similarly, the price that I may buy 100 shares of Apple for today never can reflect the market-clearing price for all Apple shares. Nor does the Dow Jones place a total value upon its basket of major corporations; daily prices merely reveal what willing buyers pay for small amounts of each company's share on the margin.

Similarly, with regard to the governance evolution problem, the device of the imaginary aborigines sitting down to draw up the original social compact from out of selfish thinking also comes up as lacking in veracity. There never were any original conceivers of a social compact birthed out of whole cloth. Instead, social arrangements evolved on the margin, driven by two factors that could only be realized by the generation of a third.

The first factor, property rights, somewhat resembles the Age of Reason concept of self-interest. Each human being possesses an innate sense of some things belonging to him or her—be it only one's own body and mind.[6] Property rights, then, rule as the primeval driver behind all human actions. Thomas Jefferson, of course, gave this primal driver a most felicitous identity: "the pursuit of happiness." Happiness takes us beyond the mere clutching of our pearls and into the high and sunny uplands of emotional and spiritual fulfillments. The other dimension to property rights goes beyond basic property as an individual right to the reality that property itself appears very unevenly distributed indeed; some individuals possessing far more than others of such properties as: intelligence, strength, moral courage, compassion—and malevolence.

The second factor consists of some stressor. If we may all sit around under palm trees upon a utopian island inhabited by just a few of us and eat unlimited breadfruit, we shall never even know what governance means—for we supposedly would have no need of it. [Of course, fruit was plentiful in Eden, and yet Adam and Eve really screwed up.] Stressors may come either from outside a human grouping—think of things such as invasions by other groups or bacterial or viral invasions from the natural

---

[6]John Locke famously wrote in his *Second Treatise on Government* that each man has a property right in the fruits of his own labor.

world—or from within that grouping, in the forms of thefts, murders, and rapes. In this regard, the biblical story of Cain and Abel represents a metaphor for all human bad behavior. The ultimate stressor may well be the penetrating, cold reality of evil itself, whether one chooses to regard evil as a force or a personality, a chaotic happening in a world devoid of meaning, or a wicked plan: As the poet saith, "What but design of darkness to appall, if design govern a thing so small."[7] In the Genesis story, Cain gets ostracized by all human communities for his primal act of murder.

Both within and without each human grouping, some behaviors appear to have always been regarded as existential threats to general human self-interest and have been dealt with according to some sense of morally-based judgment—operationalized perhaps by the divinity, or by some lessor group of moral agents. Life joins with liberty and the pursuit of happiness. What happens, then, when the moral sensibility of a property right within a small grouping of humans gets violated? Let us imagine the case of Cain who has committed murder. His family and community members feel deeply offended. The offense—a great stressor—causes perturbation amongst all group members. The gut-level responses range from desires to ostracize Cain, as happened in the Genesis account, to raging against him and destroying his entire family. For much of early human history, both unwritten and written, the gut determined the response, which took the form of retaliation. At some points, perhaps when retaliation has destroyed the vigorous members of entire families and clans, some individuals wonder if there can be a better way.

At this point, a point that arises numberless times in history, the third leg emerges: the idea that some individuals representing the tribe, or several tribes, might pass judgment upon who was to blame for a nasty behavior, and how best to punish for it. Gradually, a weight of moral opinion would build up against perpetrators of that nasty behavior. Other violations of an evolving moral code might over many years fall under the same weight of moral judgment. After perhaps centuries, or even millennia, a code of conduct evolved, along with the idea of a council determining who had actually broken the code. That council, of course, by then had become the critical third leg of adjudication. But by then, all traces of the evolutionary trajectory had devolved into a tradition—about which nobody could say *why* or *how*. By the time of Hastings, the chief adjudicatory body had long existed, as the witan. Because people everywhere are pretty much the same, the same evolutionary process no doubt

[7]Robert Frost, *Design*.

had already occurred many times before, say during the ancient Chinese dynastic period.

Hastings: A Near Perfect Storm

> When I think of the rollicking pleasures that earlier filled my life,
> Like the time I beheaded a man who was beating his naked wife.
>
> From Lerner and Loewe, *Camelot*

Our quintessential tale of Hastings becomes far more complex for us to grasp when we take into account the events that led up to the battle itself and in its aftermath. Of course, England after the battle would never be the same again—for Hastings is the story of what happened when a developing feudal, dyadic form of governance replaced a fully-evolved, triadic form. The entire Anglo-Saxon balance-of-power structure abruptly ended with the invasion. In a very real sense, Europe was the loser for this fundamental change that meant England would never be the same again—and the continental nations would go down a pathway leading to nearly continual conflict until the 1814–1815 Congress of Vienna brought an exactly 100-year hiatus to the continent. This entire period in the West possesses critical similarities to the Warring Period some 1,000 years earlier in China, and to the fifth-century BC Athens-Sparta period of conflict between a tyranny and a democracy.

One should note right up front that the defeat of Anglo-Saxon England by Norman France did not mean that the developing feudal system on the European continent possessed superiority over the English system of governance. Sometimes, regressions happen. What happened instead: the English house-carls, King Harold's own army, became worn down by two closely successive invasions—one from the Vikings into the English north, and then the successful invasion by the Normans in the south of England. Even then, Harold's house-carls and the regional fyrd likely would have withstood this second invasion had it not been for a strange loss of confidence upon Harold's part.[8]

---

[8]David Howarth speculates that Harold fell under a spell of doom when he learned that, through William of Normandy's machinations, the Pope in Rome had excommunicated the English king. This may well be so, for we know the Scandinavians possessed a deep sense and fear of fate. One might note Shakespeare's play *Macbeth* in this regard.

We have already speculated about how and why the Anglo-Saxon form of governance evolved from outside stressors. In order to round out the Hastings story, we need to understand, as well, what drove the evolution of feudal government on the European continent. What we do know right at the outset of our inquiry: A technological revolution on the mainland preceded and made possible the following developments in both warfare doctrine and governance itself—war of course being an extension of politics and diplomacy by other means.[9] That technological revolution displays itself in many museums—in the form of steel plate and ring armor, swords, and long lances. Put simply, trial-and-error advances in metallurgy for weaponry made possible the revolution in warfare doctrine that enabled the Norman victory. The Anglo-Saxons had fought with the last war's technology and doctrine, the broad axe, against opponents using the next war's armor and bow technology and doctrine—a frequently-occurring mismatch in the history of warfare.

The technology-driven revolution in the arms of war also begat another technological revolution—this time, within animal husbandry. On the continent, advances in the evolution of animal husbandry yielded the European warhorse—a large and mighty beast bred for size and strength in order to carry an armored rider. From these two revolutions came the new European doctrine of the offensive utilizing cavalry. The contrast: Harold of England's army fought on foot with the Viking-derived battle-axe. Some rode small horses, sturdy ponies really, to reach a battlefield faster; once there, they fought on foot. The Normans used massed cavalry to break through and disorganize the immobile enemy army—somewhat resembling the British use of tanks later in World War I, also to break through a static defense. Warfare frequently seesaws between defensive versus offensive doctrines in war, and technological advances drive the seesaw. One important lesson: People do what they know how to—even when it no longer works.

One might add that advances in doctrine then drive further technological advances: Harold of England personally fell victim on the field of battle to another continental innovation—the longbow. French archers could launch literally thousands of arrows shot high in the air on trajectories that would bring them viciously down upon static defenders, who only possessed their broad shields as a defense. Inevitably, arrows

[9] See Von Clausewitz, *Vom kriege*, first published in 1832 and driven by that author's Napoleonic Wars experience.

got through that defense, and hundreds, perhaps thousands, of relatively poorly armored house-carls fell victim to them. Harold succumbed to one such arrow, through his right eye. Ironically, England's Henry V used what by then became known as the "English longbow" to defeat the French army at Agincourt 300-some years later. What goes around comes around.

In conclusion, what might we say about the Feudal Revolution in governance occurring both before and even whilst the Hastings drama unfolded? It was driven by the wicked triad composed of power, greed, and chivalry, which meant cruel slaughter—the same triad that rules many lands today. In governance, a dyadic form evolved away from an earlier traditional triad of ruler-ruled-adjudicator. It eventually replaced triadic kingship chosen by a nation's elites with dyadic kingship emerging out of warfare and forcing blood inheritance upon the selection of rulers—all in an attempt to gain some dynastic stability caused in the first place by the instabilities brought through conquest. Very often in human governance, changes evolve out of attempts to the fix a condition created by forced changes in governance in the first place.

The Hastings story reflects a dichotomy between the two pure forms of national governance—the dyadic versus the triadic. Very significantly, we believe, the Anglo-Saxon triad worked very well indeed for its people for several centuries before being confronted by two powerful adversaries nearly simultaneously. Perhaps the most significant aspect of Hastings: The country stood as a powerful and successful Rule of Three governance form without being in any significant way democratic. Hastings illustrates one of our major contentions—that the basic differences in governance do not fall fundamentally into the authoritarian-democratic paradigm. Anglo-Saxon English governance was triadic without displaying any elements of democracy. Democratic government, as in ancient Athens, can readily run amuck and create the conditions for autarchy or outright tyranny. Authoritarian government can at the same time provide its citizens with Rule of Three protections against tyrannical government actions, as in the modern example of Singapore. Above all else, the Rule of Three matters.

The final word on the knights in shining armor and feudalism: The American musical stage play *Camelot* brilliantly captures the illusionary romance promulgated by chivalry, as well as the underlying ugly violence. The play sums up the lies about knighthood and kingship, emotion, and quests for conquest in these simple words: "Fie on goodness!"

Appendix B

AUGUST 1914: RUSSIANS TO THE RESCUE

> In the sudden and dreadful realization that the enemy was winning, people, searching for hope, seized upon a tale that had cropped up within the last few days and turned it into a national hallucination.
>
> Barbara Tuchman, *The Guns of August*

The New Rule of Three

In the West, the 15th-century Printing Revolution eventually permitted all manner of scurrilous pamphleteers to embark upon careers in the defamation of rulers and politicians alike.[1] The press brought political debate from out of the king's closet and into public view. By the 18th century, one unintended consequence of the revolution and its attendant blessing placed upon press freedoms involved the concomitant creation of mass communicated public opinion. Public opinion, in turn, developed so as to form a critical third leg in politics, along with the government and the populace, making up a zesty new Rule of Three. Public opinion could do more than merely shape how the mass of people reacted to government initiative. It could create swelling *opinion pandemics* as well. It could bring about government emergencies, cries for war, fears of epidemics

[1] See our Chapter Four for our discoveries about the Printing Revolution and its effects upon public discourse and governance.

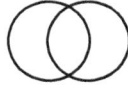

and other health crises, such as the influenza, and condemnation for the disfavored in the nation. Utilized by government, it became propaganda. It could seemingly mimic what we now know as Chaos Theory—one whiff of a matter in northernmost Scotland could become a thundering herd in London. Very likely, Adam Smith in his 1753 *Theory of Moral Sentiments* saw rumors of plagues and government intentions alike going "viral" in the newspaper letters to the editors as one of the means of giving people a "motive power" of their own on the great chessboard of life, all to overturn the policies of government.

By 1918, some three years into World War I, public opinion picked up upon the explosive Spanish flu gathering force toward becoming a worldwide pandemic, and public opinion through the press and through the verbal spread of rumor greatly magnified people's desires to escape it—thereby spreading the virus even more rapidly. Somewhere between 50 million and 100 million people eventually died of it over its three-year course of death.[2]

Just a little over three wartime years before the pandemic, another rumor went viral in Great Britain. As a form of comic relief from this excruciating matter, we pick upon this quixotic example of black humor in a public opinion virus run amuck.

1914: The Russians are Coming!

> On August 27, a seventeen-hour delay in the Liverpool-London railway service inspired the rumor that the trouble was due to the transport of Russian troops who were said to have landed in Scotland on their way to reinforce the Western Front. From Archangel they were supposed to have crossed the Arctic Sea to Norway, thence come by ordinary steamer to Aberdeen….
>
> Barbara Tuchman, *The Guns of August*

It all began near the North Sea. A Scottish Highlands gentleman thought that he had heard voices and seen shadowy figures landing upon his shorefront at night. He wrote a letter to the editor of his local newspaper. The flapping of a butterfly's wings. Another landowner responded, writing to

[2] A large number of books have been written about the Spanish flu since its disappearance. For a good present-day recounting see John Barry, *The Great Influenza.*

the newspaper that he, too, had heard and seen something, during the next night. And so it went: shadowy figures marching across the nighttime landscape, seemingly heading south. This all was happening during the period in which the press first informed the British public of near disaster facing the British Expeditionary Force in France. To many British citizens, the Russians seemed to offer the only source of rescue.

Reports continued, offering corroborative detail. A railway porter in Edinburgh reported that he had actually wiped the snow from the platform where the Russian troops had embarked. The Russians still had snow on their boots—in late August! Other citizens reported seeing men in strange uniforms aboard passing trains headed south. A 17-hour delay in a Liverpool-to-London passenger train obviously had been caused by the need to run a special train south for the Russian soldiers. Other mysterious train delays became attributed to the need for Russian troops transport.

Soon, 10,000 Russian troops were seen after midnight in London, marching along the embankment on their way to Victoria Station where they were reported embarking onto trains bound for Dover. The knowing members of the electorate, probably touching the sides of their noses, explained that the naval battle off of Heligoland Bight had been fought to protect the troop transports carrying the Russian army to Belgium. The most reliable of people had actually seen the Russians—or knew friends who had. An Oxford professor knew a colleague who had been summoned to interpret for them. A Scottish army officer in Edinburgh reported that he actually saw them striding forth in long, gaily-colored coats and big fur caps—carrying bows and arrows rather than rifles. Unsurprisingly, the Russians resembled the famed Cossacks—looking just like Victorian-era mezzotints.

One British resident of Aberdeen informed his brother that 125,000 Cossacks had marched right across his estate in Perthshire. An English army officer assured his friends that 70,000 Russian soldiers had passed through England "in utmost secrecy" to join the Brits on the Western Front. These rumors got passed on by mouth as British censorship would never permit publishing such matters. The Americans who learned of it from friends in England labored under no such limits; their press reported rumors of young American soldiers embarking at Liverpool to return home; after all, the Russians, perhaps as many as 500,000 were going to win the war for the allies. Meanwhile, dispatches from Amsterdam reported huge numbers of Russian soldiers headed for Paris to relieve the pressure on the French army; some Parisians ran to the train stations in Paris to see and greet the coming Cossacks.

The Germans, too, heard the rumors, and German generals worried about 70,000 Russian solders reportedly behind their backs—a catastrophe in the making, since they had just ordered the dispatch of the same number of German troops from the Western to the Eastern Front to help fight off a Russian invasion. These many fears lasted for a full month—a thundering herd set a-beating by the butterfly wings in Scotland. Chaos Theory in real life. In reality, during the whole of World War I, not a single Russian soldier ever set foot upon British soil.

Viral Epidemics in the News

News epidemics, and even worldwide pandemics, occur just as naturally as the viral sort. Each begins with a source, perhaps even a single source—as did the story of the Russian troops. One may even speak of transmission rates for both news and viruses, and also varying population susceptibility to the virus—and for that matter, herd immunity. In both sorts of viral infections, the setting of hard boundaries may delay, or even prevent, viral transmissions. May populations get vaccinated against such diseases? Certainly. By propaganda, and conversely, by free and open discourse in a nation's press: quarantine versus open discourse arguing both sides to a viral infection. Of course, news epidemics spread far more rapidly since the Internet Revolution. The internet may facilitate the making of a mere local news epidemic into a worldwide pandemic. What effect upon governance might worldwide, instantaneous viral transmissions have? We should all stay tuned.

The Uncertainty Principle

The professional class around the world can deal very well with risk. Be it with life insurance, the stock market, or likely cases of the common cold, and many, many other examples, the Data Revolution has greatly facilitated the calculating of risk for everything in which the odds can be known. Not so with *uncertainty*. Uncertainty exists wherever the professionals do not know what they do not know. Uncertainty constitutes the growth culture for viral and news epidemics to germinate within.

Without uncertainty, the Spanish flu would have been far less severe— and no Russian troops would ever have been speculated to have been in Great Britain.

We common folk should cut the professionals a bit of slack regarding events such as the HIV viral outbreak and the SARS and H1N1 difficulties. Not so regarding the U.S. mortgage crisis hitting the country in 2007–2008. We can excuse lack of knowledge regarding the unknown; we should never excuse stupidity.

Appendix C

Public Virtue, Private Vice

One good Man may take another's Word, if they so agree, but a whole Nation ought never to trust to any Honesty, but what is built upon Necessity; for unhappy is the People, and their Constitution will be ever precarious, whose Welfare must depend upon the Virtues and Consciences of Ministers and Politicians.

Bernard Mandeville, *Fable of the Bees*

Introduction: A Fable of the Bees

No Bees had better Government/More Fickleness, or less Content.
They were not Slaves to Tyranny/Nor ruled by wild Democracy;
But Kings, that could not wrong, because/Their Power was circumscrib'd by Laws.

Bernard Mandeville, *Fable of the Bees*

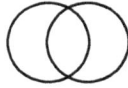

Once upon a time, a very large and spacious Hive well stocked with bees flew into a very unsettling moment: One bee, truly virtuous, pointed out that most members of the swarm, whilst professing virtuous conduct, in reality engaged in the most shameful of practices, seeking out self-enrichment at the expense of others. With millions seeking to supply each other with objects of lust and vanity, the Hive had thrived—but at what cost? Public Virtue/Private Vice reigned in the Hive. When that single virtuous bee, however, made clear the Vice reigning therein, the bees began to reform themselves, genuinely working for the interests of the Hive. Eventually, the thriving Hive lost so many bees gone elsewhere for entertainments that the Queen was forced to retreat with her much-reduced assemblage to a hollow tree. Private Virtue/Public Poverty.

Or so the remaining bees and their Queen told themselves; but was that story really true? Did the Hive's rulers really do no wrong, because their power was circumscribed about by laws? Indeed, the rulers did the Hive great wrongs, despite the laws. Whilst proclaiming their utmost loyalty to the common bees and to the rule of law, they amongst all beings in the Hive had most practiced the art of displaying Public Virtue whilst practicing Private Vices—vices harming the entire Hive. For a price, they had excused great lawbreaking bees, and they had sold the Hive's great honey treasures to another hive—again for private gain. The Hive had failed, not for want of virtuous conduct on the part of commoner bees, but for vices upon the part of the Hive's rulers. The moral of the story: Put not your trust in the virtues and consciences of Government Ministers and Politicians.[1]

The Incorrigible Public Servant

> A number of the public...servants of the crown, having lately absconded from their duty, for the purpose of...living by robbery, such of the above **public servants** as might have taken to concealments on shore for the purpose of avoiding their work, or making their escape from the colony, if they did not return within a week to their respective stations, might, upon discovery, expect the most exemplary punishment.
>
> David Collins, *An Account of the English Colony in New South Wales,* 1799

Ah, so the original of the phrase *public servant* came from the penal colony of 18th-century Australia where particularly naughty criminals transported thither from the mother country got set to performing the

[1]Our Fable finds its basis in the wicked satire of British society created by Bernard Mandeville in *The Fable of the Bees*. Whether the good doctor intended his fable as a satire upon Georgian Britain, we know not, but we take it to be so. On the serious side, Dr. Mandeville added mightily to economic understanding and influenced Adam Smith greatly, bringing him better to see the "hidden hand" of the marketplace.

nastier chores of local public service—such as, presumably, cleaning out the privies and collecting the night soil. The public servants of government today do dirty work as well, but not via manual labor; like their early Australian forebearers, however, they prefer to do no laborious work at all. Instead, they seek to profit from the vices of others who would bribe their ways into personal wealth for themselves by paying for the profligate practices of the public servant class. And so the processes of government itself become corrupted and fall into decay. Never take the term *public servant* as one of approbation. Whoever first thought to apply the nomenclature of penal colony Australia to Western heads of government surely deserves a gold medal for wicked humor.

Everywhere—East and West, amongst Cowboys and Dragons alike—we hear government ministers and major bureaucrats described as *public servants*: selfless individuals laboring long hours in the interests of others. In reality, everywhere truly stunning levels of official corruption exist—corruption unimagined in Mandeville's Hive—and will doubtlessly continue to do so in the future. We suspect that the recently identified corruption within the Ukraine has an equally squalid compatriot within the American public service corps. How else can it be that modestly-salaried ministers, legislators, and bureaucrats retire so wealthy—again in both West and East, and Middle East? *The biggest block to nations attaining peace and plenty for their peoples takes the form of official corruption.*

As another delicious play upon words in addition to *public servant*, *corruption* originally stood for something far different than the meaning ascribed to it today: It of course originally signified organic material rotting and putrefying in its breakdown into simpler organic compounds—like corpses. Corruption had a distinctly unpleasant aroma attached to it—and still does, metaphorically speaking. Continuing a biological analogy: Biological corruption sets in when certain bacteria commence attacking, breaking down, and destroying living material that has been starved of nutrients that support it. Until such a condition becomes irreversible, thorough cleansing, fresh air, and antibiotics may bring it under control. So, too, with organizational corruption: Any organization can become so corrupted by people feeding off of it that the organization must become very sick indeed, and perhaps eventually die. Countries totally given over to corruption get called *kleptocracies*—and they constitute the worst of the worst nations upon earth.

Interestingly, the application of the appellative term *corruption* in government has only a fairly recent history, emerging as it does out of Western innovations in governance over the past 300 years or so. Before that, what we today call corruption in government was very well known; it simply escaped regard as particularly egregious conduct. Instead, it was seen to constitute the normative conduct for every ruling class: Class hath its privileges. While the Western journalists began attaching the term corruption to certain vices over a hundred years ago, no such condemnations for self-benefiting maladministration appear within even today's authoritarian regimes—especially those of Latin and South American countries. It's elite business as normal in these lands.

One might note that so-called public servants can be recompensed for normal duties in two manners: paying for *inputs* or *outputs*. Modern civil servants get paid salaries—payments for inputs of work, or at least for time. Traditional bureaucrats, since time immemorial and still today, get paid for outputs: A private individual pays the civil servant for his results in favor of the citizen—commonly in the West now called graft. It is a close call as to which system generates more corruption—given that modern civil servants have plenty of time on their hands to engage in the favors marketplace, and not upon a fixed-fee basis.

The lexicon of corrupt practices includes the following dirty dozen: bribery, extortion, cronyism, nepotism, patronage, parochialism, influence peddling, graft, embezzlement, drug trafficking, money laundering, human trafficking, and general repressions of political opponents (including the use of police brutality). Notice that all of these dark-side activities require some form of market-making. Potential markets for illicit services always exist and can easily enough get activated by persons of evil intent. That said, the favored techniques for market-making in the East and West do differ.

In the West, corruption presently works like the attempts at cheating constantly played within certain athletic events and within auto and yacht racing. Sports officialdom desires to project public virtue and the image of fair play by announcing new rules to deflect certain performance advantages competitors gain by gaming some aspect of the existing rules. Its virtue signaling merely sets off a new search by the competitors to find a manner of beating those new rules. For some time now, the favorite American ploy for ministers and lawmakers has been to play by the rules domestically (mostly) whilst raking in foreign "contributions." For the East, epitomized presently by Japan, and for Russia, the game that has gotten played has been "see no evil; hear no evil; speak no evil."[2] When truly egregious conduct becomes impossible to overlook, Eastern elites then turn to some form of show trial in order to make a public spectacle of some usually minor offender—often some poor sod of a nonentity—who nevertheless will get hung in infamy—such as Comrade Rubashov in Arthur Koestler's *Darkness at Noon*. Of course, what really titillates the taste buds of totalitarian regimes occurs when a totally honest and upright citizen can get hung (sometimes literally) on a false, drummed-up charge.

The West practices this last deceit as well. Example: President Ronald Reagan's Labor Secretary Raymond Donovan got wrongly accused of fraud and had his name dragged through the mud before finally being found not guilty—all in an attempt to dirty up the President. His pleading voice should echo down the hallways of history as a reminder of just how dirty the corruption charges can get in government: "Where do I go to get my reputation back?" Character assassination writ large in Donovan's case.

Public Choice Theory and Corrupt Devices

> If men were angels, no government would be necessary.
>
> James Madison

> Hypocrisy is a tribute which vice pays to virtue.
>
> Duc de La Rochefoucauld

Given this sordid history for public servanthood, it should surprise no one that over the past 60-some years, Western professional interest has grown in challenging the rather naïve public servant model for ministerial and senior bureaucratic conduct, which holds that the behaviors of public servants—many, but not all as there are always a few rotten apples in the barrel—get shaped by selfless ethical standards directed toward the well-being of a country's people. The challenge to this now rather charming Victorian public servant model has taken the form of Public Choice Theory, which holds, among other matters, that public officials pursue

[2]This Japanese maxim of the three mystic apes refers to the common oriental practice of turning a blind eye to wrongdoing—until it gets too blatantly obvious.

goals akin to profit maximization by CEOs in the private sector. Government public servants apparently believe that they deserve the same gains as made by talented people who actual produce something; that something often takes the form of brilliant innovation. The theory arose in America during a time when the greatest public threat to private wellbeing seemed to be public servants' pursuits of larger and larger government agencies—and with the concomitant increase in public eminence, a rise in perceived personal merit and value for each agency head. Bigger agency/bigger salary, and bigger benefits package. Since that time of relative innocence, the reasons for some public servants' behaviors have only become more nefarious as the breakdown in ethical standards practiced by them has become more corrupted. There is a market for private benefits to be sold by public figures, for the gain of both. Huge private benefits for a few, minimal public losses per individual citizen; focus the gains, spread the losses—so maybe no one will much care. The growing army of those public actors who would profit from such exchanges threatens the welfare of everyone everywhere. Money is the root of all evil?

The question that shall surely shape the future history of nations more than any other: *How can public corruption get eliminated, or at least reduced to an absolute minimum*—in order for peace and plenty to prevail in all nations? After all, when a corrupt dictator bilks his people of a nation's entire economic surplus for many years, and proceeds to flee his own country with that wealth before he can get arrested, the result cannot be pretty for those from whom he has stolen practically everything. If men were angels, no government would be necessary. As things stand in reality, we should identify the means for accomplishing corrupt purposes—and then identify means for blocking such corruption.

The motives for theft by public servants require little understanding: Some men place self-interest above the public good. The methods for extracting public surpluses for private gain, however, seem muddy to the honest portion of the public and of public servanthood. So, we think that bringing clarity to the *devices* employed by corrupt politicians will be of more benefit than telling stories of their malfeasance. We should add that whilst public officials have been "truck(ing), barter(ing), and trade(ing)" public goods for private benefit long before Adam Smith coined the original phrase, technological innovations—particularly in finance—have made the methods for exercising such vice far more complex, demanding continually evolving government rules in order to combat them.

The evidence for political malfeasance itself does go back some 4,000 years, at least, being best illustrated in the ancient world by Hebrew scriptures—particularly the histories and the greater prophets. In a very real way, the leadership of the ancient Hebrew empire brought slow-motion ruin to the entire country through outrageous self-dealing—until it all ended, in a heartbeat, like bankruptcy. The hypocrites in the last reign of the Judean monarchy got disciplined quickly—with their capture, torture, and murder. So, too, for the last despot of the Babylonian empire; a disembodied hand wrote his death sentence upon a wall, and his empire—and he— promptly fell that very night (*Daniel* 5:25–26). In both Hebrew and Christian scriptures, the writers are particularly unmerciful regarding *hypocrites*—those who publicly denounce others for what they do themselves. Today, we call this "virtue signaling."

Stripping away detailed complexities, the general devices for exercising malfeasance have always fallen into three broad categories: Simple theft, *quid pro quo* arrangements, and lawfare. They appear in the Hebrew histories, and they appear today in the Western news. Theft, of course, includes such crude arts as bribery and extortion—also in the news these days. *Quid pro quo* arrangements involve exchanges of things of value—often public cash for private favors. Because both simple theft and *quid pro quos* usually involve money transfers, they can often get detected and traced back to the originators of the deal. Follow the money.

The more devious devices within this general category involve the use of blackmail, where a target becomes captured by a tempting offer for money in exchange for some favor. Once the hook has been set, the blackmailing politician, or foreign government these days, has a means of controlling his target, and of benefiting from future payoffs through threats of exposure. Blackmailers always have the opportunity to increase their demands, thereby expanding the harms that they may do. Blackmail by foreign entities, of course, potentially makes an entire nation vulnerable to the blackmail victim's initial folly in engaging in such a practice.

Lawfare involves the abuse of the law to gain political or financial benefits. Crude uses of lawfare are age old and involve such things as the invention of or the altering of documents pertaining to property rights and the obtaining of government-granted monopoly rights that destroy one's competitors, euphemistically called *rent-seeking*. Unlike most employments of simple theft and *quid pro quos*, lawfare can and often does get used as a tool for wreaking punishment upon other persons, and for the execution of vengeance upon the disliked. When a government lawyer says that "it's nothing personal," you may be sure that it is *very* personal.

The American experiment within its founding constitution sought to outlaw some of the most egregious practice within British government (but largely eliminated in the 18th century), especially bills of attainder that resulted in the execution of a political enemy and the forfeiture of the enemy's title and entire estate to the Crown—in effect placing the victim and all of his relatives in the permanent condition of outlaws, if not corpses.

Impeachments had also been used as a tool for disciplining the king by charging close members of his administration with "maladministration", and then separating their heads from their bodies. Thus the American desire to limit the scope of impeachments to truly bad conduct rather than mere policy differences. Fortunately, these practices have largely been themselves outlawed within the American experiment, except that one must wonder about the use of impeachment as a tool of character assassination within the country today, and also its possible regular usage in the future. Character assassination stands as a particularly nasty and vindictive political practice executed through lawfare—a practice that leaves an individual a lifeless shell of a person. A man may well lose his head in a less literal ways than through the axe or guillotine.

Of course, the larger difficulty with all corrupt devices takes the form of possible detection. The old saying about the criminal that was not at all sorry that he stole, but very sorry he got caught, applies here. The favored devices for escaping detection: virtue signaling in the form of *appeals for greater ethics in government generally* and *the calling for special committees* to study some unrelated problem, *sacrificing some small fry to create the appearance of justice*, and the employment of *layered complexity*. The first involves playing the loyal public servants card: Most public servants are underpaid, honest, and hard-working; don't you dare besmirch their reputations. This defensive ploy works by attacking people who would question public servants' motives. The response may include a pledge to form a committee to study some issue probably unrelated to the original deceit. Above all else, the major politician looking to cover his tracks will claim public virtue and promise to prevent any breaches of the public trust that might be made by his underlings; he will make a close examination and root out any malfeasance. All of this, of course, is like unto setting a fox to guard the henhouse.

The second ploy works by blame-shifting down the bureaucratic hierarchy; the big fish cannot be blamed for the misconduct of the little fish—say the big fish. Instead, attach blame to a minor bureaucrat for some tangential matter. This defense has the added benefit of transmitting a warning to bureaucrats generally to be more careful in their cheating. "Hang one to encourage the rest," as the Emperor Napoleon said about his weaselly admirals.

The last deceit—layered complexity—involves creating a byzantine pathway for the working out of the theft, particularly regarding the pathway for money transfers. This, of course, is a high-tech version of the old cattle rustlers' ruse: Cover your tracks. The use of foreign shell companies and offshore bank accounts all aim to confuse attempts to trace money from a buyer of corrupt practices back to the seller.

Whilst deceitful devices may bring great gains to both buyers and sellers of illicit practices, those same practices may have serious unintended consequences, ones that harm an entire nation. For instance, suppose that a corrupt dealing goes bad: one party feels cheated by the other. As men are no angels, the party feeling wronged may seek out revenge, but then merely generate another response. Soon a tit-for-tat game may result—one with escalating costs for each player and for a country as a whole. Within traditional societies the result often becomes a "blood feud" wherein eventually many players taking one side or the other create a bloody wasteland of destruction that may well last scores of years, or even centuries. Even within supposedly "civilized" nations, the leaders of political factions may also create long-lasting feuds. The feuding may even tear nations apart. Looking into future, huge opportunities for destructive feuding exist right now, within some South American countries, Middle Eastern nations, the European Union, Sicily with its timeworn mafia feuds, and—of course—within both China's claimed spheres of influence and within the United States'.

Even more unintended corruption, especially within wealthy Western democracies, comes about through their well-intentioned efforts to do good: Compassion without common sense harms all parties—givers and takers—alike. Nothing so whets a person's appetite as the offer of free government money. Then, the grifters gather around that honey pot to help themselves. Even the intended uses of free government money to help disadvantaged groups corrupt the very people they seek to aid. It does so by disenabling the working of individual liberty to shape human resolve and character.

To many people, *liberty* means doing what I want, but that is wrong; to prove it, try shoplifting or seducing another man's wife or shack up. *Liberty is the operant principle behind all learning.* Each individual, local human society possesses norms for bad conduct, but within those norms lie limited degrees of freedom—liberty. Exercising liberty always runs a person up against those norms. Sometimes, heroic individuals may succeed in reshaping whole community norms—the reshaping of human bondage norms ins the American South by Quakers and evangelical Christians being the greatest American example, and Aleksandr Solzhenitsyn in Russia. More normally, customs build up character in young men and women, thereby instilling experiential learning within them. *Without liberty, then, no real learning, or progress, can ever happen.* Unsurprisingly in Middle Ages Europe, great thinking, learning, and collection of knowledge all happened within monastic life—monks being at liberty to pursue such matters, free as they were from worldly entanglements. A social order that restricts liberty in an authoritarian manner can never yield a healthy society—only dependency and dissolute conduct. A famous remark made during the last years propping up the USSR: "They pretend to pay us, and we pretend to work."

Conversely, too much individual freedom can only yield a fractionating social order. An acting out younger generation should be seen as a canary in a coal mine: Such behaviors portend future social crises. America saw this in its infamous 1960s, especially during the rioting during the 1968 Democratic Convention in Chicago. A tension between freedom and social norms actually indicates a form of health for a natural community—so long as overt rebellion does not win out, and so long as liberty does not yield to outright freedom. Unbounded freedom always yields only chaos. In the words of the American pop singer Janice Joplin, "Freedom's just another word for nothing left to lose." Freedom of conscience, yes; freedom to do what I want, no. True liberty always bears a cost.

Boundaries Against Corruption

What, then, might be done to lessen dramatically the destructive proclivities of corrupt government officials? We will look here at three things within the realm of possibility: *reforms to public servanthood*, *reductions in the scale and scope* of large government programs, and *quid pro quo strategies* exercised over time.

We may dismiss out of hand all appeals made regarding the reformation of public servanthood, and all promises for future better behavior. Remember, setting the foxes to guard the chicken coop will never reform the foxes. Never confuse the culprits for saviors. In 17th- and 18th-century Britain, the honest ministers within government made side payments to hive off their corrupt members into retirement—all-in-all, a good deal for the commonwealth.

Reductions in the public funds made available to government grifters has great potential but faces a huge roadblock: All such efforts appear as existential threats to public servants generally and to their supporters within government agencies. All efforts in nearly all modern countries so far have failed in their endeavors to reduce the role of "free" money doled out by bureaucrats. What we suggest in this area relates to the empowering of natural local communities: First, make all possible political efforts to drive decisions regarding the obtaining and use of public monies down to the lowest possible level, local natural communities, that level closest to real human needs. Second, make all such public funding contingent upon potential recipients identifying measurable goals for funded programs. Third, appoint impartial administrators one level up in local government hierarchies to release monies and monitor expense against goals—with the requirement that this level of government repay public money spent corruptly or unwisely. Great program; good luck implementing it. After all, that's a nice piece of graft you've got there.

Critical to cutting corruption: Place into effect some forms of *safety valve*. Remember, men are no angels. Some wasteful and corrupt spending will always occur, so let's allow a little lubricant to grease the works—provided that grease gets applied to lessen, rather than to encourage, warring political factions within government and it yields at least some gain to the commonwealth. Political peacemaking always involves some sacrifice of the common good to political welfare. Here, we would like to apply for the future a lesson from the American system learned in the past. That system had evolved since the relatively early days of the Republic. Unfortunately, this spontaneous evolutionary means for minimizing government corruption got killed in our modern era by overzealous efforts to stamp out all corruption. A little corruption leavens the loaf of comity amongst the parties.

The means toward political comity that we recommend: good old-fashioned *log rolling*. Log rolling added one new dimension to simple *quid pro quo* agreements: time. Once the idea that politically motivated agreements to spend public money somewhat wastefully as *quid pro quo* agreements *over time* set in amongst the political class, a number of beneficial results evolved: First, it became important for any corrupt largesse to be spread roughly equally amongst existing political parties or factions of parties: I scratch your back today; you scratch my back in the next legislative session. The absolute amounts of such public corruption would get somewhat held in check by the squeals of dismay emanating from an opposing faction and from a watchdog press when the honeypot got too large.

Second, *quid pro quo* over time encouraged comity within legislators (at several levels of overall government)—somewhat like honor amongst thieves. Any individual legislator, or faction of legislators, violating the public trust by refusing to meet their future quid pro quo obligations would meet with condemnation also from a watchdog third leg of what would become an informal Three-Legged Stool—an application of the Rule of Three. The watchdog institution would be comprised of a watchdog free press and of adjudicating bodies established in each branch of every legislature—national, regional, and local—which would also informally allocate government money oil to the various factions.

Third, the entire evolutionary log-rolling institution would yield changes in the conduct of legislators. Attacks upon members of opposing parties would become less frequent and less severe. Public outrage over government "waste" would be contained by the watchdog institutions as well. Poison politics—in which one political move gets treated as a poison pill by another party—would also be minimized. An environment somewhat like traditional Anglo-American "good sportsmanship" should come into being. This is not to say that the contact sport of politics would resemble American touch football by any means; perhaps it would become more like English rugby: Politics is by its very nature messy, a matter of controlled violence.

A critical corollary: There can be no such thing as effective multilateral trade agreements under this set of conditions—either in a legislature or amongst nations. There are no bridges that run simultaneously to every island in a large archipelago—only bridges connecting each island to each. Multilateral agreements simply give bad actors a group to corrupt and hide within to avoid discipline.

Conclusion: Cowboys, Dragons and the Changing World Order

They went out to do good, and they did very well.

Said of 19th-century American missionaries to Hawaii

We must conclude this long epistle on corrupt governance by observing something more about the changes that have occurred within triadic versus dyadic forms of government. Thirty-some years ago, at the infancy of modern-era East-West trade relations, the American Cowboys rode into China to rustle up profitable new business; they eventually learned how to do well in the Dragon rodeo. Then, things underwent a sea-change as China became much stronger economically: The Chinese Panda face morphed into the Dragon. At some point, the Cowboys began making a killing by getting paid to benefit the Dragon at the expense of the American Eagle, where before the Cowboys had been red-white-and-blue patriots making money from American firms seeking new frontiers in the old land of the Dragon. This later era cannot last either. The selling of the American future to China has become contentious within the American electorate, and the Chinese Communist government faces internal dissensions and dissensions amongst its claimed sphere-of-interest countries. What shall become of future relations, East and West?

Here, we hold up the natural communities–trade bridges solution that we laid out in the last chapter. Rather than seeking to impose domestic ideologies on their nation's peoples, central governments would be wise to allow maximum local liberties to each natural community—allowing each community to receive inner strength through its own foundational myths and boundary-setting rules, hopefully complemented by structures of Rule-of-Three hierarchies. Then, bridges formed through trading with each other—internally within a nation and externally with other nations—will ensure the maximization of peace and plenty throughout the world. The enforcement mechanism for such an evolving world harmony would take the form of *shaming* and *shunning* those powers refusing to trade fairly and refusing fundamental, existential human rights to their citizens and those they hold in bandage.

Remember: it is far easier to build a bridge than to rebuild a nation. And a bridge can have its traffic shut down.

Bibliography: An Eclectic Choice in Readings

Andrlik, Todd. Reporting the Revolutionary War: Before It Was History, It Was News (Sourcebooks 2012).

Arendt, Hannah. *The Origins of Totalitarianism* (Schocken Books 1951).

Arendt, Hannah. *Eichmann in Jerusalem* (Viking Press 1963).

Aristotle, attrib. *Economics* (4th century BC).

Aristotle, attrib. *Politics* (4th century BC).

Axelrod, David. *Evolution of Cooperation* (Basic Books 1984).

Bailyn, Bernard. *The Ideological Origins of the American Revolution* (Harvard University Press 1968).

Behe, Michael. *Darwin's Black Box: The Biological Challenge to Evolution* (Free Press 1996).

Browning, Reed. *The War of the Austrian Succession* (Griffin 1995).

Burke, Edmund. *Reflections on the Revolution in France* (James Dodsley 1790).

Cahill, Thomas. *Sailing the Wine-Dark Sea: Why the Greeks Matter* (Anchor 2010).

Clausewitz, Carl von. *Vom Kriege* (1832).

Cohen, Stanley. *Folk Devils and Moral Panics* (MacGibbon and Kee 1972).

Confucius (and followers). *Analects* (500 BC).

Congressional Research Service. *China's Economic Rise: History, Trends, Challenges, and Implications, and Challenges for the United States* (2019).

Constitution of the United States of America (1788).

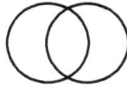

Croly, Herbert David. *The Promise of American Life* (Macmillan 1909).

Croly, Herbert David. *Progressive Democracy* (Macmillan 1914).

Cronon, William. *Changes in the Land* (Hill and Wang 1983).

Curry, Robert. *Reclaiming Common Sense* (Encounter Books 2019).

Deacon, Terrence. *The Symbolic Species: The Co-Evolution of Language and the Brain* (Norton 1997).

Economy, Elizabeth C. *The Third Revolution: Xi Jinping and the New Chinese State* (Oxford University Press 2019).

Edwards, Jonathan. *The Great Awakening*, ed. C.C. Goen (Yale University Press 1972).

Edwards, Jonathan. *Religious Affection,* ed. John E. Smith (Yale University Press 1959).

Eliot, Thomas Stearns. *Four Quartets* (Harcourt 1943).

Fischer, David Hackett. *Albion's Seed: Four British Folkways in America* (Oxford University Press 1989).

Fonte, John. *Sovereignty or Submission: Will Americans Rule Themselves or Be Ruled by Others* (Encounter Books 2011).

Frazier, George MacDonald. *The Steel Bonnets: The Story of the Anglo-Scottish Border Reivers* (Barrie and Jenkins 1971).

Fukuyama, Francis. *The End of History and the Last Man* (Free Press 1992).

Galbraith, John Kenneth. *American Capitalism: The Concept of Countervailing Power* (Houghton Mifflin 1952).

Galbraith, John Kenneth. *The New Industrial State* (Houghton Mifflin 1967).

Golding, William. *Lord of the Flies* (Faber 1954).

Harari, Yuval Noah. *Sapiens: A Brief History of Humankind* (Harper Collins 2018).

Hayek, Friedrich. *The Fatal Conceit: The Errors of Socialism* (University of Chicago Press 1988).

Hobsbawm, Eric. *Bandits* (World Publishing 1969).

Howarth, David. *1066: The Year of the Conquest* (Penguin 1977).

Hayek, Friedrich. *The Road to Serfdom* (University of Chicago Press 1944).

Hayek, Friedrich, *Law, Legislation, and Liberty,* 2 vols. (Routledge and Kegan Paul 1973).

Hayek, Friedrich. *The Fatal Conceit* (University of Chicago Press 1988).

Hegel, Georg Wilhelm Friedrich. *Phenomenology of the Spirit* (Joseph Anton Goebhardt 1807).

Hetzel, Robert L. *Monetary Policy in the Early 1980s: Working Paper 84-1* (Federal Reserve Bank of Richmond May 1984).

Hirschman, Albert O. *The Passions and the Interests: The Political Arguments for Capitalism Before Its Triumph* (Princeton University Press 1977).

Hobbes, Thomas. *Leviathan* (1651).

Homer. *The Odyssey* and *the Iliad* (1200-800 BC ??).

Huntington, Samuel. *The Clash of Civilizations and the Remaking of World Order* (Simon and Schuster 1996).

Hurst, James Willard. *Law and Markets: Different Modes of Bargaining Among Interests* (University of Wisconsin Press 1982).

Huxley, Aldous. *Brave New World* (Chatto and Windus 1932).

Jefferson, Thomas. *The Declaration of Independence* (July 1776).

Kahn, Sulmaan Wasif. *Haunted by Chaos: Chinese Grand Strategy from Mao Zedong to Xi Jinping* (Harvard University Press 2018).

Kharas, Hami and Kristofer Hamel. *A Global Tipping Point: Half the World is Now Middle Class or Wealthier* (Brookings Institute 27 September 2018).

Kirkpatrick, Jeane. "Dictatorships and Double Standards", *Commentary* (November 1979).

Koestler, Arthur. *Darkness at Noon* (Macmillan 1940).

Lee, Charles. *Cowboys and Dragons: Shattering Cultural Myths to Advance Chinese/American Business* (Kaplan 2003).

Lerner, Alan Jay and Frederick Loewe. *Camelot,* stage play (1960).

Locke, John. *A Letter Concerning Toleration* (Awnsham Churchill 1689).

Locke, John. *Two Treatises of Government* (Awnsham Churchill 1689).

Machiavelli, Niccolo. *The Prince* (Antonio Blado d'Asola 1532).

Madison, James, Alexander Hamilton and John Jay. *The Federalist Papers* (The Independent Journal 1788).

Malthus, Thomas. *An Essay on the Principle of Population* (J. Johnson 1798).

Mandeville, Bernard. *Fable of the Bees* (J. Roberts 1714).

Manent, Pierre. *Natural Law and Human Rights: Toward a Recovery of Practical Reason* (University of Notre Dame Press 2020).

MacKay, Charles. *Extraordinary Popular Delusions and the Madness of Crowds,* 3 vols. (Richard Bentley 1841).

Mill, John Stuart. *On Liberty* (John W. Parker & Son 1859).

Mill, John Stuart. *Representative Government* (Parker, Son & Bourne 1861; reprint Batoche 2001).

Miller, Perry. *Errand into the Wilderness* (Harvard University Press 1952).

Miller, Perry. *The New England Mind: The Seventeenth Century* (Harvard University Press 1954).

Milton, John. *Areopagitica: A Speech of Mr John Milton for the Liberty of Unlicenc'd Printing, to the Parliament of England* (1644).

John Milton. *Paradise Lost* (Samuel Simmons 1667).

Montesquieu, Charles-Louis de Secondat. *The Spirit of Laws* (1750).

Murray, Charles. *Coming Apart: The State of White America, 1960-2010* (Crown Forum 2012).

Nisbet, Robert. *The Quest for Community* (Oxford University Press 1953).

Orwell, George. *Nineteen Eighty-Four* (Secker and Warburg 1949).

Otto, Rudolph. *The Idea of the Holy* (1917).

Penn, William. *No Cross, No Crown* (1669).

Penn, William. *The Great Case of Liberty of Conscience Once More Debated and Defended* (1670).

Pinker, Stephen. *The Better Angels of Our Nature: Why Violence Has Declined* (Penguin 2011).

Plato. *The Republic* (380 BC).

Preston, Diana. *The Boxer Rebellion: The Dramatic Story of China's War on Foreigners That Shook the World in the Summer of 1900* (Constable 1999).

Robbins, Lionel. *An Essay on the Nature and Significance of Economic Science* (Macmillan 1932).

Robson, Alex. *Law and Markets* (Palgrave Macmillan 2011).

Roland, Nadege. *China's Eurasian Century? Political and Strategic Implications of the Belt and Road Initiative* (National Bureau of Asian Research 2017).

Rousseau, Jean Jacque. *Confessions* (1765–1770).

Sewell, Samuel. *The Selling of Joseph* (1700).

Schama, Simon. *Citizens: A Chronicle of the French Revolution* (Penguin Random House, 1989).

Sharansky, Natan. *The Case for Democracy: The Power of Freedom to Overcome Tyranny and Terror* (2006).

Smith, Adam. *The Theory of Moral Sentiments* (Andrew Millar 1759).

Smith, Adam. *The Wealth of Nations* (W. Strahan and T. Cadell 1776).

Smith, Lee. *Strong Horse: Power, Politics, and the Clash of Arab Civilizations* (Doubleday 2010).

Solzhenitsyn Aleksandr. *The Gulag Archipelago: An Experiment in Literary Investigation* (Engl. trans. 1973).

Sun Tzu. *The Art of War* (roughly 500 BC).

Tillich, Paul. *Systematic Theology,* 3 vols. (University of Chicago Press 1951–63).

Tocqueville, Alexis de. *Democracy in America* (Saunders and Otley 1835).

Tuchman, Barbara. *The March of Folly: From Troy to Vietnam* (Alfred E. Knopf, 1984).

Tuchman, Barbara. *The Guns of August* (Macmillan 1962).

Vance, James David. *Hillbilly Elegy: A Memoir of a Family and Culture in Crisis* (Harper 2016).

Veblen, Thorstein. *Theory of the Leisure Class: An Economic Study in the Evolution of Economic Institutions* (Macmillan 1899).

Webb, Jim. *Born Fighting: How the Scots-Irish Shaped America* (Broadway Books 2004).

Weber, Max. *The Protestant Work Ethic and the Spirit of Capitalism* (1905).

Yeats, William Butler. *Collected Poems* (a number of editions).

Index

I

J

S

www.ingramcontent.com/pod-product-compliance
Lightning Source LLC
Chambersburg PA
CBHW070813300326
41914CB00054B/847
* 9 7 8 9 8 1 1 2 2 8 2 6 1 *